Hispanic Education in the United States

Raíces y Alas

Eugene E. Garcia

ROWMAN & LITTLEFIELD PUBLISHERS, INC.
Lanham • Boulder • New York • Oxford

ROWMAN & LITTLEFIELD PUBLISHERS, INC.

Published in the United States of America
by Rowman & Littlefield Publishers, Inc.
4720 Boston Way, Lanham, Maryland 20706
www.rowmanlittlefield.com

12 Hid's Copse Road
Cumnor Hill, Oxford OX2 9JJ, England

British Library Cataloguing in Publication Information Available

Library of Congress Cataloging-in-Publication Data

Garcia, Eugene E., 1946–
    The education of Hispanics in the United States : raíces y alas / Eugene E. Garcia.
        p. cm. — (Critical issues of contemporary American education)
    Includes bibliographical references and index.
    ISBN 0-7425-1076-X (cloth : alk. paper) — ISBN 0-7425-1077-8 (pbk. : alk. paper)
        1. Hispanic Americans—Education. I. Title: Raíces y alas. II. Title. III. Series.

LC2669.G37 2001
371.829'68073—dc21   00-054434

Printed in the United States of America

⊖™ The paper used in this publication meets the minimum requirements of American
National Standard for Information Sciences—Permanence of Paper for Printed Library
Materials, ANSI/NISO Z39.48–1992.

Contents

1

An Introduction to "Raíces y Alas"

WHY THIS BOOK?

During my recent assignment in Washington, D.C., as the director of the Office of Bilingual Education and Minority Languages Affairs in the U.S. Department of Education, I attempted to address the challenge of engaging my professional experience and expertise as an educational researcher and my personal cultural and linguistic experiences to the tasks of addressing national educational policy. The professional in me was and continues to be nurtured in some of the best educational institutions of this country, and the nonprofessional in me was and continues to be nurtured in a large, rural, Hispanic family. I found bringing these *personas* (the Spanish term for "persons") together not as difficult as I might have expected and even came to conclude that this intersect was quite helpful to me, my colleagues, and the wide variety of audiences that I interacted with in this national role. In fact, I found that by bringing together these personas, I was able to communicate to individuals in ways that were not possible if I spoke with only one or with separate voices. The present book is my attempt to put into writing these intersecting but distinct voices and to help further our understanding of living in a diverse society, but particularly as doing so relates to Hispanics in this country. Moreover, I will emphasize the role of educational institutions that strive to serve a linguistic and culturally diverse population today and will need to serve them better in the

1

future. For there is no doubt that the historical pattern of the education of Hispanics in the United States is a continuous story of underachievement. It need not be that way in the future.

The voices in this book recognize the multiple selves that make up not only my persona but also the multiple selves that are a reality for all of us. For me, it has been useful to recognize that I am walking in varied and diverse cultures. But we all do this. We are all living with diversity, some of us more than others—but no one escapes this challenge or its advantages and disadvantages. In fact, cultural diversity has been hotly debated throughout Western history. Early Hebrew scholars debated the "us versus them"—the *Hom* and the *Goy*. Plato and Aristotle differed vehemently on the issue of whether social diversity was preferable to social homogeneity. (Plato concluded that homogeneity among peoples in a nation-state minimized political tensions and favoritism. Aristotle, his student, concluded that diversity fostered inventiveness and creativity as well as political compromises in a democracy.) Thomas Aquinas professed that likeness in reverence to God promoted unity, while Martin Luther promoted religious diversity in reverence to the same God. Today, in the United States, the English First movement is passionately concerned that multilingualism and multiculturalism might produce civil strife, while indigenous people mourn just as passionately the loss of their languages and cultures. As this country and the world shrink communicatively, economically, socially, and intellectually, our diversity becomes more visible and harder to hide. But it has been and will always be there. Our social institutions will need to address it more than in the past, particularly for Hispanics, and of specific importance will be how our educational institutions help us address it successfully.

EUGENE

In the book that follows, I will attempt to address the issues of the Hispanic educational experience from the varied voices within me. Those include that voice that often represents my intellectual upbringing and is recognized primarily by my academic credentials—what degrees I received, where and when I received them, how successful I was in those environments, what academic positions I have held, their status in the academic world, the empirical research that I have conducted, the teaching I have done, and of course what articles and books I have written. They are the educational pedigree indicators of this society. I do not apologize for such indicators or my pedigree rating. But they are more than that. They are a set of experiences and accomplishments that have at their core the attempt to expand in critical and strategic ways our broader understanding of language acquisition, teaching, learning, and schooling and their specific relevance to language-minority populations—learners who come to the educational enterprise not knowing the language of that formal enterprise—and particularly for a group of students like me who are classified as Hispanic in the present jargon of educators and demographers. I did not begin my academic pursuits with this specific population in mind but have naturally gravitated to using my professional skills to address issues of relevance to them, but not only to them. I am quite proud of the academic and scholarly accomplishments of Dr. Eugene E. Garcia—I do not apologize for them and will use them in the pages to come; but I do recognize that they are only a part of who I am.

GENE

The other parts of me are more rooted in the nonacademic world, in my social and cultural realities. I am a son, brother, husband, father, and so on. In such social and cultural roles, I have experienced a wonderful family environment, learning much from my father and mother—neither of whom ever had the opportunity to attend public or private schools. They taught me to respect my elders, my brothers and sisters, and others who were not members of my family—such as my teachers—and, most of all, to respect myself. They never gave me a formal lesson about these things. They just lived these things, in the harsh realities of poverty and the hard work any migrant or sharecropping family can understand. This teaching and learning included environments of outright racism or more subtle institutional racism in which our language, our color, and our heritage were not always met with either individual or group respect. It was from these experiences that the voice of "Gene" (a name used most often by my family and friends) emerged. It was this persona that agreed to work as an undergraduate in the migrant camps, tutoring adults in English and related subjects so that they could pass the GED. "Gene" also continued to be a member, or adopt the values, of community-based organizations, such as the GI Forum, the League of United Latin American Citizens (LULAC), the Mexican American Legal Defense Fund (MALDEF), the National Council de la Raza (NCLR), and the National Association for the Advancement of Colored People (NAACP). In this contest, I come to particularly respect and honor César Chávez, Martin Luther King Jr., and the Kennedys for their contributions to issues of social justice.

It was this persona within me that realized early on that I was different. I spoke primarily Spanish; my peers spoke only English. My family and I worked in the fields; my peers and their families hired us to work in their fields. My peers enjoyed a much higher standard of living; I recall being embarrassed that my family did not take vacations in the summer and did not have running water or flushing toilets. But most of the time these differences did not weigh heavily on my mind or on my behavior—I had lots of friends, some like me and others quite different than me. It was one of my elder brothers who first signaled something more about the meaning of these differences than the simple fact that there were differences. Someone had called him a "dirty Mexican," and he told me that these were fighting words. He went on to teach me a significant lesson: *Do not let anyone ever call you dirty.* He made it clear to me that such a statement implied that our mother did not attend to our cleanliness. My mother never sent us to school, church, or any other place dirty. All of us were required to shed our school clothes for our work clothes and vice versa on a daily basis. In short, to be called a Mexican was not derogatory, but to be called "dirty" was cause for defending the honor of our mother. I learned later that many of my peers *did* perceive calling me a "Mexican" as derogatory. That lesson came hard and stuck but did not destroy the previous lesson from my brother.

It was "Gene" who was convinced primarily by nonacademic friends to venture into local politics and seek election to a board of education in a city that was characterized by some as hostile to the language and culture of Chicanos—a label that I and my wife had chosen for ourselves. With the help of a broad sector of the community, I was actually elected, by less than 50 votes out of a total of some 6,000, to that body. And it was more likely "Gene" than "Eugene" that accepted the invitation to join the Clinton administration and Secretary of Education Richard Riley in the U.S. Department of Education. I agreed to do so in an attempt to reauthorize a set of legislative initiatives begun in the mid-1960s to assist local and state educational agencies in addressing the educational inequities that characterized the efforts of our local school with regard to learners who came to those schools from circumstances of poverty and who, like me, did not have proficiency in English. It was in these policy roles that I realized that policymakers and practitioners of education do not always act on the very best theory, proven educational practices, or even promising educational innovations. They act on purely political interests, many having nothing to do with benefiting the present or future status of children, families, or the social institutions we have created to assist them. I realized the importance of the politics of education. "Gene's" voice is often dominated by these lessons, although "Eugene" is not totally unaffected by them.

GENO

There is still one other voice that will contribute to the analysis of diversity, Hispanics, and schooling in the remainder of this book—one identified best by the endearing name that my mother chose for me, "Geno." In my large Catholic family, to baptize a child was a distinct honor, and in recognition of that honor, *los padrinos*—the godparents—were given the authority to name the child. My eldest sister and her husband were selected by my parents to serve as my padrinos. My sister was enchanted with the name "Eugene," and that is how I came to have a Greek name in a cohort of brothers and sisters named Antonio, Emelio, Cecelia, Ciprianita, Abel, Federico, Tiburcio, and Christina and born of parents named Lorenzo and Juanita. All these solid Hispanic names adjusted for biblical raíces (roots). (My youngest brother did not escape my fate—he was named Ernest. Why? Because his padrinos liked the name.) Of course, my mother could not pronounce "Eugene," and to her and my immediate family, I became "Geno."

"Geno" carries a distinct sense of cultural "Hispanic-ness," "Chicanismo," "Latino-ness," and "Raza-ness." These all reflect a deep regard for the linguistic and cultural raíces that foster who he is. This is best exemplified by a lesson from my father, again while I was young and not as understanding as I am today, as an *educado*—a term my parents used to identify an individual became formally educated. While I was growing up, winter was a time to prepare for work. And it was during one farm winter in the high plains of Colorado where I was born and raised that my father pointed to an *árbol* (tree)—a cottonwood tree as I recall—near our home. He asked simply, *"Por qué puede vivir ese árbol en el frío del invierno y en el calor del verano?"* (How can that tree survive the bitter cold of winter and the harsh heat of summer?) My father was not a man of many words—he was characterized by relatives as quiet and shy—but when he spoke, we all listened very carefully. I remember struggling to find an answer. I was also characterized as quiet and shy, but I tried to respond to my father. I rambled on for some time about how big and strong the tree was and how its limbs and trunk were like the strong arms and bodies of my elder brothers, particularly the two who were serving in the U.S. Army during the last phases of the Korean War. Then, he kindly provided a different perspective by referring to a common Spanish *dicho* (proverb): *"El árbol fuerte tienen raíces maduros."* (A strong tree has mature/strong roots.) In articulating this significant piece of the analysis that was absent from my youthful ramblings, he made very clear that without strong raíces, strong trees are impossible—and we do not even see the raíces. In a Spanish class many years later, a teacher extended this lesson further by pointing me to a more elaborate dicho: *"Del árbol caído, todos hacen leña."* (From a fallen tree, anyone/everyone can make firewood.) What became clear to me at that moment was the more substantive lesson my father was framing—if you have no raíces, how can you withstand the tests of the environment that surely will come and prey on your vulnerabilities?

Without those raíces, any tree can be transformed from a beautiful living organism to a fallen entity. For me as an individual with a set of cultural raíces, if my raíces were to die and I were to be stripped of the integrity that lies in those raíces, then I would also disappear.

For many Hispanics in this country, their raíces have been either ignored or stripped away in the name of growing strong. Many have been directed to stop speaking Spanish, to perceive their culture as one less-than, and to assimilate as quickly as possible so they can succeed in American society. And, unfortunately, many have suffered the fate of the rootless tree—they have fallen socially, economically, academically, and culturally. Like that fallen tree, they have been transformed and forever lost the individual and cultural integrity that their ancestors once thrived on, even in circumstances of poverty and social hostility.

But for "Geno," my mother made it very clear, strong raíces and their concomitant integrity and self-respect were not enough. As a mother, she wanted the very best for all her children, certainly not the long and painful fieldwork that she had endured for a lifetime. She wanted us *bien educados*—to have a set of formal educational skills. She made very clear that children needed *alas* (wings) as well, like the alas she insisted we children grew every night on falling to sleep so as to fly to heaven to be with God. All children, she said, were angels. Victor Villaseñor's mother, in recent stories by this Chicano author, elaborates further on this notion. His mother made it just as clear that the children flew to God each night and stationed themselves as stars in His heaven. Both mothers express a special regard for the sanctity of childhood and required children to have alas to perform their related roles. My mother made it clear that she could not provide the kind of alas that God and a good education could provide. She knew that the teachers and schools would have to take me further than she could personally. Education would provide the strong and elaborate alas for me to succeed where she often felt she had failed. God can provide you with strong spiritual alas, she reminded us—always go to church and follow His teachings. And go to school—strong alas like those of the *águila* (eagle) are what you need to raise your family and provide for them all that we have been unable to provide for you.

For Hispanics in this country, the emphasis on building alas in school has strategically focused on teaching English language skills: "Teach them English well, and they will succeed." Yet all educators realize that in today's information age, education must provide strong linguistic, mathematical, scientific, and technological skills. English literacy is important, but it is not enough. Yet Hispanics have been educationally shortchanged in these areas.

WHAT'S IN A NAME? WHAT'S IN A CULTURE? WHAT'S IN AN EDUCATION?

My sister looked forward to her first day at school. Her older brothers and sisters, this brother yet unborn, reminded her that school was important, even though they went to work while my mother accompanied her. Her school was a small one-room schoolhouse, and it, like the teacher, was held in high esteem by the local community—a rural Colorado community of farm and ranch owners and laborers. While her siblings had picked up some English, they spoke primarily Spanish, and my mother spoke only Spanish. Our European and indigenous ancestors, dating back before the arrival of the Pilgrims on Plymouth Rock, decided to stay in the territory seceded to the United States by Mexico in the Treaty of Guadalupe Hidalgo in the mid-1800s. They had retained the Spanish of their ancestors.

My sister will never forget her first day of school. She was asked by the teacher, "What is your name, little girl?" My sister responded, "Ciprianita." The teacher tried to pronounce the name and then respectfully requested, "Can I call you Elsie? It is my favorite name." In that one instant, my sister's linguistic and cultural heritage was politely and unintentionally challenged, and in my mother's presence, her child's "raíces" were metaphorically severed. The teacher's intent was positive. She meant no harm. It did not seem like a significant incident since scenes like these were common then (as they are today).

But my sister to this day still goes by the name of Elsie and tells this story with tears in her eyes. Changing a student's name, without consideration of the consequence, was a common occurrence. This incident marked an important attribute of schooling for her and other Hispanic children like her who came to school not speaking the schooling language, English. The most positive interpretation of this practice is that it reflects the general educational philosophy that who you are—poor, rich, Anglo, or Hispanic—does not matter in school. Everyone is treated as equals, and changing a name really is not that important. The most negative interpretation is that the practice signals an unwillingness to respect a student's cultural and linguistic background and sets the stage for still other practices that do the same. It might also suggest to the student and the family that they may not belong.

For Elsie and our family, the interpretation of this one action was somewhere between these interpretations. Elsie never did well in school, nor did she graduate from high school. And my mother often refused to do school visitations with any of us. However, neither my mother nor Elsie lost the notion that education was important. My mother continued to send

Elsie and all her children to school. Elsie left school when she felt that other things in her life, particularly work, were more important.

I had a similarly important day in my own school life. Like many of my senior high school classmates, I was called to the counselor's office to learn about my Scholastic Aptitude Test (SAT) scores. At the time, I must admit that I did not completely understand the significance of those scores.

However, I do recall taking the test on Saturday morning after having been high point man on our high school basketball team the night before. We had taken a bus to the game some 70 miles away from our town, and I did not arrive home until after midnight, having "celebrated" my accomplishment and the team's victory. I recall the principal of our high school congratulating me on my athletic performance as I entered the cafeteria for the test and how I daydreamed a bit of my future career in the National Basketball Association during the exams. Overall, I do not recall much about the test.

The counselor gave me a strange look as he handed me my SAT results report and provided me with his analysis. I had not scored too badly on my math, in the upper 500s, but my verbal score was low, only in the upper 400s. I recall his honest and respectful conclusion: "You'll do okay, but you will never be a college professor." Because of my low verbal scores, I lost my offer to attend the U.S. Naval Academy, which had very strict regulations about the minimum SAT requirements. Instead, I accepted an athletic tuition scholarship at the local community college. Of course, today I am a professor at one of the most respected universities in the nation, the University of California, Berkeley.

As I share these stories with Hispanics in this country, heads begin to nod, suggesting, "That happened to me or my family members." It is far too common a reaction. We were and are different. Many of us speak a language different from most teachers, and they want us to be like them, and, in most cases, even when we want to do exactly that, something gets in the way. Unfortunately, we often pay a heavy academic price. *It need not be that way.*

I learned early on about my differences. Our family and extended family were very close physically and emotionally. We gathered at least weekly with my several *tíos* (uncles), *tías* (aunts), and *primos* (cousins) to share food, religion, and general companionship. We had little social contact with *gabachos* (Anglos; this was not used as a derogatory term) other than in school or in the workplace—they were the bosses and we were the workers. We had no ethnic label for ourselves; we were not "Hispanic," "Mexican," "Mexican American," or "Chicano"—we were the Garcías, the Candelarias, the Vigiles, the Herreras, and so on. One of my nephews was asked as a little boy if he was "Chicano," and he responded, "No, I'm Catholic." When family members married, it was understood that the new couple would move in with us until they got on their feet. We even had our own family baseball team, made up of cousins. We could take on any ga-bacho team, and such friendly rivalries brought us even closer. The family was the first and last resort for support, assistance, and even recreation—it was the primary source of socialization and identity.

The family raíces were very strong and helped all of us to survive and even prosper. As an extended family, we negotiated work contracts with large farms to accomplish such related work as thinning sugar beets and picking peaches, apples, and pears. We worked hard and together in such work without serious dissension, without lack of "workforce continuity," and with clear accountability. Unfortunately, this cooperation did not help when it came to education. Our family valued education, but the adult members had not prospered in the schools. None had the opportunity to even attend a school on a continuous basis. But those same adults clearly understood the resources of a formal education. My father would say to all of us, *"Núnca te pueden quitar la educación."* (They can never take away your education—what you have learned.) My father and the extended family set out to teach us all they could—respect for family, respect for elders, respect of others, hard work, persistence, patience, the importance of our spirituality, and so on. But they could not teach us literacy, mathematics, science, and the entire culture of schooling. Yet my mother made it very clear that we would need schooling if we were to have the "wings" to carry us beyond the labor of the fields, the inadequacies of our economic situation, and our constrained intellectual circumstances. She spoke of her children needing *"alas del águila"* (wings of an eagle). She understood that the schools could provide us with those broad and strong wings.

It was in seeking those wings that I first realized the disadvantage of my differences. My home language was never spoken at school or even acknowledged. One of my tíos told us how he was punished for speaking Spanish on the school grounds, so we were careful never to do that. The very raíces of my past existence outside of school was specifically dis-counted. I realized that I did not do things that had value in the school culture. I did not take summer vacations—we worked the hardest and lon-gest in the summer. I did not go to visit Grandma—she lived with us. (For some reason, this was not as valuable as visiting her.) I did not visit the library—we lived 10 miles from the nearest library, and the only vehicle we had was shared for purposes of making a living. I was always individ-ually respected—I was never accosted by any teacher for my individual presence as a student. And I was treated "equally." But the linguistic and cultural milieu in which I was socialized and lived was not given equal respect. It was most always considered irrelevant or sometimes negatively regarded. (I recall the high school football coach responding to a group of us "Mexicans"—that was his term for us—after we informed him that we could not come to the required, pre–fall semester football practices because we were all picking peaches with our families. "You are either football players or peach pickers, you decide," he said. That stopped our football team participation. There was no choice for us. As a young student, I was quiet and complacent, accommodating to the classroom and school but never feeling a part of it, never thriving there. *It need not be that way.*

When I tell this story to gabachos, the obvious question arises, "Then how do you account for your success?" My answer is that I was the only one who did succeed. In my immediate family, less than 50 percent of us graduated from high school, and no others went on to postsecondary education. I am the exception, not the rule. My success can most likely be attributed to my family, who always supported me in my educational endeavors (I was the "baby" of the family, the one who profited from the experiences of those who went before); the athletic ability that won me scholarships; and key teachers who did respect me and my raíces and who insisted on high standards. But I am the exception. Among my school *compadres* (companions), I can name several who are in prison, some who died in the Vietnam War, some who are presently on welfare, a few who graduated from high school, fewer who attended college, and none who completed college. Unfortunately, the same is true of my own extended family.

Educational improvement for Hispanics in the United States rests on several presuppositions:

- Access to formal education continues to hold the promise of enhanced physical, economic, social, and cultural well-being.
- To honor diversity is to honor the social complexity in which we live—to give the individual and where he or she has developed a sense of integrity.
- To unify with others in this nation is absolutely necessary, but to insist on it without embracing diversity is to destroy that which will allow that unity—individual and collective dignity.

On the first of these presuppositions, there is little disagreement. However, concerning the subsequent points, there is significant disagreement. Linda Chavez, in her 1991 book *Out of the Barrio: Toward a New Politics of Hispanic Assimilation,* offers a rather different view of what will assist Hispanics in the future and why the well-being of Hispanics has been declining:

Every previous group—German, Irish, Italians, Greeks, Jews, Poles— struggled to be accepted into the social, political and economic mainstream, sometimes against the opposition of a hostile majority. They learned the language, acquired the education and skills, and adapted their own customs and traditions to fit into an American context. Assimilation proved an effective model for members of these ethnic groups, who now rank among the most successful Americans, as measured by earnings and education. But a quarter of a century ago another model emerged and challenged assimilation as a guide to the behavior of ethnic groups. This model originated in the civil rights movement of the 1960s. (Chavez, 1991, 2)

The civil rights movement, Chavez argues, and the concomitant legislation and government emphasis on assuring equity along racial lines encouraged Hispanics to maintain their language and culture, their separate identity, in return for rewards apportioned them as a disadvantaged minority group. She further maintains that Hispanic leaders promoted the disadvantage syndrome so that their organizations could profit from the local, state, and federal resources aligned with the civil rights efforts. In this scenario of the Hispanic circumstance in this country, Hispanics' failure to assimilate is to be judged as the cause of limited economic, social, and educational advances. The failure to assimilate, in turn, is placed on the influence of Hispanic leaders who are envisioned, much like the pied piper, as leading mesmerized followers to their own demise, all for their own personal gain.

Chavez is not alone in identifying the "failure to assimilate" as a reason for Hispanic student underachievement. Richard Rodriguez, in his 1982 autobiography *Hunger of Memory: The Education of Richard Rodriguez—An Autobiography* paints a troubled self-portrait of a successful academic career based on his forced assimilation at the hands of dutiful nuns. He suggests that at least part of his educational success required him to leave behind what was "Mexican." Learning English early on, he argues, allowed him access to the best literature and broader understandings of U.S. society than his Mexican parents' Spanish language or culture could provide. Moreover, having assimilated and become successful, his individual identity and accomplishments were compromised by his identification as a Mexican American, a disadvantaged minority group member. He wanted only to be identified as an individual and was opposed to being a member of any ethnic group. This assimilation set him free as an individual, but he perceived himself continually constrained by society's efforts to place him in an advantaged group, as an ethnic minority with a good education. He accuses individuals and social institutions of awarding him privileges (scholarships, fellowships, and jobs) on the basis of his ethnicity, not because of the merits of his work. The result, he concludes, was a perversion of good intentions gone very wrong—frustrating, confusing, and negatively affecting ethnic group members themselves.

Who is right? Linda Chavez, Richard Rodriguez, or Eugene/Gene/ Geno? Or are others who have debated the advantages of moving societies into homogeneity (from Plato to Thomas Aquinas to Bill Bennett) or promoting heterogeneity (from Aristotle to Martin Luther to Paulo Freire) right? This debate is not new either in this country or worldwide, at this time or in early literary histories. Nor is it confined to the main subject of this book—Hispanics. The Afrocentrism debate is alive and well in the U.S. African American community. Its promoters suggest that only recognizing and addressing the Afrocentric-based principles and knowing African history will enhance the well-being of the U.S. African American community. Its detractors argue that it is nothing more than disguised reverse racism. It places blame on others for the negative well-being of this community and misdirects and further inflames racial divides.

This debate is an emotional one. It can get personal and dirty. However, that does not mean that I wish to avoid it here. I only wish to bring some sensibilities and empirical information to light regarding this debate and its direct relationship to the education of Hispanic children in today's schools. I am convinced that new conceptual frameworks regarding human development, teaching, learning, and schooling, along with new research-and-development efforts in classrooms and schools, can help in the analysis of this ongoing and critical set of debates. This is the main task of this book. I will admit that it will get personal at times—just like the earlier pages in this book and much like the insightful writing of Richard Rodriguez. In addition, it will get philosophical and political, just like the important contributions of Linda Chavez. But it will be primarily a broader work of educational theory and research—neither of which is exemplified in the work of Chavez or Rodriguez.

In the search for sensibility, simple answers to complex questions are always prized. Chavez and Rodriguez provide the basis for a simple answer to the question regarding Hispanic student underachievement: the individual and social/economic influence on the individual not to assimilate. It is just not that simple. My approach will "complexify" this understanding. This is not to suggest that the search for simple, straightforward "explanations" is to be disregarded. Einstein is credited, rightly or wrongly, as saying that "we need to simplify explanations but avoid making them too simple." Therefore, my approach attempts to bring into perspective numerous contributing "causes" that alone cannot account for a phenomenon. By articulating these interactive ingredients, a better understanding of a phenomenon can be gained. We should not fear complexity. Rather, we should attempt to use it to better our own analytical processes. In complexifying the issue of Hispanic student circumstances, we can move away from superficial "tip-of-the-iceberg" analysis and more fully understand the course of events through more comprehensive articulations of these circumstances. In that way, the phenomenon becomes treated more integratively and becomes more comprehensible. Once comprehensible, it becomes more possible to act in ways that affect undesired outcomes exposed in the analysis.

2

Culturally Diverse We Are, Equal and United We Are Not

INTRODUCTION

The continuing attention to educational reform in the United States is a marvel, with some 10 to 20 national reports being published annually, ranging from preschool to higher education. These reforms have focused our attention on many variables that today influence our educational institutions and others that will inevitably affect our future "schooling" endeavors.

Allow me to turn to several issues that have underlined this continuous attention to the education of our children:

- Societies—past, present, and future—rest on the fundamental educational capabilities of their individual members. In our present, we must prepare our children for the future.
- Our own society finds itself at a significant competitive disadvantage, with that disadvantage increasing relative to the "new" global economic context. In that developing economy, international trade will be the focus. Presently, 1 in 10 U.S. jobs is related directly to international trade. In the next two decades, it is estimated that over 50 percent of U.S. jobs will be related to international trade—or the global economy. We will no longer "make and sell" for and to ourselves.

- Education has become a major activity of noneducational institutions, with only one-third of formal educational endeavors occurring within primary, secondary, and postsecondary educational institutions.
- Today's sixth-graders will likely average 7 to 10 job changes in their working lifetime along with two to three career changes. My father was an agricultural worker and died an agricultural worker. I have had four jobs, though only one profession. My daughters will likely change jobs 10 times and change professions two or three times.
- Only 8 percent of tomorrow's jobs will require less than a high school education, while 35 percent of these jobs will require at least a high school education, and a whopping 60 percent of tomorrow's jobs will require three or more years of postsecondary education.
- Eighty percent of new jobs will be in the information and service sector of the economy. Employees in these sectors must be flexible, computer literate, creative, and highly communicative (preferably in more than one language) and have good "people skills."
- We have sustained major value shifts in the last three decades. Women in this country can choose something other than education or nursing as a profession. In addition, we are being transformed by "new" sexual, recreational, health, environmental, and familial value shifts.

Under these new and developing circumstances, what is the role of the school? It seems evident that schools cannot provide adequate job training skills. The job market is much too volatile, and employers themselves have found it necessary to provide highly tailored job-related training. Therefore, schooling must take on several responsibilities, some similar to and some significantly different from those in the past and present:

1. Schools must serve children well with regard to the development of academic skills. We need all individuals to be communicative and literate linguistically, mathematically, and technologically.
2. Schools must shift their emphasis to the development of broader "living" processes that will enhance human relationships, critical thinking, and civic responsibility.

In essence, in the new curriculum of 2000 and beyond, schooling must become collaborative, highly social in nature, and process oriented. Memorizing facts to regurgitate to a teacher has never been part of quality education. It will become even less valued as facts become more easily accessible via electronic memories. Students' lives, even more than our own, will face continuous social, economic, and technological change. However, these students as adults must be able to react to these changing situations: They must act as well-informed individuals, reasonably with reflection and analysis, no matter what the specific employment, civic, or cultural context.

It is this cultural context that I wish to address in greater detail in this book. In short, we are a country of incredible cultural and linguistic diversity. Yet we are singularly nationalistic, "American" to the core, but, as of yet, unaccepting of the diversity among us. Recent sociological perception data suggest that over the last three decades, "majority" Anglo adults have not changed their view of minority populations—they continue to be perceived as less intelligent, lazy, and of lower moral character. This is absolutely frustrating considering that within these three decades we have witnessed a civil rights movement, a women's movement, and an equal educational opportunity initiative. Millions of dollars and, more significantly, millions of person-hours have been dedicated to addressing the inequalities and human injustices of our age. The University of California, Berkeley, where I am a professor, now has rethought its commitment to intellectual excellence by eliminating affirmative action. The reason: Affirmative action discriminates against Anglo students and favors underrepresented minority students. Anglo students and their parents raised the issue of "reverse discrimination" in a situation where minority students remain significantly disadvantaged with regard to University of California participation: General eligibility of high school seniors is at 15 percent, while Latino (4 percent), African American (4.5 percent), or American Indian (1.5 percent) eligibility rates are significantly lower. It is highly significant that these feelings of reverse discrimination exist in California's elite Anglo student body. These students have directly benefited the most from our enriched educational system.

In a nationwide survey of families, researchers have found evidence of serious disruptions of family relations occurring when young children learn English in school and lose the use of the home language. This study revealed that while language-minority parents recognize the importance of English and want their children to learn it at school, they do not want it to be at the expense of the home language. Many of the parents expressed a concern that their children will lose their native language and become estranged from their families and cultural heritage. Others reported that their children had already lost or were losing the native language.

An interviewer told the story of a Korean immigrant family in which the children had all but lost the ability to speak their native language after just a few years in American schools. The parents could speak English only with difficulty, and the grandmother who lived with the family could neither speak nor understand it. She felt isolated and unappreciated by her grandchildren. The adults spoke to the children exclusively in Korean. They refused to believe that the children could not understand them. They interpreted the children's unresponsiveness as disrespect and rejection. It was only when the interviewer, a bilingual Korean–English speaker, tried to question the children in both languages that the parents finally realized that the children were no longer able to speak or understand Korean. The father wept as he spoke of not being able to talk to his children. One of the children commented that she did not understand why her parents always seemed to be angry.

It may take years before the harm done to families can be fully assessed. One family that has been in the United States for nearly 20 years showed how breakdowns in family communication can lead to the alienation of the children from their parents. The four children, who are now teenagers, have completely lost their ability to speak or understand Spanish. The children are ashamed of Spanish, it was reported. They do not acknowledge it when their parents speak it, even though it is the only language the parents know. The mother says her 17-year-old son is having problems in school. He is often truant and is in danger of dropping out. She has tried to influence him but cannot because he does not understand her. A recent attempt at discussion ended in physical violence, with mother and son coming to blows when words failed them. Have we come a long way? I am afraid not.

THE CHALLENGE

The United States has long been a country of incredible cultural and linguistic diversity. This trend of ethnic and racial population diversification continues most rapidly among its young and school-age children. Nationwide, white non-Hispanic student enrollment has decreased since 1976 by 13 percent, or a total of five million students. As the overall total of the U.S. student population has decreased from 43 million to 41 million students (pre-K to grade 12) since 1976, the following demographic student indicators have become educationally significant:

1. Minority enrollment as a proportion of total enrollment in elementary and secondary education rose from 24 percent in 1976 to 34 percent in 1996.
2. As a proportion of total enrollment, Hispanics increased from 6.4 percent in 1976 to 12 percent in 1996. The number of Hispanic students increased from almost 3 million in 1976 to more than 4.5 million in 1996, an increase of 52 percent.
3. During this same period, Asian/Pacific Islander students increased from 535,000 to 1,158,000, an increase of 116 percent (National Center for Education Statistics, 1998).

The demographic transformation that has become more evident since the 1990s was easily foreseen at least that long ago. Our future student growth is as predictable: In a mere 40 years, white students will be a minority in every category of public education. Unfortunately, these emerging majority ethnic and racial background students continue to be placed "at risk" in today's social institutions. The National Center for Children in Poverty (1998) provided a clear and alarming demographic window on these "at risk" populations. Of the 21.9 million children under six years of age in 1990, who will move slowly through society's institutions—family, schools, the workplace—five million (25 percent) were living in poverty. Although less than 30 percent of all children under six years of age were nonwhite, over 50 percent of these children in poverty were nonwhite. In addition, these children continue to live in racial/ethnic isolation. Some 56 percent lived in racially isolated neighborhoods in 1966, 72 percent resided in such neighborhoods in 1994, and 61 percent of these children in poverty live in concentrations of poverty where 20 percent of the population is poor.

With regard to schooling, high school or equivalent completion rates are alarming for these emerging majority student populations. In 1994, the high school completion rate for the U.S. population was 81.1 percent for 19-year-olds, 86.5 percent for 24-year-olds, and a very respectable 86 percent for 29-year-olds. For blacks and Hispanics, the rate of completion in all age-groups was close to 60 percent (U.S. Department of Education, 1998). With regard to academic achievement, in 1997, 30 percent of 13-year-old-students were one grade level below the norm on standardized achievement levels. However, this differed significantly for emerging majority and white students: 27 percent for white students, 40 percent for Hispanic students, and 46 percent for black students.

Much more eloquent than any quantitative analyses of this situation is a recent unsolicited letter from a new high school English teacher in Los Angeles communicating the circumstances of educating students in an urban setting to a previous colleague:

Hi . . .
   Here's the report from the Western Front. Please pass it around.
   What I initially perceived to be innovative use of year-round scheduling seems to be more mechanization run amok. Although they apparently were able to split the kids into three separate tracks with different vacations with little or no problem, the track system has virtually NO academic benefit, at least the way it operates here. There are about 600 9th and 10th graders per track and about 200 11th and 12th graders per track. Look at the dropout rate (near 50% if not more). And the school just received a 3-year accreditation rather than a 7-year so things are pretty bad.
   In short, this school and school district are nightmares.
   For instance, there is no attendance accountability or follow-up except for homeroom. No period-by-period reporting of attendance to the central office.

The only phone calls home are for kids who miss homeroom. So kids can—and do—just show up for homeroom and "ditch" all their other classes, and unless a teacher inquires, but no one bothers, absences are invisible to the central computer and administration. I have about 20 students on my rolls that never saw this semester, even once. Or kids can pick and choose which classes to go to and there is no central administrative accountability.

Reading and writing levels are grotesque. I have only four students who are operating above grade level who could function in an honors program. That's out of 150 on the rolls.

Teacher support is nil. I still don't have a stapler or even file folders for portfolio writing assessment. The trash is emptied maybe once a week. The floors are filthier than some bars I've been in, and the bathrooms and stairwells stink. Half the lights are out in most classrooms and every third and fourth light works in the dark hallways. The school, in addition to being year-round, which presents logistical difficulties for a good periodic cleaning, is also used for a night adult school. That means it is being used for twice the time [of] an ordinary building. But it gets worse. Zero maintenance. Zero, zero, zero. Except for in the main office area, I have yet to spy a custodian doing anything during the day.

The dress code is not enforced . . . gangster wear is the norm, not the exception . . . and the administration, besides making occasional announcements, do nothing . . . thus none of the teachers care to stir the pot by even trying to enforce dress codes. Tardies are not enforced. This is LA and despite that kids are wandering through the halls and all over the campus all the time. There is one computer lab for Math, four or five computers in the library and that's about it. The textbooks left for me to use were 1980 copyright 10th grade lit books, and there were only enough for a classroom set. And, of course, all except one of the short stories was about teenage white (male) characters, and these kids Just Don't Relate to that. Plus, despite this being a major ESL school, no supplementary resources "enrichment" materials exist that I can find that contain black or brown or multi-national short stories or poems. . . . They do know the main players in the OJ drama, but one must be careful here when making allusions to that. The Maya Angelou books were in pieces. The book accountability procedures here are non-existent.

The administrators don't deal with discipline . . . there is a dean system here. The administrators do assign lockers, handle student picture IDs, write attendance excuses and other similar executive tasks. The principal is an elegant looking woman who looks like an aging movie star . . . and mentally, she is like the "Sunset Boulevard" movie character waiting for her closeup with Mr. DeMille.

There is one counselor per 1,000 students, an ESL program for half the students that doesn't seem to be upticking tests scores or achievement. Half the kids don't bring ANYTHING to school let alone pens and paper; forget assigning homework. I have 21 students with perfect attendance and no discipline problems. Half of them turn in work that is perhaps 4th or 5th grade level; the others don't turn in anything at all. But they are all there every day.

I asked other teachers what to do about grades. Well, if they make it every day, pass them with a D even if they don't do anything. Other kids I see one day and then don't see them again for two weeks. The sixth period English class has 37 students on the roll and I have an average of 14–17 in daily regular attendance.

There are few AP classes but few students pass the tests. Kids who miss school for field trips and football games are not listed on an excuse sheet nor is there any other official notification. They just tell you they were on a field trip and you mark the grade book accordingly. I guess.

Very few—perhaps 10%—of the kids are black and so far the only white kids are from Armenia or Russia with the occasional native white kids spotted here and there. The black kids were jubilant over the OJ verdict; the other (mostly brown) kids were split, but I could see no pattern there. Among grown-ups, middle class blacks seemed chagrined or outraged over the verdict but the lower class, high school–educated security guards were also jubilant. Most teachers were outraged over the verdicts, but the white ones were especially quiet about it. On the day of the verdicts, I had an incredible number of absences. Perhaps some stayed home for fear of riots, but the next day, one kid TOLD ME he stayed home in case of a riot so he could get some FREE STUFF. It was a canceled Christmas. This really works my white male middle class nerves . . . and the other teachers report the same experience. The Rodney King riots were in the immediate vicinity of the school . . . fires burning everywhere, they said, and this is in the mid-Wilshire area which is where all the hoity toity northwest Austin types of buildings and residences are, despite the "port of entry" school population.

I asked the Union Steward if all the schools in LA were as screwed up as this one. He said that he has taught only at LAHS but that he hears it is the same way but the sad thing is that it doesn't have to be that way. Indeed. The English teachers here are solid, intelligent and superb. But they all tell me to forget everything I know and just do the best you can with what tools you have and forget how it could be. The faculty has rich experience, but I have never seen so many good ideas from attendance to technology disappear into such a black hole of central administrative and school administrative ennui.

These kids are sweet. What lives they have led. So many from El Salvador, fleeing the government violence. The native speakers are incredibly poor, but sweet kids. One kid, who works harder than any kid I have ever seen, literally just got off the boat from Korea in August. Another kid, from El Salvador, is as bright as the brightest I ever had. . . . I would give anything to get that kid out of here. . . . I have had the weird experience of having collaborative group work on short stories conducted in spoken languages other than English and then each group reports back to the entire class in English. But kids are kids. It's too bad this system here just processes them through, like the Pink Floyd mechanized conveyor belt "We don't need no education" song, but on a bad drug trip. (Garcia, 2001)

The qualitative description of education presented here is further affirmed for Hispanics by quantitative descriptions. This portrait of educational vulnerability has been a historical reality for Hispanic children in the United States. This population identifier, "Hispanic," is a relatively new census-related term. Of course, it has little appreciation for the diversity among such identified U.S. populations. That is, it is quite evident that such identified populations (Mexicans, Mexican Americans, Puerto Ricans, Cubans, Chicanos, Latinos, and so on) are quite heterogeneous linguistically and culturally both within and between such identified categories. However, educational interest spawned by a significant record of educational underachievement has generated educational programs, educational research, and a wide range of intellectual discussion regarding the "at risk" educational circumstances of these populations. Combined with the contemporary educational "zeitgeist" that embraces excellence and equity for all students, best reflected in the 1983 *A Nation at Risk* and the more recent national goals statement, *Goals 2000* (1994), attention to the underachievement of Hispanic students has been significant. The major thrust of any such educational effort aimed at these populations has been centered on identifying why such populations are not achieving and how schools can be "reformed" or "restructured" to meet this educational challenge.

The demographic attributes of Hispanic students in the United States are important. The initiatives targeted at these students have at times been synonymous with the schooling endeavors aimed at "poor," "lower class," "immigrant," "limited-English-proficient," "at-risk," "underachieving" and "dropout" students. As Gonzalez (1990) has documented, these children are usually perceived as the "foreigners," "intruders," or "immigrants" who speak a different language or dialect and hold values significantly different from the American mainstream. These perspectives have led policymakers (including the U.S. Supreme Court) to highlight the most salient characteristic of the student (the racial, national origin, and language differences) in their attempts to address the historical academic underachievement of these populations. The following discussion will include an expanded discussion of "vulnerability" factors both within and outside the schooling arena along with demographic data of particular relevance to the schooling of this growing population of students:

1. An overall demographic assessment of factors related to the schooling of cultural diverse populations, including issues of poverty, family stability, and immigrant status.
2. An in-depth discussion of academic-related issues, including comparative data with regard to dropouts, academic performance, and overall high school completion.
3. A particular analysis of the challenges associated with the growing

number of Hispanic language-minority students—students who come to school with no or limited proficiency in English.

The U.S. Census Bureau, in its attempts to provide clarifying demographic information, never fails in confusing us. With regard to documenting the racial and ethnic heterogeneity of our country's population, it has arrived at a set of highly confusing terms that place individuals in separate, exclusionary categories: white, white non-Hispanic, black, and Hispanic (with some five subcategories of Hispanics). Unfortunately, outside the census meaning of these terms, they are for the most part highly ambiguous and nonrepresentative of the true heterogeneity that the bureau diligently seeks to document. Therefore, it is important to note at the outset of this discussion that these categories are useful only as the most superficial reflection of our nation's true diversity. I do not know many census-identified "whites," "blacks," or "Hispanics" who truly believe they are "white," "black," or "Hispanic," but given the forced-choice responses allowed them in census questionnaires, they are constrained by these choices. Racially and culturally, we are not "pure" stock, and any separation by the Census Bureau, the Center for Educational Statistics, or other social institutions that attempts to address the complexity of our diverse population representation is likely to impart a highly ambiguous sketch.

Having consented to this significant restriction with regard to efforts aimed at documenting population diversity in this country, I must still conclude that an examination of the available data in this arena does provide a fuzzy but useful portrait of our society and the specific circumstances of various groups within our nation's boundaries. That sketch is one of consummate vulnerability for nonwhite and Hispanic (usually referred to as "minority") families, children, and students. On almost every indicator, nonwhite and Hispanic families, children, and students "at risk" are likely to fall into the lowest quartile on indicators of "well-being": family stability, family violence, family income, child health and development, and educational achievement. Yet this population has grown significantly in the last two decades and will grow substantially in the decades to come. Table 2.1 summarizes these factors for census-derived information related to Hispanics.

DIVERSE IN AMERICAN SCHOOLS WE ARE

At the student level, the most comprehensive report with regard to this growth trend was published in 1991 by the College Board and the Western Interstate Commission for Higher Education, *The Road to College: Educational Progress by Race and Ethnicity.* This report indicates that the

Table 2.1 Hispanic Demographics

I. General Demographic Character

A. Of the 30.4 million Hispanics in the continental United States, the following characterizes the population's ethnic diversity:

Country/Area of Origin	Number	Percentage
Mexico	19.5 million	64.3
Puerto Rican	3.8 million	10.6
Central/South American	3.0 million	13.4
Cuban	1.1 million	4.7
Other Hispanics	1.6 million	7.0

B. 96% of Hispanics are concentrated in California (31%), Colorado (14%), Texas (29%), and Arizona (22%). Other top states occupied by Hispanics are Florida (14%), Nevada (15%), and New York (14%).

C. Average age in 1993 is 26.75 years (compared to 35.5 for whites). Hispanic age increased by 2 years since 1983.

D. 200,000 Hispanics immigrate legally to the United States yearly, 40% of all legal immigrants. (An estimated 200,000 Hispanics immigrate illegally.)

E. The Hispanic population grew 35% since 1990 compared to 8% growth in the general U.S. population. The census projects that Hispanics will be the largest minority group by the year 2005.

F. 17 million Hispanics report speaking Spanish in the home.

G. 90% of Hispanics live in metropolitan areas, 52% in central cities.

II. Indices of "Vulnerability"

A. Median family income has increased by 5.8% from 1995 to 1996 (to $24,906). In the past, the median income fluctuated for Hispanics (1982, $23,814; 1991, $24,614; 1992, $23,912), remaining below non-Hispanics (1982, $35,075; 1991, $38,127; 1992, $38,015). Since 1972, Hispanic median family income has decreased because of the increasing representation of immigrants in the Hispanic population.

B. In 1996, 29.4% of Hispanic families lived below the poverty line compared to 27.2% in 1982.

C. In 1993, 1,239,094 Hispanic families (23.3%) were maintained by female heads of household (an increase of 0.5% from 1983, which was 22.8%, or 827,184). 48.8% of these households lived below the poverty line. The child poverty rate for Hispanics has increased more than for any other group and is about currently equivalent to that of African Americans.

D. 72.9% of Hispanics hold unskilled and semiskilled jobs compared to 50.8% of non-Hispanics.

III. Education

A. Approximately 50% of Hispanics leave school prior to graduation (70% leave by 10th grade). In 1997, about half of Hispanics aged 25 and older did not complete high school.

B. 38% of Hispanics are held back at least one grade.

C. 50% of Hispanics are overaged at grade 12.

D. 90% of Hispanic students are in urban districts.

E. 82% of Hispanic students attend segregated schools.

F. Hispanics are significantly below national norms on academic achievement tests of reading, math, science, social science, and writing at grades 3, 7, and 11, generally averaging one or two grade levels below the norm. At grade 11, Hispanics average a grade 8 achievement level on these tests.

G. Hispanics are placed in special education services six times more often than the general student population.

Sources: Council of Economic Advisers (1998), Reddy (1993), U.S. Bureau of the Census (1990, 1993b, 1997a, 1997b), U.S. Department of Commerce, Census Bureau (1996a, 1996b, 1996c, 1996d), U.S. Immigration and Naturalization Service (1994).

U.S. nonwhite and Hispanic student population has increased from 10.4 million in 1985–86 to 13.7 million in 1994–95. These pupils constitute 34 percent of public elementary and secondary school enrollment in 1994–95, up from 29 percent in 1985–86. White enrollment, meanwhile, rose by just 5 percent, from 25.8 million to 27 million, and their share of the student population dropped from 71 percent to 66 percent in 1994–95. According to this study, in 1994, nonwhites and Hispanics make up the majority of high school graduates in California, Hawaii, Mississippi, New Mexico, and the District of Columbia. By the year 2000, the nation's seven most populous states have joined this group.

Figures 2.1 and 2.2 graphically display this astounding student demographic shift. Figure 2.1 presents actual nonwhite and Hispanic K–12 public school enrollments from 1976 to 1986 and projected enrollments (calculated using the derived changes in enrollment from 1976 to 1986 as a base) by decade through 2026. Figure 2.2 presents similar data by focusing on the percentage of total nonwhite and Hispanic student enrollments. Each figure depicts the dramatic transformation of our nation's student body. Nonwhite and Hispanic student enrollment will grow from 10 million in 1976 to nearly 45 million in 2026. These students will grow from 23 percent to 70 percent of our nation's school enrollment during this relatively short time period. *In 2026, we will have the exact inverse of student*

Figure 2.1. K–12 public school enrollment projections: Total versus nonwhite and Hispanic enrollment.

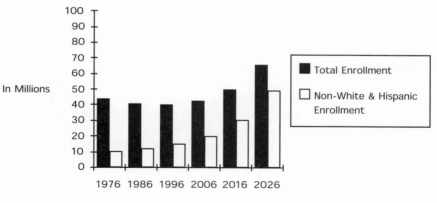

Source: U.S. Department of Education, Office for Civil Rights, *Directory of Elementary and Secondary School Districts and Schools in Selected Districts: 1976–1977,* and 1984 and 1986 Elementary and Secondary School Civil Rights Survey. As cited in U.S. Department of Education, National Center for Education Statistics (1991, 68).

Figure 2.2.   K–12 public school enrollment projections: Percentage of nonwhite and Hispanic enrollment.

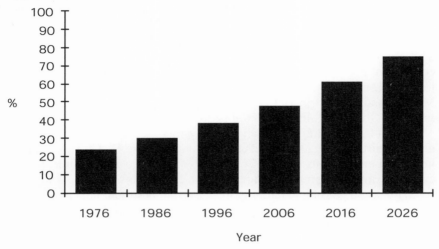

Year

Source: U.S. Department of Education, Office for Civil Rights, *Directory of Elementary and Secondary School Districts and Schools in Selected Districts: 1976–1977,* and 1984 and 1986 Elementary and Secondary School Civil Rights Survey. As cited in U.S. Department of Education, National Center for Education Statistics (1991, 68).

representation as we knew it in 1990, when white students made up 70 percent of our enrolled K–12 student body.

Figure 2.3 provides a more concentrated assessment of Hispanics population growth from 1970 through 2050. Hispanics were about 1 of every 20 Americans in 1970 and 1 of every 12 Americans in 1990 and are projected to be 1 of every 5 Americans in 2050.

Moreover, Hispanics are distributed widely throughout U.S. schools. Figure 2.4 provides some indication of their distribution in 10 states, with a range of 10.7 percent in Illinois to 45.8 percent in New Mexico. This population of students have remained in rural areas in the same proportion over the past 20 years while growing significantly in the urban and metropolitan areas (see fig. 2.5). The most significant growth has been in the central cities.

In the decades to come, it will be virtually impossible for a professional educator to serve in a public school setting, and likely in any private school context, in which his or her students are not consequentially diverse—racially, culturally, and/or linguistically.

Children and Family Well-Being

Although this book's primary agenda deals with educational concerns, such concerns cannot be appropriately addressed without attending to re-

Figure 2.3.   Hispanic population, 1970–2050: Percentage of total population.

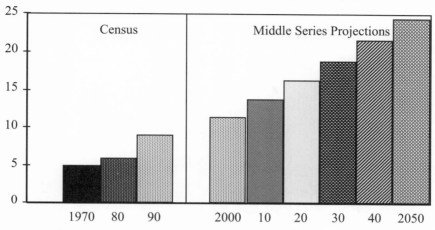

Source: U.S. Bureau of the Census (1995).

lated indicators of children and family well-being. Children who are healthy and who live in safe and secure social and economic environments generally do very well in today's schools. Poor students are three times more likely to become dropouts than students from more economically advantaged homes. Students who do not reside in these environments are placed "at risk" in today's and likely tomorrow's schools. The previous documentation regarding the dramatic demographic realities of present and future student enrollments would be more informed by addressing these nonschool but related economic and social circumstances of our emerging majority culturally and linguistically diverse students. Unfortunately, on a number of related measures of children and family well-being, the circumstances are bleak for this growing body of students.

According to the National Center for Children in Poverty in its 1990 report *Five Million Children,* 14 million children and youth under the age of 18 (approximately 20 percent of our total population in this age category) resided in circumstances of poverty in 1986. This was an increase of some two million since 1975. Of this increased total, 6.5 million, or 45 percent, were nonwhite and Hispanic. Projections indicate that unless poverty is checked in very direct ways, the number of children and youth in poverty will nearly triple by the year 2026, and almost three-fourths of those children and youth will be nonwhite with more than half Hispanic.

The overall family circumstances of these children over the next decades are also alarming. Given that most elementary school–age children presently reside in families headed by persons under the age of 30, evidence indicates that these families will be economically disadvantaged as mea-

Figure 2.4.   Hispanics as a percentage of total population and of public school enrollment for the United States and selected states, 1997.

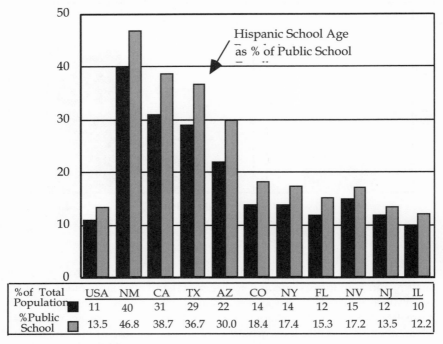

%of Total	USA	NM	CA	TX	AZ	CO	NY	FL	NV	NJ	IL
Population	11	40	31	29	22	14	14	12	15	12	10
%Public School	13.5	46.8	38.7	36.7	30.0	18.4	17.4	15.3	17.2	13.5	12.2

Source: U.S. Bureau of the Census (1997).

sured by the median income for families headed by persons under the age of 30. All families in this category have experienced and are projected to experience a decrease in economic capability. Particularly vulnerable again will be families headed by persons who are nonwhite and Hispanic. By 2026, the median family income for nonwhite and Hispanic families is projected to be $10,000 per year below the national average. Children in families with income below the poverty level are nearly twice as likely as their more advantaged classmates to be held back a grade level and as young people from low-income families enter the labor force to earn additional income for themselves or their families. While work experience during adolescence can have positive effects, recent research indicates that working more than half time during the high school years can undermine academic performance. As for those students from non-English home environments, over 90 percent in 1991 met poverty guidelines that allowed them to receive free or reduced-price lunches (Developmental Associates, 1993).

The inevitable conclusions that can be drawn from this "well-being"

Figure 2.5.   Percentage of public school students who are Hispanic by metropolitan area.

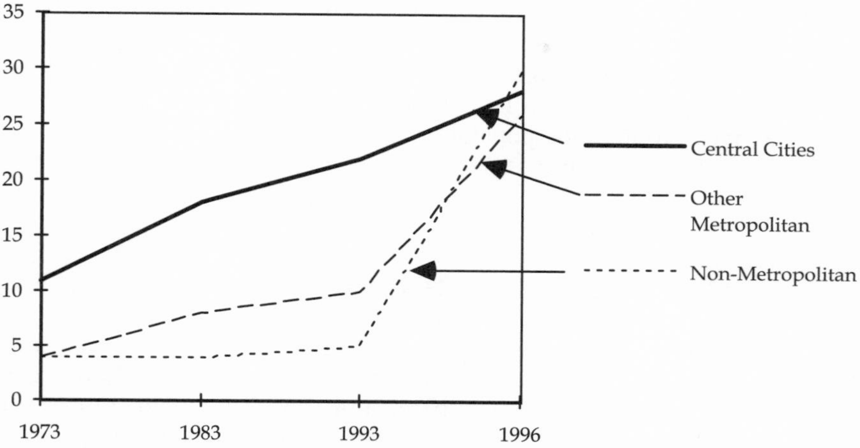

Source: U.S. Department of Commerce (1996).

data are that school-age children and their families, particularly those from Hispanic ranks, will be placed in future economic and social situations that will enhance their social, economic, and educational vulnerability. Today's educators and, even more significantly, educators of the future will be challenged by a growing cultural and linguistic diverse student body that will come to school from situations that are already identified as educationally disadvantageous. Even though educators will have little to do with ameliorating those situations, they cannot be ignored in the academic setting.

Academic Well-Being

Dropout Rate

In our present society, one major indicator of public school success is completion of high school. The second national educational goal adopted by the 1990 Education Summit in Charlottesville, Virginia, and placed into legislation in 1994 with the passage of Goals 2000 aimed to increase the high school completion rate to 90 percent by the year 2000. Unfortunately, the dynamics of school completion are not well understood, and the cause-and-effect relationships are unclear. Much confusion stems from the variety of methods utilized to document the school completion phenomenon. The National Center for Educational Statistics (NCES) considers this complexity in its reports by enumerating a set of dropout rates:

Event rates report: Within a single year, the percentage of students who left high school without finishing work toward a diploma. This is a measure of the actual event of dropping out.

Status rates report: At any given point in time, the percentage of the population of a given age range who either (1) have not finished high school or (2) are not enrolled. This measure reflects the current status of a given group in the population at large (not just students).

Cohort rates report: Over a given time period, what happens to a single group of students. This measure reflects changes in any given group over time.

Status and cohort reports provide a view of high school completion since they take into consideration what happens to students after they leave school. These type of reports indicate that high school completion rates for ages 16 to 24 have generally declined in the last 20 years. In this age group, the status rate went from 16 percent in 1968 to less than 13 percent in 1989 (Kaufman and Frase, 1990). In 1989, about four million persons in the United States aged 16 to 24 were high school dropouts. Roughly, then, 87 percent of all U.S. students receive their high school diploma or its equivalent by the age of 24. Unfortunately, this is not the case for subsets of students. Measured by either event or status measures, nonwhite and Hispanic students drop out at two to three times the rate of white students. During the period 1989–90, about 8 percent of Hispanic students dropped out of school each year, an event rate almost twice as high as that for whites; 7 percent of black students dropped out during that same period. More revealing are the status report data. In 1990, among the population aged 16 to 24, only 67 percent of Hispanics had completed high school or its equivalency, while 86 percent of blacks and 88 percent of whites were in this category. These same data indicate that high school completion rates are highest in central cities and metropolitan areas and lowest in suburban areas. Figure 2.6 provides a capsule look at Hispanic educational attainment.

For Hispanic students, particular educational attainment with regard to immigration and English-language proficiency is revealing (see figs. 2.7 and 2.8). In 1989, foreign-born 16- to 24-year-old Hispanics were twice as likely to not have completed high school as first- or second-generation U.S.-born Hispanics (fig. 2.7). However, even first- and second-generation Hispanics were twice as often identified as not completing a high school education as the general U.S. population in that same size cohort. Having been born in the United States was not an indicator of substantive high school completion. Similarly, reported English proficiency is related to the dropout rate for Hispanics (fig. 2.8). Eighty-three percent of Hispanics aged 16 to 24 who reported knowing English "not very well" were identi-

Figure 2.6.   Educational attainment, 1998.

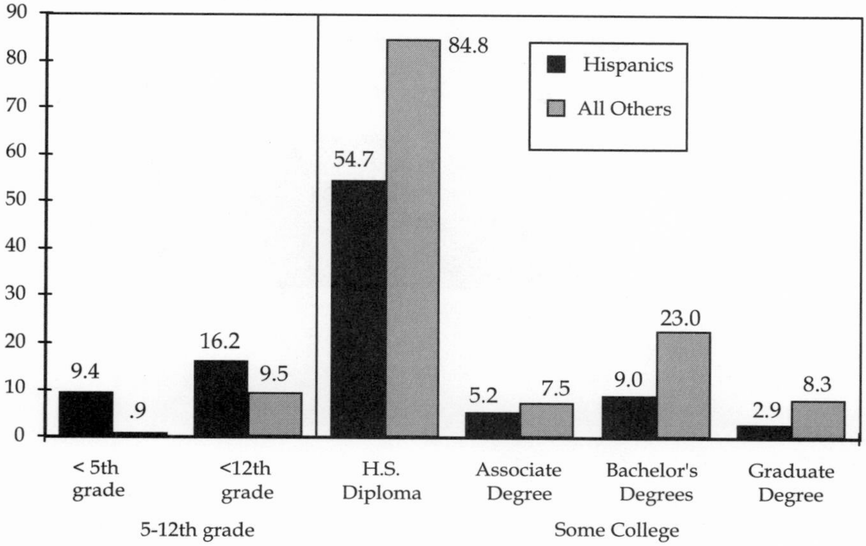

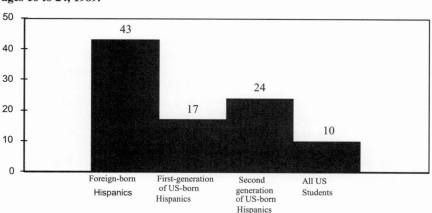

Source: U.S. Department of Commerce (1998).

Figure 2.7.   Percentage of Hispanics who had not completed high school, ages 16 to 24, 1989.

Source: U.S Department of Education (1998).

Figure 2.8.   Status dropout rate for Hispanics who do not speak English at home, ages 16 to 24, 1990.

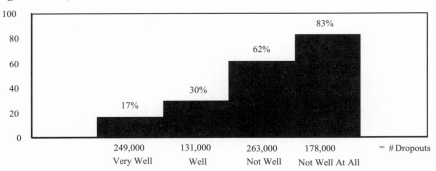

Source: U.S. Bureau of the Census (1993a).

fied as status dropouts, while 17 percent of Hispanic students who reported knowing English "very well" were identified as dropouts in the same age cohort. Unfortunately, the 17 percent rate is still almost twice as high as the national average.

A study by the U.S. General Accounting Office (1994) reports that Hispanic dropout rates varied by country of origin: 36 percent for Central American, 34 percent for Mexican American, and 12 percent for South American and Cuban cohorts. In short, immigration status, including country of origin and English-language proficiency, is related to Hispanic student dropout rates, but they alone cannot account for the rate of Hispanic student dropouts, which is twice that of the general population.

In a national study of middle school dropouts, Rumberger (1995) reported that the single most powerful predictor was whether a student was held back in an earlier grade. Hispanics are held back a grade level at three times the rate of the general student population. When broken down by ethnic group, a more complex set of relationships emerged. Specific factors were associated with some groups but not for others. For example, misbehavior, changing schools, and low grades increased the probability of dropping out for blacks and whites but not Hispanics. Yet the rate of absenteeism was associated with dropping out for all groups. Such findings continue to suggest that simple answers to the causes of dropping out are not easy to come by.

For Hispanics, socioeconomic status, immigration status, being held back a grade, and English-language proficiency seem to be most associated with noncompletion of high school in the present schooling environment. These types of conclusions regarding the associated factors for Hispanics' dropping out have been used to explain the phenomenon and to prepare particular solutions (Chavez, 1991). But such conclusions are based on the *characteristics of school dropouts* rather than on the *schooling of these dropouts*. Only when two sets of analysis come together with the *characteristic of Hispanic graduates* and the *schooling of those graduates* will we better understand this phenomenon. Later in this book, an effort is made to do exactly that.

Academic Achievement

Having determined that high school completion is problematic for the students of concern in this book, how do these students do while they are in school? The NCES has again generated a set of data that addresses this question. The most revealing data concern the modal grade level achievement as measured by standardized measures of academic achievement over several years, 1983 to 1989. This measure attempts to assess the relative number of students who are not achieving at the "normal" and expected level. Overall, these data indicate that the percentage of students one or more years below modal grade level has increased for boys and girls and for whites, blacks, and Hispanics at each age level over the period reported. However, an interesting pattern emerges for whites as compared to blacks and Hispanics. At the age of eight, there is little difference between whites (24.5 percent), blacks (25.1 percent), and Hispanics (25.0 percent) with regard to academic nonachievement. But, at the age of 13, the discrepancy is quite significant: whites 28.8 percent, blacks 44.7 percent, and Hispanics 40.3 percent. From roughly third grade to eighth grade, academic achievement drops off significantly for blacks and Hispanics as compared to whites. Moreover, this effect is more attenuated for boys than girls. The unfortunate result is that 40 percent or more of black and Hispanic students are one grade level or more below expected and normal achievement levels by the eighth grade. This revelation, in concert with the previously discussed high school completion and dropout data, raises substantive educational concerns. Figure 2.9 provides math and reading achievement data on the 1990 National Assessment of Educational Progress (NAEP) for whites, Hispanics, and blacks.

The data indicate that math and reading achievement in Hispanic and black students is two to three times less on NAEP measures of moderately complex procedures and reasoning but not dissimilar to whites on NAEP measures of beginning skills and understanding. Such data suggest that the academic and intellectual quality of education that Hispanics and blacks receive is substantially different. More bad news for Hispanics.

But there is good news in another longitudinal study that tracked NAEP achievement from 1975 to 1990 for 13- and 17-year-olds (Rand Corporation, 1994). Figures 2.10 to 2.13 depict significant trends indicating educa-

**Figure 2.9.   NAEP mathematics (a) and reading (b) assessments for 17-year-olds,
1996. Data are average scores and percentages at levels 200 and 300.**

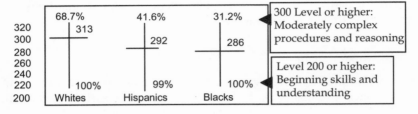

NAEP Mathematics assessment 1996 for 17-year-olds
Average score, and % scoring at 200 and 300 levels

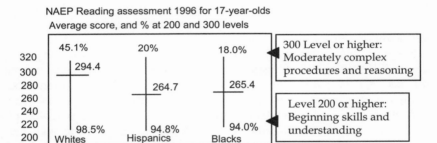

NAEP Reading assessment 1996 for 17-year-olds
Average score, and % at 200 and 300 levels

Source: Campbell et al., 1996.

tional achievement gains by Hispanics. Specifically, higher gains in verbal
and math scores were observed for Hispanics and blacks than for whites
from 1975 to 1990 (figs. 2.10 and 2.11). In addition, the gap in math and
verbal achievement between Hispanics and whites and between blacks and
whites was significantly reduced from 1975 to 1990. Although it is difficult to attribute this "good news" to any specific variable, the authors of
this study suggest that enhanced resource investments in education may
account for such results. They come to that conclusion by controlling statistically for the differences of socioeconomic status and family background characteristics.

Financial Resources

Educational financing in the United States is not without its national, state,
and local complications. On the average, 90 percent of any educational

Figure 2.10.   Change in NAEP verbal scores by racial/ethnic group for 13- and 17-year-old students, 1975 to 1990.

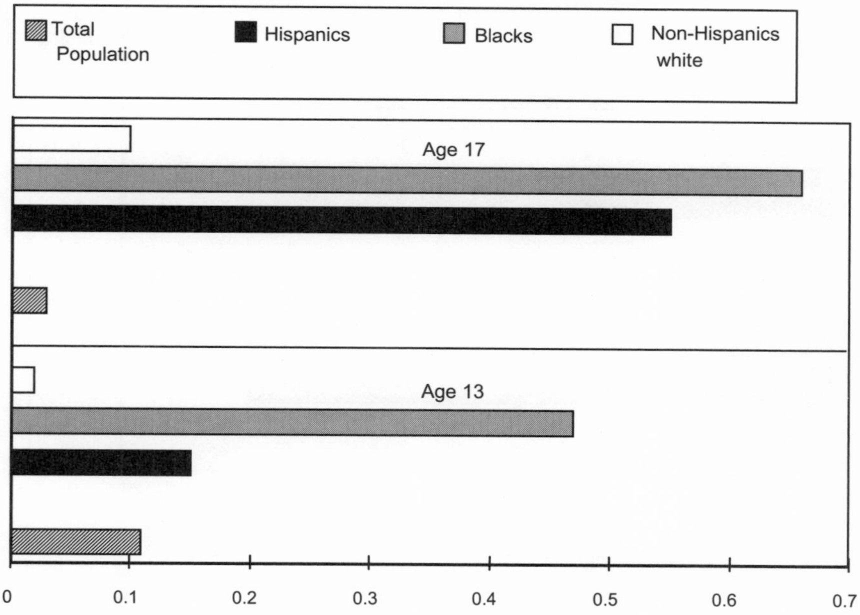

Source: Rand Corporation (1994).

expenditure consists of tax dollars flowing directly from local or state sources. Less than 10 percent of these expenditures come from federal sources. Although funding for education increased substantially in the United States during the 1980s, education spending actually declined slightly as a proportion of the gross national product to just over 3.5 percent, the lowest for all "developed" countries. Nevertheless, in real terms, overall state and local spending rose 26 percent between 1980 and 1988. However, the federal share actually decreased by 2 percent.

Keep in mind that nonwhite and Hispanic children reside primarily in central city and metropolitan areas in highly populated pockets of racial and ethnic segregation immersed in neighborhoods of concentrated poverty (Kozol, 1991). These children are likely to attend troubled schools with fewer resources and larger classes (National Commission on Children, 1991). Moreover, these children have been more negatively affected than others by recent changes in educational funding policies. The reduction of federal assistance to education, including that for compensatory education and desegregating school districts, has reduced the fiscal resources directly available for the education of these children (Levin,

Figure 2.11.   Change in NAEP mathematics scores by racial/ethnic group for 13- and 17-year-old students, 1975 to 1990.

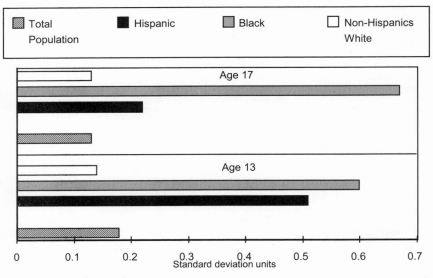

Source: Rand Corporation (1994).

Figure 2.12.   Comparison of differences between racial/ethnic groups in NAEP verbal scores, 1975 and 1990.

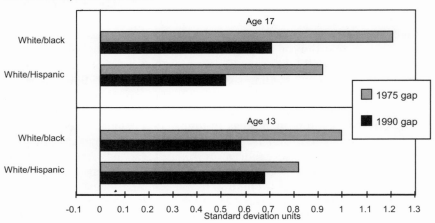

Source: Rand Corporation (1994).

Figure 2.13.   Comparison of differences between racial/ethnic groups in NAEP mathematics scores, 1975 and 1990.

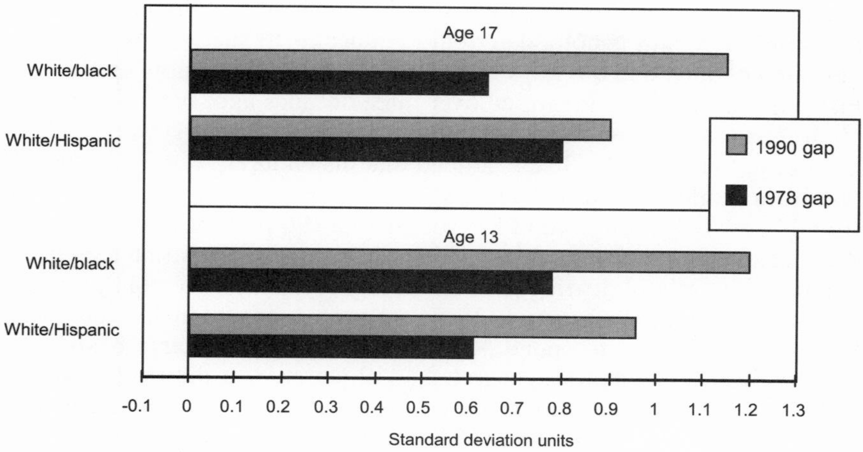

Source: Rand Corporation (1994).

1986). Districts that cannot be integrated because they lack white students are not eligible for enhanced funding available to establish science and math magnet schools, an emerging federal funding priority (Oakes, 1990). In such schools, educational personnel have not accepted the educational buzzwords of the 1980s—"restructuring," "reform," "teacher empowerment," "site-based management," "teacher competencies," "outcome accountability," "national goals," and so on. Instead, they are concerned about the bare necessities, for example, windows, books, typewriters, heat in buildings, working bathrooms, lighting, and a renovated building (Kozol, 1991; Rose, 1989).

These schools have been transformed into institutions that must spend valuable time seeking the resources for basic survival. They are much like developing countries that beg for grants, loans, and so on from one source after another. These schools "beg" from city, state, federal, business, and charity sources. They do so only because the basic resources are not provided by present funding structures and formulas. In fact, those structures and formulas are working to their disadvantage. These students attend schools in cities and taxing entities in which competition for tax dollars is great. These same communities have high unemployment and underemployment and are pressed to provide a higher level of related social services. These communities are competing to retain businesses. These variables directly affect the resources that can be directed to education.

Most directly, students in these schools are relatively underfunded, even in times that argue for "fairness" in school financing. Our society makes quite clear that we abhor the notion of social privilege. We strongly believe in an aspect of the "American Dream" in which an individual's or his or her family's wealth is not a deterrent to educational success. Yet such beliefs are not upheld in the ways in which we allocate educational resources. Fiscal disparities were identified over three decades ago. In a now famous 1968 legal case, Demetrio Rodriguez, a parent of the Edgewood School District in San Antonio, Texas, argued that his children were underfunded relative to children in an adjacent school district, only a few miles away from his own. The Edgewood School District (96 percent nonwhite) residents paid a higher tax rate than residents of that nearby district, a predominantly white school district and community. Yet they were able to generate only $37 for each pupil. With resources provided by the state, Edgewood was able to spend $231 per student on a yearly basis. The neighboring school district generated $412 per student drawing on its locally lower tax rate and, with resources from the state, was able to generate a yearly per pupil expenditure of $543. This amounted to over a 100 percent differential.

Professional Educational Personnel

The previously given demographic information has indicated that diversity in our schools is a recent but explosive and long-term phenomenon. Teachers, administrators, and other educational professionals receiving their training over a decade ago were not encumbered by the challenges facing preservice teaching candidates today. They did not "need" to be ready to respond to the challenge presented by a highly diverse student body. Moreover, few individuals from the ranks of the emerging majority succeeded academically themselves a decade ago and so were not and are not in the teaching profession. In fact, for the 1993–94 school year, of the 2.6 million public and private school teachers and the 103,000 school administrators, over 88 percent were white, and less than 12 percent were nonwhite and Hispanic—8 percent black, 3 percent Hispanic, and less than 1 percent American Indian, Native Alaskan, and Asian or Pacific Islander. In this same academic year, nonwhite and Hispanic academic enrollment was over 30 percent.

It remains evident that the vast majority of school teachers and administrators are white and will continue to be white in the near future, while the proportion of nonwhite and Hispanic students continues to increase rapidly. Although it is difficult to identify specific attributes of teachers that have served a diverse student body effectively, recent efforts have attempted to do so. Unlike earlier reports that have identified and described effective programs, recent efforts have sought out effective programs and/

or schools and then attempted to describe the specific instructional and attitudinal character of the teacher. Dwyer (1991) identifies four domains that "good" teachers excel in: content knowledge, teaching for student learning, creating a classroom community for student learning, and teacher professionalism. Villegas (1991) has extended these four domains when the student population served by the teacher is culturally and linguistically diverse. She suggests that "good" teachers in these classroom contexts are required to incorporate culturally responsive pedagogy.

A concern for the effectiveness of teachers is not new. From the earliest days of education program evaluation, the quality of the instructional staff has been considered a significant feature. Unfortunately, for programs serving "minority" students, the evaluation of "effectiveness" has been consumed by a concern regarding the significance of the multicultural aspect of the curriculum and, for many Hispanic students, the use or nonuse of the students' native language and the academic development of the English language. Very little attention is given to the attributes of the professional and paraprofessional staff that implement the myriad of models and program types omnipresent in the service of these students. Typically, attention to the characteristics of such a staff is restricted only to the years of service and the extent of formal educational training received. Yet most educational researchers will grant that the effect of any instructional intervention is directly related to the quality of that intervention's implementation by the instructor(s).

A recent report issued by the California Commission on Teacher Credentialing verified that a disproportionate number of poor and minority students are taught during their entire school career by the least qualified teachers because of high teacher turnover, larger numbers of misassigned teachers, and classrooms staffed by teachers holding only emergency (temporary and not state-approved) credentials.

It is important to note that professional teaching organizations such as the National Education Association (NEA), the American Federation of Teachers (AFT), and the National Association for the Education of Young Children (NAEYC), to name a few of the largest professional educational organizations, have addressed the specific need for teachers to receive special training in areas that relate to teaching the growing diverse student body. Certification agencies, such as the National Council for Accreditation of Teacher Education and the California Commission on Teaching Credentialing, have included particular provisions related to "multicultural" education that institutions of higher education must implement if they are to be accredited as teacher training institutions and their graduates considered positively as candidates for state teacher credentialing.

Is this presently an acceptable situation for meeting our growing need to train and assess the competencies of teachers who more and more will face the challenges of a diverse student population? Unfortunately, because of the explosion of this diverse population and our own professional unpreparedness (we are learning how "best" to do it at the same time that we are doing it), the limited number of expert teachers available, and the diversity of students and therefore programs that serve these students, the training and assessment of teachers is highly problematic.

In summary, the teaching expertise of those professionals charged with meeting the challenges of educating Hispanics is highly questionable. These individuals have not been well prepared. We are far from achieving the instructional expertise that will effectively meet the growing challenges. However, that challenge is not dissipating, and many educators will likely be called on directly to assist in developing and implementing educational initiatives that will meet that challenge. These educators will not just be actors in this domain; they will be strategically involved in writing the script.

CONCLUSION

Making sense of demographic data within the realm of education and related domains is like trying to make sense out of the U.S. economy only by exploring the vast array of statistics that we as Americans compile about our nation's economic well-being. As we all know, no one can obtain a clear understanding of the "economy" simply by examining those statistics, no matter how comprehensive, strategic, or ingenious those numbers are. The same is true for the education of Hispanic students in this country. However, much like the economy, education is an important part of our social fabric. Most of us have been to school, just like most of us work and decide how to spend our money, and we utilize educational and related educational statistical patterns, much like we use economic statistics, to help us understand the nature of the enterprise through the description of the status or well-being of the economic indicators. In the statistical analysis presented in this chapter, a representation of specific educational indicators for Hispanics has been presented with the understanding that such a description can add some depth but not a total understanding to the challenge that today's and tomorrow's educators face with regard to this population.

Following with the "economy" metaphor, what do these descriptive data tell us about that challenge? It is unmistakable that the number of students who will populate our schools, that will fuel the "economy," will be radically different with regard to race, culture, and language within a relatively short period of time. In less than two decades, half our students will be nonwhite and Hispanic, with half those students speaking a language other than English on their first day of school. A teacher will likely be responsible for the education of a more diverse student body than any teacher at any time in the history of formal education since the turn of the 20th century. This will be true at all levels of education. These growing populations of students will undertake their schooling with several "economic handicaps." They are and will be coming "to the workplace" from social and economic circumstances that will likely leave them more vulnerable to the various "instabilities and unpredictabilities" that they will encounter in the "marketplace." Those unpredictabilities are a result of an increased global competitive climate in which educational success is an absolute must and a world in which our fundamental knowledge base is growing exponentially.

These students are likely to be underresourced, lacking important infrastructure. They are likely to have been "prepared" by individuals who do not meet the highest productivity standards. Moreover, many of these students will require learning in a language that is not their own. They will need to acquire the knowledge of the "economy" along with the language and culture in which that "economy" is immersed.

Yet these same data unequivocally indicate that the future of the economy rests with them. As they emerge as the majority, their success is our success and their failure our failure. They must succeed. To think of disbanding education in this country is analogous to thinking of disbanding the economy—it cannot be done. Can education rise to this challenge and accommodate students it has historically underserved but needs so desperately in the future? The remainder of this book will address important aspects of this question. It is important to add that type of depth to the understanding of this challenge.

3

It Doesn't Have to Be "Either/Or"

My wife and I joined the "Chicano movement" in 1970. She was working to support me while I "studied" my way through graduate school at the University of Kansas. She was from a little town in southern New Mexico known as Central, near the larger but still small town of Silver City. She had grown up in a "Chicano" family, spoke both Spanish and English (although her Spanish was better than mine), and had very strong "roots" in the culture of that family and community. We were married in 1969. We were both a long way from our families. However, we managed to find family-like support. We found the local Hispanic Catholic parish—Our Virgin of Guadalupe Church. There, and through other "Chicano" acquaintances we had made at our jobs and ones I made playing softball, we were adopted by new Chicano families. We became part of the Escobar, Rodriguez, and Renteria families. We joined the "Chicano movement," far from the heart of that movement in California, Texas, and Colorado, because we identified with its cause—equal educational opportunity—as it related to us and our "new family" in Kansas.

But we also had other friends who were like family and had other causes: the Guesses, the Baers, the Livingstons, and so on. These individuals worked with us in pursuit of educational opportunities for mentally retarded children. We all felt strongly that much more could be done. We believed in that cause—equal educational opportunity—for the children we served. We worked to support the Special Olympics and often brought institutionalized, "retarded" children home with us on weekends.

It was not unusual for us to attend a cocktail party with one group of friends or family on a Friday night and on that same weekend attend a *quinceñera* (a traditional Mexican celebration of a young girl's entrance into adult society) on a Saturday. At one gathering, we would speak mostly English and at the other mostly Spanish. The music we enjoyed in one gathering ranged from classical to rock and in the other from *Mariachi* to *Norteñas* and sometimes rock but never classical. We moved comfortably between "cultures." While there were similarities across those "cultures" and significant differences, we did not have to choose between them. We were respected and enjoyed, and we prospered and received support from each one. It was not an "either/or" situation. In short, this type of existence is the ideal for Hispanics in the United States. During a time when the U.S. Congress holds hearings on "English Only" laws, proponents of such laws would have us believe that homogeneity in language and culture must be promoted by the government. Some of these same proponents often argue for keeping government out of people's lives, but not on this issue. Yet individuals like me, representing most Hispanics in this country, move back and forth comfortably between languages and cultures, most of the time without many problems. Often it is a linguistic, social, and economic advantage to be able to do so.

I find it discomforting when the executive director of the organization English First proposes that citizens must know English before they can vote. My mother did not speak English, through no fault of her own, yet she was committed enough about her participation in this country's democracy to vote in every presidential election—sometimes for the Democratic candidate and sometimes for the Republican one. This shows more commitment on her part than the 40 percent of U.S. citizens who do not vote but do speak English. She was born in this country, as were her parents; she worked hard all her life, raised 10 children, and taught us more than anyone about respecting others. How can someone like this be the target of disrespect in a democracy committed to "equality and justice for all"? My mother's experience can shed light on the debate over English as an official language. Simply stated, the argument is made that if she had learned English, she would have been a better and more participatory citizen. Yet my mother voted, contributed to her community, and raised four sons who served in the armed forces, and no child of hers is on the "government dole." I know English-speaking mothers who have sons in prison and sons and daughters on welfare. Is English-language proficiency, then, a significant determining variable for good citizenship? What my mother could have profited from was better educational opportunities.

I realize that at the center of this discussion are strong personal feelings about my culture. What follows attempts to move beyond that. It is an effort at a more thoughtful, comprehensive, and integrated "complexification" of the issues of "culture" and its conceptual meaning in today's diverse societies. It is also an overview of how Hispanics in this country have been treated in the "culture wars"—from Americanization to bilingual and bicultural education.

HISPANICS IN THE UNITED STATES AND THE CONCEPT OF CULTURE

When we speak of "the culture" to which an individual belongs, our reference is generally to the system of understandings (values, prescriptions, proscriptions, beliefs, and other constructs) and characteristics of that individual's society or some subgroup within his or her society—that is, ethnic minorities, social classes, countercultures, generations, sexes, and occupational groups. This is the traditional notion of culture employed by functionalist anthropologists in their analyses of the behavioral patterns and normative customs of groups.

The culture concept, with its technical anthropological meaning, was first defined by Edward Tylor in 1871 as "that complex whole which includes knowledge, belief, art, law, morals, custom, and other capabilities and habits acquired by man as a member of society" (Kroeber and Kluckhohn, 1963, 81). Since Tylor's time, a great variety of definitions of culture have been advanced by anthropologists. These definitions commonly attempt to encompass, as did Tylor's, the totality (or some subset of the totality) of humanity's achievements, dispositions, and capabilities. And virtually every anthropologist considers culture to be something that is learned as it is transmitted from generation to generation.

Most definitions of culture include another social dimension: the notion that culture is something that members of a group share in common. A recently published anthropology textbook states, for example, that behaviors and ideas may be considered cultural only insofar as they are shared among members of a social group. This formulation is useful for anthropological comparisons between societies or subgroups within societies. Its basic assumption, however, is that of uniformity in the cultural equipment of individual members of societies and their subgroupings. In this formulation, the ontological locus of culture is some kind of group.

At the same time, all anthropologists acknowledge that members of all sorts and sizes of societies display differences in their behaviors and ways of thinking and valuing. That is, societies are characterized to some extent by intracultural heterogeneity. But such discussions remain most often at the level of the group, as in statements about the "looseness" or "tightness" of societies' cultural systems. When these researchers proceed to write their ethnographies, they tend to ignore interindividual variations as they abstract what they apparently consider to be "an essential homogeneity from the background noise of insignificant diversity" (Schwartz, 1978, 49).

Along these lines, anthropologist Ralph Linton defined culture as "the sum total of ideas, conditioned emotional responses and patterns of habitual behavior which the members of (a) society have acquired through instruction or imitation and which they share to a greater or less degree" (quoted in Kroeber and Kluckhohn, 1963, 82). Although acknowledging that cultural items (ideas or learned behavioral habits) need not be totally shared by everyone in a group, in this concept it is, nevertheless, the property of sharing that defines the domain of culture.

This emphasis on shared traits is relevant to any consideration regarding a definition of culture. But such an emphasis on shared traits leaves little if any room for the conceptual recognition of each student's individuality within the framework of the culture concept. Individuality becomes the domain of psychology, relevant only to discussions of personality, while the culture concept is reserved for behavioral and ideational features of the individual's group.

The relevance of this problem lies in the possible consequences of the group-oriented culture concept for the perceptions and expectations of teachers in their interactions with children of a different culture than their own. It is easy to understand the contention that a group-oriented notion of culture may serve to detract the teacher's attention from the process. The connection between teacher–student interaction and the culture concept derives from the fact that assumptions about the student's "culture," whether right or wrong, may serve to stereotype the student and thus preclude the flexible, realistic, and open-minded quality of teacher–student interaction needed for effective instruction. This possibility becomes more apparent when one realizes that the educational process is fundamentally a process of social interaction.

Imagine a situation where a teacher is perplexed by some action or response on the part of a student who "is not like him or her." If the teacher has studied some of the anthropological characteristics of the student's ethnic culture, he or she may leap to an interpretation of the student's behavior in terms of idealized or modal characteristics attributed to that culture. To construe an individual's behavior solely on the basis of generalization about group traits is to stereotype the individual, no matter how valid the generalizations or how disinterested one's intentions may be. It would be better for the teacher to pursue the meaning of the student's behavior in the way ethnographers most often come to understand the people they study. Even though they write about cultures in collective terms, they come to know about them through observations of individuals. Of course, the teacher's efforts to understand the individual student could (and should) benefit from knowledge of cultural orientations that are widely or typically held in the student's ethnic community. But this fund of knowledge should be viewed only as background information. The question of its applicability to the particular student should be treated as inherently problematic. Many investigations of culture and schooling also caution educational personnel against hasty "ethnographic/cultural" generalizations on the grounds that all linguistic–cultural groups are continuously undergoing significant cultural changes.

Thomas Carter's early research (1968), along with that of Ogbu and Matute-Bianchi (1986) and Steele (1994), on expectations on student learning and classroom behavior—namely, that Chicano students may sometimes actualize in their behavior the negative expectations held for them by educators—confirms the concerns expressed here.

The Individual-Oriented Culture Concept

Fortunately, anthropological theory contains a parallel individual-oriented conception of culture developed and used by a number of psychologically oriented anthropologists. As Ted Schwartz notes, these theorists "invoked the individual in critical response to the superorganic view of culture, which often chose metaphors which would lead one to imagine culture as floating somehow disembodied in the noösphere or, at best, carried by human beings as a conductor might carry an electric current containing information" (Schwartz, 1978, 49).

An early expression of the individual-oriented concept of culture is seen in the work of a now forgotten anthropologist, J. O. Dorsey. Edward Sapir wrote the following about Dorsey's orientation:

> Living as he did in close touch with the Omaha Indians, [Dorsey] knew that he was dealing, not with a society nor with a specimen of primitive man . . . but with a finite though indefinite number of human beings who gave themselves the privilege of differing from each other not only in matters generally considered as "one's own business" but even on questions which clearly transcended the private individual's concerns. (quoted in Pelto and Pelto, 1975, 1)

Advocates of the individual-oriented approach to culture frequently describe a society's culture as a "pool" of constructs (rules, beliefs, and values) by which the society's members conceptually order the objects and events of their lives. The participation of individuals in this pool is seen as variable. Spiro (1951), for example, has distinguished between the cultural "heritage" of all members of a society (that which has been made available to them by their predecessors) and each individual's particular cultural "inheritance" (that portion of the group's heritage that he or she has effectively received, or "internalized," from the past). An individual also manipulates, recombines, and otherwise transforms his or her inherited constructs. This, together with the outright creation of new constructs, is a major source of culture change. The individual's own portion of a society's culture is termed by Goodenough (1981) as a "propriocept," by Wallace (1970) as a "mazeway," and by Schwartz (1978) as an "idioverse." This constitutes for these anthropologists the ontological locus of culture.

For some of the anthropologists employing an individual-oriented concept of culture, the private system of ideas of individuals *is* culture. Other individual-oriented anthropologists, however, reject the implication in such a notion of "individual cultures." As they see it, the contents of one subjective system cannot be considered a culture. Like Schwartz, these theorists consider a cultural system to consist of all the constructs available to a society's members. Nevertheless, the society is itself not the locus of culture; its individual members are. The culture is a distributive phenomenon in that its elements are widely distributed among the individual members of a society. A major implication of this distributive model of culture is a rejection of the traditional assumption of cultural homogeneity; it implies that each individual's portion of the culture differs in some ways from those of the other members of society.

For purposes of understanding "Hispanic" culture, it seems most appropriate to simultaneously recognize a Hispanic's ethnic culture (i.e., such individuals share with their ethnic peers constructs that are not shared with out-group members) and those characteristics that define each person as a relatively unique individual (all individuals are in some ways different from their ethnic peers). It also permits recognition of traits shared with members of the larger culture, such as those acquired through acculturation.

Acculturation is a crucial variable in the analysis of Hispanics, and its process contributes significantly to the existence of the heterogeneity of "Hispanic" cultures. Writing of Hispanic culture, Bell, Kasschau, and Zellman (1976) note, for example, that among Hispanics "many have ancestors who came to North America several centuries ago, but others are themselves recent immigrants. Hence, a simple cultural characterization of [this] ethnic group should be avoided" (vii). These authors also caution against a simplistic view of the process of acculturation, noting that acculturation may not be linear in the sense that one simply loses certain Hispanic attributes and replaces them with alternative attributes. The process may be characterized by more complex patterns of combination and by ongoing recombination than by simple substitution and, in addition to the fact of degrees of acculturation among individuals, would contribute to the cultural heterogeneity of the Hispanic population, that is, the relative uniqueness of its members.

I might add that some people are likely to respond to the individual-oriented conception of culture with the question, What about customs? Chicanos, for example, might point out to us that they recognize certain *costumbres* (customs) that distinguish them as a group from the larger society and from other Hispanics. This points to a realm of culture that is highly shared and more likely to belong to the public sphere than to the individual's subjective orientation. Referring to the "layered" nature of culture, anthropologist Benjamin Paul (1965) has observed, "What we call customs rest on top and are most apparent. Deepest and least apparent are the cultural values that give meaning and direction to life. Values influence people's perceptions of needs and their choice between perceived alternative courses of action" (146).

What I wish to emphasize here is the problematical nature of the variability and sharing of values and other constructs as internalized by individuals. The individual's participation in culture reflects his or her unique set of life experiences. This variable participation and the relative uniqueness of the individual that it engenders are important for education, as are the generalized cultural differences between ethnic groups. Educators must deal with both. This is true for all students but is particularly relevant for educators who serve learners—those who have internalized a different set of experiences—who come from a culture(s) significantly different than their own.

AMERICANIZATION

Historically, "Americanization" has been a prime institutional education objective for Hispanic children (Elam, 1972; Gonzalez, 1990; Garcia, 1994a). Schooling practices were adopted whenever the population of these students rose to significant numbers in a community. This adaptation established special programs and was applied to both children and adults in urban and rural schools and communities. The desired effect of "Americanizing" students was to socialize and acculturate the diverse community. In essence, if schools could teach these students English and "American" values, then educational failure could be averted. Ironically, social economists have argued that this effort was coupled with systematic efforts to maintain disparate conditions between Anglos and "minority" populations. Indeed, more than anything else, past attempts at addressing, for example, the "black, Hispanic, Indian, and Asian educational problem" have actually preserved the political and economic subordination of these communities (Spencer, 1988a). Coming from a sociological theory of assimilation, "Americanization" has traditionally been recognized as a solution to the problem of immigrants and ethnicity in the modern industrialized United States. Linda Chavez (1991, 1995a) continues to champion this solution today for Hispanics.

"Americanization" was intended to merge small ethnic and linguistically diverse communities into a single dominant national institutional structure and culture. Thomas and Park (1921a) argued that the immigrants' "Old World" consciousness would eventually be overcome by "modern" American values. Although I will not provide here a detailed review of the literature regarding the historical circumstances of the many immigrant populations that came to the United States, I will rely on recent analysis by Spencer (1988a), Gonzalez (1990), and Moreno (1999). According to Gonzalez (1990), there were important distinctions between European immigrants and other immigrant experiences regarding assimilation. First, the "Americanization" of the non-European community has been attempted in a continuously highly segregated social context. Hispanic students are more segregated today than three decades ago. Second, assimilation of these groups had both rural and urban aspects, whereas the European experience was overwhelmingly urban. Third, this assimilation was heavily influenced by the regional agricultural economy, which retarded a "natural" assimilation process. Finally, immigrants from Mexico, Puerto Rico, and other Latin American countries could not escape the effects of the economic and political relationship between an advanced industrialized nation, the United States, and semi-industrialized, semifeudal nations and territories, the latter increasingly under the political and economic sway of the United States. This relationship led to a very constrained immigration pool with only farm and low-skilled labor immigrating continuously to this country. None of the contributory European nations had such a relationship with the United States, and thus their national cultures tended to be judged more on an equal footing with nations or territories struggling to realize their interests against the nationalism of a rising world power. This factor alone would have made for a significant modification in the objectives and manner in which "Americanization" was applied to Hispanic background communities.

It can be argued that "Americanization" is still the goal of many programs aimed at culturally diverse students (Weis, 1988; Rodriguez, 1989; Garcia, 1999; Trueba, 1999). Unfortunately, "Americanization" for these students still means the elimination not only of linguistic and cultural differences but also of an undesirable culture. "Americanization" programs seem to assume a single homogeneous ethnic culture in contact with a single homogeneous "American," and the relationship between the two is not that of equals. The dominant community, enjoying greater wealth and privileges, claims its position by virtue of cultural superiority (Ogbu,

1987a). In one way or another, nearly every culturally diverse child—Hispanic, Asian, African American, and even white, non-English-speaking immigrants—whether born in the United States or elsewhere, is likely to be treated as a foreigner, an alien, or an intruder. The Los Angeles school superintendent voiced a common complaint in a 1923 address to district principals: "We have the [Mexican] immigrants to live with, and if we Americanize them, we can live with them." Unfortunately, even today the objective is to transform the diversity in our communities into a monolithic English-speaking and American-thinking and -acting community. This attitude was recently articulated by Ken Hill, a California superintendent who has received national and state distinction for his efforts in a district serving a large number of African American, Mexican American, and Asian American students: "We've got to attend to the idea of assimilation and to make sure that we teach English and our values as quickly as we can so these kids can get in the mainstream of American life" (Walsh, 1990). Hill is echoing the "Americanization" solution articulated over and over again for 70 years. It is important to note that the dropout rate for nonwhite students in Hill's school district was recently reported as over 40 percent.

The "Americanization" solution has not worked. Moreover, it depends on the flawed notion of group culture. The "Americanization" solution presumes that culturally different children are as a group culturally flawed. To fix them individually, we must act on the individual as a member of a cultural group. By changing the values, language, and so on of the group, we will have the solution to the educational underachievement of students who represent these groups. In essence, the groups should "melt" into one large and more beneficial "American" culture. The previous discussion regarding group- versus individual-oriented concepts of culture suggests that our educational efforts have been responding quite ignorantly with regard to the processes in which individuals and groups come together to form culture and how that understanding should inform educators. The challenge facing educators with regard to Hispanic students is not to "Americanize" them. Instead, it is to understand them and act responsively to the specific diversity that they bring and the educational goal of academic success for all students.

Language in the Americanization Effort

While the United States has never declared a national official language, the primacy of English in public affairs has been well established since the time of the earliest colonies (Crawford, 1999). This is so despite the reluctance on the part of the British colonial authorities and, later, leaders of the early republic to legislate matters of language—considered traditionally one of the most fundamental freedoms of civilized societies. English was considered a language of political, economic, and social power and prestige; its preeminence in the United States, as elsewhere, has been reinforced in recent times by its establishment as a language of technology. The association of English with technological advance, combined with the worldwide concern for "development" and "modernization," has been a major factor in the spread of English as an additional language in a large number of nonnative English-language societies. This recognition of English as a language of international importance reinforces the high status it enjoys domestically; this also serves as a partial explanation for the relative indifference that U.S. English speakers demonstrate toward their own monolingualism, regarded by some as a very serious national problem (Stanford Working Group, 1993).

Observers of U.S. language behavior minimize the role that sentimental attachments play in the attitudes of U.S. English speakers toward their language. Compared with other modern-language communities, English speakers tend not to see their language as particularly beautiful, expressive, or tied to the dominant political ideology (Ruiz, 1988). Instead, they have developed a strongly utilitarian or instrumental view of their language. Ultimately, this view has been elaborated into an orientation that sees English as an essential instrument of opportunity and eventual success: "Without a high proficiency level in English, one should not expect a good education or a good job." (Ruiz, 1985) In English proficiency lies the power to produce social goods for both individual and society. Therefore, in the United States, language is primarily a means to political power, economic attainment, and social prestige rather than a good in itself. In this orientation to language-as-means, a prerequisite concern centers around the issue that any language development not diminish the power of English. Some of the major public policy issues of the last decade have their roots in this concern: the "literacy crisis" declared by the National Commission on Excellence in Education in 1983, the need to teach English to language-minority populations and the birth of bilingual education as a means to do so, and the concern to "protect" and "enhance" the place of English in public life. Each of these language issues has targeted Hispanics in a major way.

In this debate, with Hispanics on center stage, the process of language policy development is embedded in one or more of three basic orientations: language-as-problem, language-as-right, and language-as-resource (Ruiz, 1990):

1. *Language-as-problem* construes the targets of language policy to be a kind of social problem to be identified, eradicated, alleviated, or in some other way resolved. Local vernaculars and their communities

are the most common "beneficiaries" of language policies aimed at moving them into dominant mainstream. In the officially received view, in the view of the outside community, and frequently in the view of the local community itself, the local vernacular is an important determinant of poverty and disadvantage; doing away with the problem involves doing away with the local language and replacing it with the dominant standard. This policy of subtractive multiculturalism is often regarded as benign by the dominant society—a way of providing for equality of opportunity. The often cited experiences of Hispanics punished for speaking Spanish at school or American Indians prohibited from speaking their native language at Bureau of Indian Affairs (BIA) boarding schools serve as examples. Contrast these examples with those of English who were encouraged and rewarded for learning Spanish as a foreign language in school and English-speaking missionaries who learned indigenous languages to convert the Indians.

2. *Language-as-right* often is a reaction to these sorts of policies from within the local communities themselves. It confronts the assimilationist tendencies of dominant communities with arguments about the legal, moral, and natural right to local identity and language; it refutes the notion that minority communities are somehow made "better" through the loss of their language and culture. The language-as-right orientation is most visible, however, when the dominant language-as-problem orientation is taken to extremes: When language diversity is seen as a problem *in itself,* calling for language eradication *as a condition of individual and social betterment,* legal and quasi-legal remedies are regarded by minority communities as the last step before war or surrender. The Navajo tribe has made it very clear that it has the right as a sovereign with the United States to retain its language.

3. *Language-as-resource* is an orientation that has received very little emphasis. It presents the view of language as a social resource; policy statements formulated in this orientation should serve as guides by which language is preserved, managed, and developed. To the extent that the language-as-resource orientations draws attention to the social importance of all communities and their languages and to the extent that it promotes tolerance and even acceptance of minority languages, it holds promise for reducing social conflict in a way that the other two cannot match. U.S. English and other advocates of an English Language Amendment (ELA) in the United States are proposing a significant language policy change. At the moment, U.S. policy approximates the following formal or "official" stance regarding English: a geographically widespread national language that

is not the declared, official language. It is not clear to me that there are benefits in the proposed policy change and how those benefits would outweigh the problems created by disengaging the present, very successful policy of language laissez-faire (Ruiz, 1990, 11–24).

By way of summary and conclusion, allow me to offer a set propositions by which we might understand language officialization, the ELA, and its problems, particularly for the circumstances of Hispanics in the United States:

1. *Language officialization is generally associated with nation building.* This suggests that officialization movements are evidence of the perception of instability. This is understandable in emerging nations struggling to establish a national identity. The emergence of language officialization movements in the 1980s, however, a period of unparalleled English hegemony domestically and internationally, is a puzzle. It was and continues to be also a time of extreme growth in immigration, Spanish-language speakers, and economic uncertainty. It was not a time of nation building. It suggests, perhaps, that the actual "risk" perceived by ELA movers is something beyond language.

2. *Language officialization is usually attended by some corpus planning.* This is merely a restatement of the language planning axiom that status planning and corpus planning should proceed more or less simultaneously; there are numerous examples of such simultaneous development. It is therefore important to ask what corpus planning activities are proposed by ELA advocates in the United States. There seem to be none. This language officialization movement seems to be not about language at all but about society. Language serves as a symbol for diversity and the diffusion of power; the perceived threat is not language but, rather, language communities and their potential to disturb existing relations in society. This sort of movement has correlates in other societies (Tollefson, 1986).

3. *Language officialization is usually poorly planned as to articulation and implementation.* In the best language planning circumstances, articulation and implementation are problematic. An important failure of ELA movements in the United States is the lack of thought as to how language officialization can be made consistent with our jurisprudential traditions (especially those dealing with free speech) and as to what the anticipated effects of the policy change might be, that is, the detailed consequences of officialization. Therefore, the movement can be seen as ideological and not instrumental (Ruiz, 1990).

Proponents of an ELA in the United States profess a concern for national unity; to that end, they seek to constrain the language behavior of non-English speakers. They could benefit. Although deliberate attempts to create national identity derives from a "values" position, forcing individuals to restrict their native language realization is not a very effective way of promoting national unity. Instead, that a sense of national identity is more likely to develop when it is not forced but allowed to emerge out of functional relationships within the society. This is that Hispanic experience in the US: Hispanics have retained their language and culture, shifted into English and have come to identify themselves as "Americans." (Ruiz, 1990)

The conflicts surrounding language politics and Hispanics are intense, much more so than if the questions involved were about merely education and meaningful participation. Perhaps it is important to recognize that this political debate, unlike most, can have important implications for what this nation is to become. As articulated by Ruiz (1984), at the root of any new language policy will be some fundamental assumptions about the future of the United States: that it will marshal its public and private resources to create a more viable and tolerant cultural pluralism, or not; that the nation's considerable language resources will be actively developed and conscientiously maintained, or not; that equal educational opportunity and quality of education will be seen as compatible, or competitors; and that the nation will begin to recognize its interdependence with the rest of the world, or else remain relatively isolated, hopeful that its military and technological influence and the power of its language are sufficient to maintain its preeminence. The posture that the United States takes toward the language question may well signal the orientation it brings to these other, more general social concerns. It is my own conclusion that we can have English and other languages play important roles in our society. They do so today. It does not have to be "either/or."

THE HISPANIC LANGUAGE-MINORITY STUDENT AND BILINGUAL EDUCATION

Like my brothers and sisters, I attended my first day of school as a predominantly Spanish speaker. More correctly, I was a Spanish/English bilingual speaker—the English came from my older brothers and sisters, who had learned English in a variety of settings, including their schools. My school's and teacher's practice, if not their policy, was one of neutrality with regard to my native language. For many of my aunts and uncles who had attended school, their experience was one of subtraction and replacement. That is, schools and teachers insisted that they stop speaking Spanish and replace it with English. Under such policies and practices, it was not atypical to request Spanish-speaking parents to refrain from speaking Spanish to their children and to switch to English instead. Such requests are similar to those that, in the late 1960s, some schools sent to parents, asking that they help their children in the "new math" or to those today regarding computer literacy, even though parents have no expertise in this new "language" of mathematics or information technology.

Whether the policy was subtractive or neutral, educational endeavors that I encountered never considered my language ability outside of English as a resource until I reached high school. At that level and beyond, knowing another language was considered an advantage. I was even requested by my Spanish teachers to help the disadvantaged English speakers acquire Spanish. But even then, my Spanish was not the Spanish of academic prestige. My Spanish was considered inferior to that of the teachers, most of whom had learned Spanish as a second language and who could not be understood well either in their Spanish-language classroom or in any Spanish-language community, including those in my own hometown. It is still difficult for me and many other Hispanics in the United States to understand these contradictions: Spanish is not good when you are young, but it is good when you are an adult; your native Spanish is not good, but those of nonnative speakers who are less communicative than you is good. Something is wrong with this picture.

The picture can be right only if there is something intrinsically bad about acquiring two languages when young—that is, it interferes intellectually or linguistically with development and learning—and if only one kind of Spanish is the "best." Neither of these conclusions holds any water. One need only observe that children around the world "normally" acquire more than one language without any intellectual or linguistically negative effects. If that is not enough, there is a rich research literature in psychology and linguistics that destroys such conclusions (Hakuta, 1986; McLaughlin, 1995). And, of course, no one Spanish-language dialect is more pristine or grammatically correct than another—Spaniards and Latin Americans have agreed on that for at least a century.

Yet I can attest to confronting this myth about my bilingual ability and Spanish-language ability, and so can other Hispanics in the United States. More than I ever thought possible, attempts to formally adjust our educational policy and practice to adhere to what we know continue to face the same long-standing negative perceptions, particularly with regard to policies and practices that promote native languages as a resource through programs we have come to label bilingual education. Linda Chavez (1991) articulates this position: "The history of bilingual education in the Hispanic community is marked by false hope and intrigue; it is a case study in the use of legislative, judicial, and administrative authority to promote an unpopular policy among an unsuspecting public" (8).

Implicit in this conclusion is that bilingualism is somehow detrimental to Hispanics and the public at large. My own experience argues against such a serious allegation. But that is not enough. Allow me to expand on the shallowness and unrepresentativeness of such a conclusion.

Policy

The education of students who come to our schools speaking a language other than English, language-minority students, has received considerable research, policy, and practice attention in the last two decades. The Department of Education as well as private foundations have supported specific demographic studies and instructional research related to this population of students, from preschool through college. The U.S. Congress has authorized legislation targeted directly at these students on six separate occasions (1968, 1974, 1984, 1987, and 1994), while numerous states have enacted legislation and developed explicit program guidelines. Moreover, federal district courts and the U.S. Supreme Court have concluded adjudication proceedings that directly influence the educational treatment of language-minority students. This significant attention has allowed answers to some questions of importance that were unanswerable less than a decade ago. The following discussion will highlight these questions and their respective treatment in light of emerging information regarding Hispanic language-minority students.

Who Are These Students?

I was a language-minority student when I entered elementary school in 1952. I spoke Spanish as my first language, and my home language was Spanish, although my older brothers and sisters had mastered significant English proficiency, as had I. In the present system of labels for such children, I would have been classified as limited English proficient (LEP). As one searches today for a comprehensive definition of the "language-minority" student, a continuum of definitional attempts unfolds. At one end of the continuum are general definitions, such as "students who come from homes in which a language other than English is spoken." At the other end of the continuum are highly operationalized definitions, "students scored in the first quartile on a standardized test of English language proficiency." Regardless of the definition adopted, it is apparent that these students come in a variety of linguistic shapes and forms. The language-minority population in the United States continues to be linguistically heterogeneous with over 180 distinct language groups identified. Even in the largest language-minority ethnic group, members of this "Hispanic" group are monolingual Spanish speakers, while others are to some degree bilingual. Other non-English-speaking minority groups in the United States are similarly heterogeneous. Not inconsequential are the related cultural attributes of this population of students, making this population not only linguistically but also culturally distinct. Describing the "typical" language-minority student, as you may have already surmised, is highly problematic. However, put simply, we might agree that the student is one who (1) is characterized by substantive participation in a non-English-speaking social environment, (2) has acquired the normal communicative abilities of that social environment, and (3) is exposed to a substantive English-speaking environment, more than likely for the first time, during the formal schooling process.

Estimates of the number of language-minority students have been compiled by the federal government on several occasions (O'Malley, 1981; Development Associates, 1984, 1993; Waggoner, 1991). These estimates differ because of the definition adopted for identifying these students, the particular measure utilized to obtained the estimate, and the statistical treatment utilized to generalize beyond the actual sample obtained. For example, O'Malley (1981) defined the language-minority student population by utilizing a specific cutoff score on an English-language proficiency test administered to a stratified sample of students. Development Associates (1984) estimated the population by utilizing reports from a stratified sample of local school districts. Therefore, estimates of language-minority students have ranged between 2,500,000 (Development Associates, 1993) to 4,600,000 (U.S. Bureau of the Census, 1991) with the following attributes:

1. The total number of language-minority children, ages 5 to 14, approximated 1.52 million in 1976, approximated 2.5 million in 1993, and was projected to increase to 3.40 million in the year 2000.
2. The majority of these children reside throughout the United States, but with distinct geographical clustering. For example, about 75 percent of language-minority children are found in Arizona, Colorado, California, Florida, New Jersey, New Mexico, New York, and Texas.
3. Of the estimated number of language-minority children in 1993 for students in grades K through 6, 76 percent are Spanish-language background, 8 percent Southeast Asian (e.g., Vietnamese, Kampuchean, and Hmong), 5 percent other European, 5 percent East Asian (e.g., Chinese and Korean), and 5 percent other (e.g., Arabic and Navajo).
4. For the national school districts sample in the 19 most highly impacted states utilized by Development Associates (1993), 17 percent of the total K–6 student population was estimated as language minority in these states.

Regardless of differing estimates, a significant number of Hispanic students from Spanish-language backgrounds are served by U.S. schools. Moreover, this population is expected to increase steadily in the future. The challenge these students present to U.S. educational institutions will continue to increase concomitantly.

What Types of Educational Programs Serve These Students?

For a school district staff with Hispanic language-minority students, there are many possible program options: "transitional bilingual education," "maintenance bilingual education," "English as a second language," "immersion," "sheltered English," "submersion," and so on (these are definitions developed as program types by the Government Accounting Office in 1987). Ultimately, staff will reject program labels and instead answer the following questions:

1. What are the Spanish- and English-language characteristics of the students, families, and communities we serve?
2. What model of instruction is desired?
   a. How do we choose to utilize Spanish and English *as mediums of instruction*?
   b. How do we choose to handle the instruction of Spanish and English?
3. What is the nature of staff and resources necessary to implement the desired instruction?

These program initiatives can be differentiated by the way they utilize the native language and English during instruction. Development Associates (1993) surveyed 333 school districts in the 19 states that serve over 80 percent of language-minority students in the United States. For grades K through 5, they report the following salient features regarding the use of language(s) during the instruction of language-minority students:

1. Ninety-three percent of the schools reported that the use of English predominated in their programs; conversely, 7 percent indicated that the use of the native language predominated.
2. Sixty percent of the sampled schools reported that both the native language and English were utilized during instruction.
3. Thirty percent of the sampled schools reported minimal or no use of the native language during instruction.

Therefore, two-thirds of the schools sampled have chosen to utilize some form of bilingual curriculum to serve this population of students. However, some one-third of these schools minimize or altogether ignore native-language use in their instruction of language-minority students. Recall that some two-thirds to three-fourths of language-minority students in this country are of Spanish-speaking backgrounds. Programs that serve these students have been characterized primarily as "Bilingual Transitional Education." These programs transition students from early-grade, Spanish-emphasis instruction to later-grade, English-emphasis instruction and eventually to English-only instruction.

For the one-third of the students receiving little or no instruction in the native language, two alternative types of instructional approaches likely predominate: ESL and immersion. Each of these program types depends on the primary utilization of English during instruction but does not ignore the fact that the students served are limited in English proficiency. However, these programs do not require instructional personnel who speak the native language of the student. Moreover, these programs are suited to classrooms in which there is no substantial number of students from one non-English-speaking group but instead may have a heterogeneous non-English-background student population.

School district staff have been creative in developing a wide range of language-minority student programs. They have answered the previous questions differentially for different language groups (e.g., Spanish, Vietnamese, and Chinese), different grade levels within a school, and different subgroups of language-minority students within a classroom and even different levels of language proficiency. The result has been a broad and at times perplexing variety of program models.

What Federal and State Policies Have Been Generated?

The preceding discussion has attempted to lay a foundation for understanding who the language-minority student is and how that student has been served. The discussion turns now to educational policy: first, federal legislative and legal initiatives, and second, state initiatives.

Federal legislative initiatives. The U.S. Congress set a minimum standard for the education of language-minority students in public educational institutions in its passage of Title VI of the Civil Rights Act of 1964 prohibiting discrimination by educational institutions on the basis of race, color, sex, or national origin and by the subsequent Equal Educational Opportunity Act of 1974 (EEOA). The EEOA was an effort by Congress to specifically define what constitutes a denial of constitutionally guaranteed equal educational opportunity. The EEOA provides, in part,

> No state shall deny equal educational opportunities to an individual on account of his or her race, color, sex, or national origin, by the failure by an

educational agency to take appropriate action to overcome language barriers that impede equal participation by students in its instructional programs. (20 U.S.C. sec. 1703 [f])

This statute does not mandate specific education treatment, but it does require public educational agencies to sustain programs to meet the language needs of their students.

The U.S. Congress, on six occasions (1968, 1974, 1978, 1984, and 1987), has passed specific legislation related to the education of language-minority students. The Bilingual Education Act of 1968 (BEA) was intended as a demonstration program designed to meet the educational needs of low-income children with limited English-speaking ability. Grants were awarded to local educational agencies, institutions of higher education, or regional research facilities to develop and operate bilingual education programs, native history and culture programs, early childhood education programs, adult education programs, and programs to train bilingual aides; make efforts to attract and retain as teachers individuals from non-English-speaking backgrounds; and establish cooperation between the home and the school.

Five major reauthorizations of the BEA have occurred since 1968, in 1974, 1978, 1984, and 1987 and a major reauthorization in 1994. As a consequence of the 1974 Amendments (Public Law 93–380), a bilingual education program was defined for the first time as "instruction given in, and study of English and to the extent necessary to allow a child to progress effectively through the education system, the native language" (Schneider, 1976). The goal of bilingual education continued to be a transition to English rather than maintenance of the native language. Children no longer had to be low income to participate. New programs were funded, including a graduate fellowship program for study in the field of training teachers for bilingual educational programs and a program for the development, assessment, and dissemination of classroom materials.

In the Bilingual Education Amendments of 1978 (Public Law 95–561), program eligibility was expanded to include students with limited English academic proficiency as well as students with limited English-speaking ability. Parents were given a greater role in program planning and operation. Teachers were required to be proficient in both English and the native language of the children in the program. Grant recipients were required to demonstrate how they would continue the program when federal funds were withdrawn.

The BEA created new program options, including special alternative instructional programs, that did not require the use of the child's native language. These program alternatives were expanded in 1987. State and local agency program staff were required to collect data, identify the population served, and describe program effectiveness.

New National Educational Policy in 1994 and 2000

From this broader context, specific changes in policy with regard to these students developed in the reauthorization of 1994. Typical rationales for changes in national policy are often related to crisis intervention: There is a problem, and it must be addressed quickly, usually with more political and philosophical rhetoric than action. The past national policy for serving linguistically and culturally diverse students and their families was driven to a large extent by the "crisis" rationale. Accordingly, crisis policies in this arena have been shortsighted, inflexible, and minimally cohesive and integrated; they are not always informed by a strong knowledge base— conceptual, empirical, or one related to the wisdom of practice. Past articulations of Title I and Title VII of the Elementary and Secondary Education Act (ESEA), both prime examples of the crisis intervention approach related to providing services to Hispanic language-minority students, have suffered from these disadvantages.

New policies emerging specifically under the 1994 reauthorization of ESEA, while recognizing the acute need to serve this student population, also recognized the following in developing new policy:

1. The new knowledge base—theoretical, empirical, and practice based—was central to any proposed changes.
2. Policies and programs must be cohesive in order to effectively integrate services that are to be provided, this cohesiveness reflecting the partnership between national, state, and local educational policies and programs.
3. The demographic (growing number of students) and budgetary (limited resources) realities that were present and would likely remain operative throughout the near future must be acknowledged.

New policy directions, primarily those related to Title I and Title VII, have been implemented in line with the presuppositions mentioned previously (for a comprehensive description of the policy foundations for this reauthorization, see Teachers College Record, 1995).

Knowledge Base

The foundation established by recent findings has documented effective educational practices related to linguistically and culturally diverse students in selected sites throughout the United States. These descriptive studies identified specific schools and classrooms serving language-minority students that were academically successful. The case study approach adopted by these studies included examinations of preschool, elementary, and high school classrooms. Teachers, principals, parents, and students were interviewed, and specific classroom observations were conducted that assessed the "dynamics" of the instructional process.

The results of these studies (August and Hakuta, 1997) provide important insights with regard to general instructional organization, literacy development, academic achievement in content areas (e.g., math and science), and the views of the students, teachers, administrators, and parents. Interviews with classroom teachers, principals, and parents revealed an interesting set of perspectives regarding the education of the students in these schools.

In summary, effective curriculum, instructional strategies, and teaching staffs reflect the understanding that academic learning has its roots in sharing expertise and experiences through multiple avenues of communication. Effective curricula provide abundant and diverse opportunities for speaking, listening, reading, and writing, along with scaffolding in order to help guide students through the learning process. Further, effective schools for language-minority Hispanic students encourage them to take risks, construct meaning, and seek reinterpretation of previous knowledge within compatible social contexts that utilize the language and culture of the student as a learning platform. Under this knowledge-driven curriculum, skills are tools for acquiring knowledge, not ends in themselves. The curriculum recognizes that any attempt to address the needs of these students in a deficit or "subtractive" mode is counterproductive. Instead, this knowledge base recognizes, conceptually, that educators must be "additive" in their approach to these students, that is, adding to the rich intellectual, linguistic, academic, and cultural attributes and skills they bring to the classroom. Moreover, programs for these students are integrated and comprehensive. They are not segregated, and they consider the development of English and the mastery of academic content equally important. Separate educational goals are not articulated for these students—they are the same as they are for all students. Yet federal efforts to assist local school districts, particularly in programs that may be perceived by parents as inappropriate for their students, inform parents of the nature and goals of the programs, and parents voluntarily agree to their students' participation.

Wisdom of Practice

In the heat of battle in Congress and in the political process overall, policy development can become centralized within interest groups and among professional policymakers. Therefore, new national policy initiatives have been crafted in consultation with diverse constituencies. For linguistically and culturally diverse communities, the usual players were consulted.

These included the National Association for Bilingual Education; the Mexican American Legal Defense Fund, which has made specific, major legislative recommendations; and other educational groups that have made recommendations related to their own interests and expertise.

This new legislation was also organized around broader efforts at school reform. Of particular significance was the Carnegie Foundation for Advancement of Teaching's report *The Basic School: A Community for Learning.* This report acknowledged the notion that there are key components of an effective school that need to be brought together in an integrated and cohesive manner. A good teacher alone, in a good classroom guaranteeing effective teaching and learning, is not enough. Good schools are effective teaching and learning communities that undermine the significance of the early schooling years and place a high priority on language and a knowledge with cohesiveness. *The Basic School* is an idea based on best practice, a comprehensive plan for educational renewal, and has as its goal the improvement of learning for every child. This same idea is at the core of new federal education policy.

Of particular significance was the work of the Stanford Working Group. This group, funded by the Carnegie Corporation of New York, consulted widely with many individuals representing a broad spectrum of theoretical, practical, and policy-significant expertise. In published reports and in various forums, the group put forward a comprehensive analysis and articulated precise recommendations for policy and legislation related to linguistically and culturally diverse populations. Thus, new policy proposals were shaped in consultation with others. To do otherwise would be to negate the importance of shared wisdom from various established perspectives. Moreover, any proposed changes, if they are to be effective, must be embraced by those individuals and organizations presently in the field.

Cohesiveness

The enacted policy selections have also attempted to view the provisions of the services to students in a comprehensive and integrated manner. Through the introduction of new legislation in Goals 2000, the U.S. Department of Education has set the stage for the state-by-state development of educational standards. Then, with the passage of the Improving American Schools Act (IASA) and the reauthorization of ESEA, specific goals and standard initiatives were aligned with specific resource allocation policies. This alignment recognizes that the integration of federal, state, and local government efforts must occur in order to enhance effectiveness and efficiency. Moreover, the federal role must allow flexibility at the state and local levels while requiring that all children achieve at the highest levels.

Title VII reauthorization—services to students with limited English proficiency as a component of the IASA—is also highly congruent with the alignment principle. As such, Title VII is not seen as yet another intervention aimed at meeting an educational crisis in American education. Instead, it is a key component of the integrated effort to effectively address the educational needs of students.

Demographics and Budget Realities

Since the 1990s, large increases in the number of LEP students in the schools have occurred. In the last six years, that increase approached 70 percent, or about one million students. There is no reason to believe that this trend will subside. However, it is important to recognize that the national presence and the diversity of this population is substantial. In the last decade, 10 states have been added to the number of states with more than 2 percent of their students having limited English proficiency. Today, 20 states can be counted as such, half of which have student populations that vary between 5 and 25 percent. Moreover, the diversity of non-English-language students served is substantial. Presently, over 180 language groups are represented in programs funded under Title VII.

Unfortunately, the fiscal resources that can be consolidated to meet the growing and diverse demands of this population are not likely to increase in any significant way. National, state, and local funding for these populations has not grown in proportion to the increase of those populations. Critics of bilingual education, such as Linda Chavez and Congressman Bill Light of New York, have indicated that bilingual education costs taxpayers anywhere from $5.5 billion to $15 billion yearly. How they arrive at those figures is a mystery since federal funding for bilingual education programs in the 1990s ranged between $125 million and $200 million yearly. A 4 percent increase in these federal funds was requested by the Clinton administration in 1996 and 2000. No major increases in this program area will likely be requested in the near future. Although new legislation in the IASA regarding the disposition of Title I funds to high-poverty areas should bring more resources to Hispanic language-minority students, such funding will still be limited. This means that present resources must be utilized more efficiently.

Specific Changes in Title I and VII

The Title VII legislation of 1994 was part of a cohesive policy change initiated by the U.S. Department of Education. Title VII, as articulated in the legislation, continues to serve the mission of leadership and capacity building with regard to educational services, professional development, and research related to linguistically and culturally diverse populations.

However, federal resources and related services for language-minority students are packaged in a comprehensive and integrated manner, one that recognizes the significance of Goals 2000, Title I, and other IASA programs as well as state and local education efforts. The needs of Hispanic linguistically and culturally diverse children are not only recognized but also directly responded to in new federal legislation. Title I legislation, for example, was modified deliberately to serve as a major source of federal educational programming for Hispanic language-minority students.

Within this integrated federal framework, several important changes characterize Title VII. Direct assistance to local and state educational agencies has been the core federal services to LEP children in the nation's schools. Under the new legislation, previous "targeted" funded initiatives that were changed yearly have been replaced by new and consistently funded programs: development and enhancement grants, comprehensive school grants, and comprehensive district grants. This new configuration recognizes the complexity of educational responses for language-minority students as well as the necessity for locally designed and integrated programs. A new required state review of proposals was enacted to reinforce the implementation of state plans for these students.

After 20 years of efforts to develop a teaching force prepared to meet the needs of Hispanic language-minority students, this area remains a major challenge. Professional development programs in the reauthorized Title VII of 1994 place renewed emphasis and resources on professional development, including a new career-ladder program. In addition to these continuing efforts to prepare teachers, opportunities for professional development through doctoral fellowships remain in place. To continue the development of a strong research and theoretical base, opportunities for postdoctoral studies were created.

These changes were framed by a federal commitment to the value of bilingualism and the belief that all children can achieve high standards. Resources to develop more "two-way" bilingual programs have been prepared by Secretary of Education Richard Riley. The new policy has attempted to strengthen services from federal resources for language-minority students not only through Title VII but also through Title I and related federal K–12 education funding, thus opening the possibility of several million additional dollars in funding to meet the great need for services to linguistically and culturally diverse students, particularly the large number of Hispanic students.

Federal Legal Initiatives

The 1974 U.S. Supreme Court decision in *Lau v. Nichols* (414 U.S. 563) is the landmark statement of the rights of language-minority students, indicating that students with limited English proficiency must be provided with language support:

> [T]here is no equality of treatment merely by providing students with English instruction. Students without the ability to understand English are effectively foreclosed from any meaningful discourse. Basic English skills are at the very core of what these public schools teach. Imposition of a requirement that, before a child can effectively participate in the education program he must already have acquired those basic skills is to make a mockery of public education. We know that those who do not understand English are certain to find their classroom experiences wholly incomprehensible and in no way meaningful.

The Court of Appeals for the Fifth Circuit, in *Castaneda v. Pickard* (1981), set three requirements that constitute an appropriate program for language-minority students:

1. The theory must be based on a sound educational theory.
2. The program must be "reasonably calculated to implement effectively" the chosen theory.
3. The program must produce results in a reasonable time. The courts have also required appropriate action to overcome language barriers. "Measures which will actually overcome the problem" were called for by the *U.S. v. Texas* case, and "results indicating that the language barriers confronting students are actually being overcome" were mandated by the *Castaneda* case (628 F. 2d et 1010). Therefore, local school districts and state education agencies have a burden to assess the effectiveness of special language programs on an ongoing basis. Other court decisions have delineated staff professional training attributes and the particular role of standardized tests.

State Initiatives

Through state legislation (and legislation in the District of Columbia) 12 states mandate special educational services for language-minority students, 12 permit these services, and one prohibits them. Twenty-six states have no legislation that directly addresses language-minority students.

State program policy for language-minority students can be characterized as follows:

1. Implementing instructional programs that allow or require instruction in a language other than English (17 states).
2. Establishing special qualifications for the certification of professional instructional staff (15 states).

3. Providing school districts with supplementary funds in support of educational programs (15 states).
4. Mandating a cultural component (15 states).
5. Requiring parental consent for enrollment of students (11 states).

Seven states (Arizona, Colorado, Illinois, Indiana, Massachusetts, Rhode Island, and Texas) impose all these requirements concurrently.

Such a pattern suggests continued attention by states to issues related to language-minority students (for details, see Garcia, 1998). Of particular interest is a subset of states that, when taken together, are home to almost two-thirds of this nation's language-minority students: California, Florida, Illinois, New York, New Jersey, and Texas. In these states, bilingual credentialing and ESL or some other related credential or endorsement are available. However, in only three of the six states is such credentialing mandated. Therefore, even in states that are highly "impacted" by language-minority students, there is no direct concern for the specific mandating of professional standards. Valencia (1991) has suggested that with the segregation of language-minority students, particularly Chicano students in the Southwest, state school systems are not equally affected by these students. These students tend to be concentrated in a few school districts in the state, and even though their academic presence is felt strongly by these individual districts, they do not exert this same pressure statewide.

RETURN TO "AMERICANIZATION" POLICIES

"English Only"

In 1996, the U.S. House of Representatives passed H.R. 123, the English Language Empowerment Act of 1996, by a vote of 259 to 169. But the Senate has not acted on similar legislation. This legislation would permit states to craft "English Only" laws that could restrict the use of languages other than English in the provision of any form of government services, including education. It would also restrict the federal government in the same way and would prohibit elections from being conducted in languages other than English. Such a national legislative provision would have important effects on the use of Spanish in bilingual education programs that serve Hispanic students.

Future action on this federal legislation seems to be related to a recent Supreme Court decision regarding a case in Arizona that failed to act before adjournment, thus killing the bill. On March 4, 1997, the Supreme Court declined to rule on the constitutionality of Arizona's English Only amendment—in effect, dismissing the case after eight years of litigation without ruling on its merits. Article 28 of Arizona's constitution—also known as Proposition 106, adopted by voters in 1988—requires all levels of state and local government to "act in English and no other language." Two lower federal courts have overruled the measure as a violation of the First Amendment right to freedom of speech for state employees and elected officials. The Supreme Court threw out those decisions on procedural grounds.

For now, the practical impact will be negligible. A 1989 opinion by Arizona's attorney general minimized the restrictive impact of Article 28, arguing that it would not prohibit employees from using languages other than English "to facilitate the delivery of government services." A separate challenge to Article 28, *Ruiz v. Symington,* is under consideration by the Arizona Supreme Court, and the measure has already been ruled unconstitutional by a lower state judge. So, until that case is resolved, the English Only amendment will not be enforced. Any decision by the Arizona Supreme Court could, of course, be appealed to the U.S. Supreme Court, further delaying a final disposition of the case.

The English-Only State Initiative

A new California state initiative is the most recent effort for state action to restrict the use of a language other than English in the delivery of educational services to non-English-speaking children. The new ballot measure, identified as "English for all Children" and passed by 61 percent of the vote on June 2, 1998, proposes the following:

1. To require all children to be placed in English-language classrooms and to educate English-language learners through a prescribed methodology identified as "structured English immersion."
2. To prescribe a methodology that would be provided as a temporary transition period not normally to exceed one year.
3. To allow instruction in the child's native language only in situations in which a waiver is granted, done so in writing and done so yearly by parents requiring a school visit by a parent.
4. To prohibit native-language instruction only if the student already has mastered English and is over 10 years of age and such instruction is approved by the principal and the teacher.

In addition, this "English Only" initiative allows native-language instruction only through an exclusionary and complicated process: 20 or more parents at each grade level at each school would have to request waivers; they would then have to annually request and personally come to the school to negotiate written consent to continue native-language instruction. Moreover, teachers, administrators, and school board members would be held personally liable for fees and damages incurred by the child's parents and guardians. These provisions, taken together, are the most restrictive measures proposed yet for serving language-minority students either nationally or within any state by way of legislation or the courts. The initiative is presently being adjudicated in both state and federal court venues. It is anticipated that the results of these court rulings will have substantive effects on the future on bilingual education policy and its practice both inside and outside the state of California. As you might surmise, this articulation of policy and practice returns the education of many non-English-speaking Chicanos/as to the earlier days of "Americanization" policy, practice, and theory. Yet such policy and practice is completely nonaligned with recent federal policy, effective classroom practices, and new theoretical formulations for these same students.

SCHOOLING PRACTICES

The Debate

The debate regarding the education of culturally and linguistically diverse students in the United States has centered on the instructional use of the two languages of the bilingual student. With regard to the schooling process, the broader issue has been the effective instruction of a growing population of ethnic minority students who do not speak English and therefore are considered candidates for special educational programming that takes into consideration this language difference. Discussion of this issue has included cross-disciplinary dialogues involving psychology, linguistics, sociology, politics, and education. (For a more thorough discussion of these issues, see Cummins, 1979; Trioke, 1981; Baker and de Kanter, 1983; Garcia, 1983a, 1994c; Willig, 1985; Rossell and Ross, 1986; Hakuta and Gould, 1987; August and Garcia, 1988; Baker, 1990b; Stanford Working Group, 1993; Chavez, 1995a; and August and Hakuta, 1997). The central theme of these discussions has to do with the specific instructional role of the native language.

At one end of this debate are supporters of native-language instruction. Proponents of this specially designed instructional strategy (Transitional Bilingual Education) recommend the utilization of the student's native language and mastery of that language prior to the introduction of an English curriculum. This approach suggests that the competencies in the native language, particularly as related to academic learning, provide important cognitive and social foundations for second-language learning and academic learning in general—"you really only learn to read once" (Hudelson, 1987). At the other end of this debate, introduction to the English curriculum is recommended at the onset of the students' schooling experience with minimal use of the native language. This specially designed approach (immersion) calls for English-language "leveling" by instructional staff (to facilitate the understanding on behalf of the student with limited English proficiency) combined with an English-as-a-second-language component. In essence, the earlier the student confronts English and the longer the time it is confronted, the greater the English linguistic advantage (Baker and de Kanter, 1983; Rossell, 1992).

Each of these approaches argues that the result of its implementation will be short-term linguistic advantages, which will lead to more long-term psychological, linguistic, and educational advantages resulting in direct social and economic advancement (Cardenas, 1986; Rossell and Ross, 1986). Simply put, each of these approaches suggests that a simple twist of the educational curriculum (particularly in the early years), one that focuses on the language of the curriculum, will fix the problem. Thus, it has been the case that policy and practice have been driven by this debate and by its related assumptions regarding the importance of the language character of the linguistically diverse student.

The native-language debate has ignored the contributions of Freire (1970), Bernstein (1971), Cummins (1979, 1986), Heath (1986), Levin (1988), Moll (1996), Ogbu (1999), and Trueba (1999), who have suggested that the academic underachievement of such students must be understood within the broader context of society's treatment of minorities in and out of schools. That is, no quick fix is likely under the social and schooling conditions that mark the Hispanic language-minority student for special treatment of his or her language difference without considering the psychological and social circumstances in which that student resides. This is not to suggest that the linguistic character of this student is insignificant. Instead, it warns us against the isolation of this single attribute as the only variable of importance. This more comprehensive view of schooling includes an understanding of the relationship between home and school, the sociocultural incongruities between the two, and the resulting effects on learning and achievement (Garcia, 1999). Much of this book will explore the specific implementation of this type of educational intervention for Hispanics. These interventions are more comprehensive and address more than the issue of English-language development.

CONCLUSION

I have attempted to highlight important policies to provide a broad understanding of issues of importance to the schooling of language-minority students. As indicated previously, the knowledge base in this area continues to expand but should in no way be considered complete or overly comprehensive. In addition, it would be an error to conclude that the data and theory that emerged have been primary factors in determining the educational treatment of language-minority students. However, it does seem appropriate to identify here the possible program, policy, and future research implications for non-English-speaking Hispanic students derived from research and theory as highlighted by the previous discussion:

1. One major goal regarding the education of Hispanic language-minority students should be the development of the full repertoire of linguistic skills in English in preparation for participation in mainstream classes. Future research should delineate alternative routes that will allow for effective achievement of this goal.
2. Time spent learning the native language is not time lost in developing English. Children can become fluent in a second language without losing the first language and can maintain the first language without retarding the development of the second language. Presently, it is not clear what processes or mechanisms facilitate this positive transfer. Identifying such processes is the challenge awaiting future research.
3. Language-minority education programs should have the flexibility to adjust to individual and cultural differences among children. Furthermore, educators should develop the expectation that it is not abnormal for some students to need instruction in two languages for relatively long periods of time. We do not yet know how much time in the native language positively influences academic outcomes in the second language. This type of research will greatly enhance educational outcomes for language-minority students.
4. Educators should expect that young children will take several years to learn a second language to the level of a native speaker. At the same time, they should not have lower expectations of older learners, who typically can learn languages quite quickly and often end up speaking those languages as well as younger learners do. The clear distinction between "young" and "older" learners requires further academic related research.
5. A major problem for minority-group children is that young English-speaking children share the negative stereotypes of their parents and of society at large. Any action that upgrades the status of the minority child and his or her language contributes to the child's opportunities for friendship with native English-speaking children. Future research with these children must link issues of ethnic identity, general self-concept, and specific academic self-concept.

In summary, theoretical (and to some extent research) support can be identified for educational interventions that choose to utilize language in a variety of distinct ways within an educational program for Hispanic students. It seems necessary to conclude that the present state of research and theory with respect to the language and the education of culturally and linguistically diverse students does allow for more specific conclusions. Of course, I would recommend that educational professionals, in their quest to intervene for the betterment of these students, carefully scrutinize relevant theory and research and utilize that analysis to design, implement, and evaluate interventions of significance to their particular educational circumstances. It is fair to request from such designers and implementers to provide a clear theoretical and research foundation, one that in turn can receive the necessary careful scrutiny. What is evident today, and what will become more evident in the chapters to come, is that Hispanics need not lose their language or their culture as they add English and other cultural attributes to their repertoire: It need not be "either/or."

4

Hispanics:
A Growing Immigrant People

In my small hometown, it was not unusual to know almost every student in one's school and all the families in one's extended neighborhood. My neighborhood was highly segregated, with mostly Hispanic families and only a few white families, all of us living at the poverty level or below. Almost all Hispanic families spoke Spanish as their primary home language, were Catholic, and had several family members, from 5 to 10 children, along with grandparents, aunts and uncles, and cousins sharing their home. Some families were characterized by circumstances that made them significantly different from my family and many others in our neighborhood. Some families, like the Gallegos, had been recently "reconstructed," bringing family members from Mexico after one or more male members of the family had come to the region to work in the fields. They were clearly, in my mother's words, "los Mexicanos." We did not see ourselves as "Mexicanos"; we had no allegiance to Mexico or any formal or informal ties with Mexico. We did not even know about "*el diez y seis de septiembre*" or "*el cinco de mayo,*" both of which are significant celebrations related to the liberation of Mexico from Spain and France, respectively. Each of these days is celebrated with specific Hispanic family and community events as well as by the general population in the form of special fiestas, sales, parades, and so on. Moreover, the Hispanic population of this small city has grown by more than 500 percent, much of that growth attributable to "Mexicanos." Much like most of the southwestern United

States and some other eastern and midwestern states, this phenomenon of immigrant Hispanic growth has been repeated over and over again.

In addition to "los Mexicanos," my neighborhood was also partly home to a cadre of families that were with us only at certain times during the year. These families, like the Montano and the Sanchez families, worked alongside my family in the summer crops, then left to harvest potatoes and onions in Idaho and apples in Washington. The whole family packed their belongings in their cars and trucks and left without any notice, only to return when the snow began to fall. I envied Jimmy Montano and Richard Sanchez because they did not have to go to school and they had wonderful stories of travel and adventure to recount regarding their trips through the mountains, deserts, and river valleys. My fifth-grade teacher, Mr. Martinez (the only Hispanic teacher I had during all my K–12 schooling), worried out loud about all the school these students missed (he was raised in a migrant family), while most of us wished we could be with them and made sure to corner them after they returned so that we could share in their adventures. Today, in my return to the old neighborhood, I do see Jimmy and Richard on occasion, and I know their families are still following the crops.

I have my own "migrant–immigrant" roots. My own family came to reside in the valley of the Colorado River because one of my uncles migrated and then immigrated with his family from New Mexico to work in the late summer crops of the valley. My family followed, migrating several summers to work the fertile valley, returning home, and then permanently immigrating to the valley.

It is these immigrant and migrant conditions that characterize up to 40 percent of the Hispanic population in the United States. They are not exclusionary categories, as a portion of immigrants are also migrants, and not all Hispanic immigrants or migrants are of Mexican origin. Laosa (1996a) has documented the "migrancy" of many Puerto Rican citizens from the island to the mainland, while Rumberger and Larson (1996) have documented the urban as opposed to rural "migrancy" of large segments of the Hispanic population in California. Whoever they are as immigrants and migrants, it is important that any discussion regarding Hispanics, and particularly Hispanic students in this country, take into consideration the related effects of these immigrant and migrant conditions.

IMMIGRATION AS A VARIABLE IN
HISPANIC POPULATIONS

The experience of immigration is not new to generations of Americans. However, for Hispanics, it has, and continues to be, an ongoing experience with particular attributes that influence present generations of immigrants as well as important lingering effects for second and third generations. Educationally, Eddie Ruth Hutton described the essence of such an experience for first-generation Mexican immigrants back in 1942:

> Manuel Segovia, Esperanza Guadarrama, Cheepe Ochoa, Tibursio Torres, Mariá Carrión. Strange names these and a hundred others representing the hundreds of strange boys and girls—first-generation Mexicans who each year enter the high schools of the Southwest.
>
> Most of these children come from the poorer homes in which diet and health are given little consideration. They are torn between the conflicting social customs instilled in them by their Mexican parents and those imposed upon them by a new society. They are apologetic for the peculiarities of their families, yet fearful of the alien social order in which they find themselves. (Hutton, 1942, 45)

This experience has changed very little for today's generation of Mexican immigrants and for many other Hispanic immigrants. Lucas (1997) characterizes the experience of these first-generation immigrants, particularly school-age children, as manifested in confronting a set of critical transitions. Most U.S. students undergo a set of important and critical transitions: from home to school and from childhood to adolescence. Immigrant children move through these same critical transitions as well as those associated with transitioning to a new culture and language. How the individual confronts and moves through these transitions, individually and collectively, is the focus of the following discussion.

After a hiatus of half a century, a wave of immigration is once again transforming the United States. With over a million immigrants, legal and illegal, entering the United States each year, the foreign-born constitute the fastest-growing segment of our population, having reached 24.5 million in 1996, roughly 10 percent of the population, the highest proportion since World War II. Even more striking than the scale of immigration is its makeup. Since the passage of the Immigration Act of 1965, which eliminated national origin quotas, Asia and Latin America have replaced Europe as the main sources of newcomers to the United States. The largest groups come from Mexico (accounting for 27.2 percent of the 1996 foreign-born population), China, Cuba, India, and Vietnam (see table 4.1).

New immigrants to the United States come with diverse languages, cultures, and experiences, even within these larger groups. Asian immigrants, for example, include people from more than 13 countries in South, Southeast, and East Asia as well as the Pacific islands. A single nationality can include several ethnic groups, each with a distinct language and culture. A Laotian immigrant might be an ethnic Lao or a member of the Hmong, Mien, or Khmu ethnic minorities. An Asian Indian immigrant might be a

Table 4.1   0–24-Year-Old Population by Race, Ethnicity, Age, and Nativity, 1990–2015

Race/Ethnicity	Nativity	Age	1990		2015	
			Sum of Pop.	Pop. Percentage	Sum of Pop.	Pop. Percentage
Asian	Native	0–3	378,243	0.43%	987,159	0.96%
		4–6	269,645	0.30%	678,564	0.66%
		7–14	557,188	0.63%	1,585,929	1.55%
		15–17	141,946	0.16%	523,002	0.51%
		18–24	278,201	0.31%	1,115,011	1.09%
	Native Total		1,625,223	1.83%	4,889,666	4.78%
	Immigrant	0–3	43,884	0.05%	57,820	0.06%
		4–6	61,115	0.07%	87,217	0.09%
		7–14	306,215	0.35%	380,363	0.37%
		15–17	179,688	0.20%	198,386	0.19%
		18–24	571,553	0.64%	661,359	0.65%
	Immigrant Total		1,162,455	1.31%	1,385,144	1.35%
Asian Total			2,787,679	3.15%	6,274,810	6.13%
Black	Native	0–3	2,142,789	2.42%	2,686,026	2.62%
		4–6	1,544,405	1.74%	1,938,823	1.89%
		7–14	4,106,058	4.63%	4,847,044	4.73%
		15–17	1,453,867	1.64%	1,739,785	1.70%
		18–24	3,340,018	3.77%	3,987,481	3.90%
	Native Total		12,587,137	14.20%	15,199,159	14.85%
	Immigrant	0–3	13,756	0.02%	22,576	0.02%
		4–6	13,532	0.02%	26,707	0.03%
		7–14	74,519	0.08%	106,818	0.10%
		15–17	37,137	0.04%	52,736	0.05%
		18–24	147,065	0.17%	168,664	0.16%
	Immigrant Total		286,009	0.32%	377,501	0.37%
Black Total			12,873,146	14.53%	15,576,660	15.22%
Mexican	Native	0–3	1,183,503	1.34%	1,879,099	1.84%
		4–6	808,994	0.91%	1,280,956	1.25%
		7–14	1,893,185	2.14%	2,934,491	2.87%
		15–17	547,356	0.62%	963,557	0.94%
		18–24	1,043,164	1.18%	2,075,965	2.03%
	Native Total		5,476,202	6.18%	9,134,069	8.92%
	Immigrant	0–3	80,125	0.09%	108,138	0.11%
		4–6	90,310	0.10%	150,058	0.15%
		7–14	318,843	0.36%	565,925	0.55%
		15–17	191,402	0.22%	278,886	0.27%
		18–24	867,766	0.98%	1,009,054	0.99%
	Immigrant Total		1,548,446	1.75%	2,112,961	2.06%
Mexican Total			7,024,648	7.93%	11,246,130	10.99%

Other Hispanic	Native	0–3	572,379	0.65%	108,138	1.83%
		4–6	391,314	0.44%	1,273,944	1.24%
		7–14	888,243	1.00%	2,918,427	2.85%
		15–17	282,982	0.32%	985,282	0.94%
		18–24	665,541	0.75%	2,064,601	2.02%
	Native Total		2,800,459	3.16%	9,084,066	8.87%
	Immigrant	0–3	31,070	0.04%	41,134	0.04%
		4–6	38,299	0.04%	60,558	0.06%
		7–14	203,508	0.23%	266,158	0.26%
		15–17	104,851	0.12%	143,714	0.14%
		18–24	404,946	0.46%	498,028	0.49%
	Immigrant Total		782,674	0.88%	1,009,591	0.99%
Other Hispanic Total			3,583,133	4.04%	10,093,658	9.86%
White	Native	0–3	9,897,590	11.17%	9,363,405	9.15%
		4–6	7,491,780	8.45%	6,910,146	6.75%
		7–14	19,274,383	21.75%	18,114,086	11.69%
		15–17	6,863,637	7.75%	6,958,099	6.80%
		18–24	18,199,024	20.54%	16,960,258	16.57%
	Native Total		61,726,414	69.66%	58,305,993	56.95%
	Immigrant	0–3	29,117	0.03%	34,446	0.03%
		4–6	35,104	0.04%	54,990	0.05%
		7–14	145,619	0.16%	239,203	0.23%
		15–17	81,494	0.09%	124,960	0.12%
		18–24	327,843	0.37%	422,050	0.41%
	Immigrant Total		619,177	0.70%	875,649	0.86%
White Total			62,345,591	70.36%	59,181,642	57.81%
Grand Total			88,614,196	100.00%	102,372,899	100.00%

Source: Vernez et al., 1999.

Punjabi-speaking Sikh, a Bengali-speaking Hindu, or an Urdu-speaking Muslim.

While the great majority of Hispanic immigrants share a common language and to some extent a common culture, this group also displays a great diversity that is due to the various ancestries (European, African, and Native American) and nations represented. Recent Hispanic immigrants have arrived chiefly from Mexico, El Salvador, Guatemala, Nicaragua, and Honduras. Caribbeans, arriving in smaller numbers, come mostly from Haiti, the Dominican Republic, Jamaica, and Cuba. Today's immigrants also vary in their social and educational backgrounds and personal experiences. They come from the elite as well as the most disadvantaged sectors of their societies. Some left to escape poverty, others were fleeing war or political persecution, and others were attracted by the hope for better educational and economic opportunities. Some came directly to the United States; others arrived after harrowing escapes followed by years in refugee camps.

Immigration today is part of an increasingly transnational phenomenon. The "new immigrants" are key actors in a new transnational phenomenon (Portes, 1996; Suarez-Orozco, 1997). Immigration today is characterized by much more back-and-forth movement—of people and of goods. Suarez-Orozco (1998) summarizes this difference:

> Compared to many Hispanic immigrants today, the European immigrants of the 19th century simply could not maintain the level and intensity of contact with the "old country" that is now possible. Furthermore, the ongoing nature of Hispanic immigration to the United States constantly "replenishes" social practices and cultural models that would otherwise tend to ossify. (p. 9)

Hispanic immigration is generating a growing Spanish-speaking mass media (radio, TV, and print) and new ways in which Hispanics identify themselves (Rumbaut and Cornelius, 1995).

Likewise, immigrants are emerging as actors with influence in the political process. Mexican politicians began to understand the political realities of millions of Mexicans working and living in the United States. Mexican dual nationality—whereby Mexican immigrants who become nationalized U.S. citizens would retain a host of political and other rights in Mexico—is influencing the "new immigration" as well.

For various psychosocial reasons that I cannot explore here, immigrants are agents of change. There is little doubt in my own experience that they profoundly change their host communities. In large cities such as Los Angeles and small communities such as Watsonville, California, a Sunday afternoon walk through part of town resembles, in sights, sounds, and food, a walk in Mexico City or Guadalajara. As Suarez-Orozco (1998) notes:

> Another feature of the new immigration to the United States is that immigrants today are entering a country that is economically, socially, and culturally unlike the country that absorbed, however ambivalently, previous waves of immigrants. Economically, the previous waves of immigrants arrived on the eve of the great industrial expansion in which immigrant workers and consumers played a key role. Immigrants today are part of a thoroughly globalized economy. (p. 11)

Porter (1996) indicates that low-skilled immigrants may be locking themselves into the low-wage sector in large numbers. These types of jobs do not offer prospects of upward mobility.

New immigrants are entering American society at a time when what we might term a "culture of multiculturalism" permeates the public space (Garcia, 1999). Only recently has there been this emphasizing of "ethnic pride." Nathaniel Glazer's recent book, *We Are All Multiculturalists Now,* admits this new reality. Some observers are afraid that these new cultural models and social practices tend to undermine "old-fashioned" assimilation, American style (Chavez, 1995b).

It is not evident how the new "multiculturalism" will affect the new immigrants. Today employers in Miami, Florida, the American city with the largest concentration of speakers of foreign languages, have trouble finding competent office workers with the ability to function in professional Spanish (Fradd, 1997b). Immigrant children today are likely to rapidly learn English (or at least a version of it) while losing their mother tongue (Snow, 1997).

We are not alone in addressing issues of large scale immigration. Over 100 million immigrants worldwide and an additional 30 million refugees make immigration today a global issue. Throughout Western Europe, increased immigration is now evident. Facing large-scale immigration as well as the American-dominated global culture, many French wonder just what will happen to French culture in the context of these onslaughts. Strikingly, the same question is being asked today throughout the United States (Chavez, 1995b). As Suarez-Orozco (1998) suggested,

> new information technologies, new idioms of communication, new patterns of capital flows, and a new ease of mass transportation are subverting many of the new boundaries that delineated much of the 20th century. These new social forces are engendering unprecedented opportunities but also stunning contradictions, paradoxes, and anxieties. The systems of meaning and security that structure our identities and give us a sense of rootedness and continuity with our social space are undergoing profound transformation, in part because of substantial increases in immigration. (p. 13)

IMMIGRANT STUDENTS IN AMERICA'S SCHOOLS

While immigrants have affected all aspects of American life, nowhere is the changing demography of the United States more keenly felt than in education. First- and second-generation immigrant children are the fastest-growing segment of the U.S. population under age 15 (Fix and Passel, 1994). With over 90 percent of recent immigrants coming from non-English-speaking countries, schools are increasingly receiving students who do not speak English at home and who have little or no proficiency in English. There has been an increase of almost one million immigrants in U.S. public schools (grades K–12) in the last 10 years, approximately 5.5 percent of the public school student population (Rumbaut and Cornelius, 1995). Recall that it is difficult to determine the number who are considered limited English proficient (LEP), the term used by the federal government and most states, because states determine the number of LEP students in different ways (Gandara, 1995). However, conservative estimates indicate that over 2.1 million public school students in the United States are identified as LEP. They account for 5 percent of all public school students and 31 percent of all American Indian/Alaska Native, Asian/Pacific Islander, and Hispanic students enrolled in public schools. The largest proportion of this population (over 79 percent) are native Spanish speakers (Goldenberg, 1996). California has been particularly affected. The number of students classified as LEP in the state's public schools more than tripled, from nearly 400,000 in 1981 to nearly 1.3 million in 1995 (Garcia, 1999). Although these students were reported to speak one or more of 54 different primary languages, some 80 percent speak Spanish as their native language.

Along with an increase in sheer numbers of immigrant students who are at various stages of learning English, schools are also faced with an increasing number of students needing extra academic instruction in addition to English-as-a-second-language (ESL) classes. Approximately 20 percent of LEP students at the high school level and 12 percent at the middle school level have missed two or more years of schooling since the age of six; 27 percent in high school and 19 percent in middle school are assigned to grades at least two years lower than age/grade norms.

Because newcomers to this country tend to concentrate in certain areas, the responsibility for educating immigrant students is not evenly shared across the country. Accordingly, 82 percent of the immigrant student in K–12 public schools live in only five states: California, Texas, New York, Florida, and Illinois. More than 40 percent are in California. Dade County, Florida, is an example of a school system struggling to serve a sudden, relatively recent influx of immigrants. Approximately a quarter of the 330,000 students in Dade County in the fall of 1996 were born outside the United States, and the county adds an average of 1,322 foreign-born students a month to its rolls. At the same time, employment opportunities draw immigrants to smaller cities and even rural areas as well, creating new challenges for schools in those areas (Lucas, 1997).

An increasingly diverse student population is hitting the schools at the same time as a record number of students in general (the baby-boom echo, a term used by demographers referring to children of the original baby boomers) are entering school. In the fall of 1996, over 51 million children entered school, a new national record. The U.S. Department of Education predicts that numbers of students enrolled in school will not level off until 2006, when they reach 54.6 million, almost three million more than in 1996. The greatest increase over the next decade will be in high school enrollments, projected to increase by 15 percent. Thus, schools already struggling with the influx of immigrant students are also facing the strains of high overall enrollments.

Understanding the Immigrant Student Population

The term "immigrant" includes those students (including refugees) born outside the United States but not those born and raised within the United States. Owing to restrictive immigration laws, most new arrivals to the country from the 19th century through the first half of the 20th were from Europe. Following an overhaul of America's immigration laws in the mid-1960s, however, this pattern changed dramatically and has contributed to a new period of large-scale immigration to the United States, which shows no signs of abating soon. Immigrants to America now come from all over the world, with the nations of Asia and Latin America supplanting those of Europe as primary sources of new arrivals.

There are two very important educational dimensions to this new pattern of immigration. First, recent immigrants are simultaneously more educated and less educated than native-born Americans—a higher percentage of immigrants than native-born Americans have a bachelors or graduate degree, while a higher percentage of immigrants than native-born Americans also have not completed high school. Second, recent immigrants with high levels of education are disproportionately from several nations in East and South Asia, while those with little schooling are largely from a number of Latin American countries. This is of great significance educationally. It is quite evident among immigrants that children from families in which the parents have a great deal of education tend to achieve at much higher levels in school than children from families in which the parents have little formal schooling (Rumbaut, 1997). Low levels of educational attainment are especially consequential for Mexican immigrants. They represent our largest immigrant group and one of the least well educated.

The large differences in education levels among immigrant groups are clearly illustrated in 1990 census data. Among 25- to 29-year-old adult immigrants (a segment with many families with preschool or school-age children), 43 percent of the Asians had a bachelors degree or more, while only 12 percent had less than a high school diploma. In contrast, just 4 percent of the young adult immigrants from Mexico had completed a college degree, while 62 percent had not completed high school. These percentages were 12 percent and 33 percent, respectively, for other Hispanic young adult immigrants. These general patterns have continued among new immigrants in the 1990s.

With immigration expected to continue at high levels for a long time to come, Rand, the respected research and policy organization, has developed projections for the student-age population in 2015. Consistent with other forecasts of racial/ethnic change, Rand's projections suggest that there will be very large increase in the number of Asian and Latino children and youth in that period, substantial growth in the number of African American youngsters, and a slight drop in the number of whites (see table 4.2). For Hispanics, a growth of 40 percent in the age-groups of 0 to 25 is highly significant. This population is likely to be in schools and will make up approximately 20 percent of the 0- to 24-year-old population in 2015, while in 1990 they made up only 12 percent of this population. Moreover, the white population will drop from approximately 70 percent of the 0- to

Table 4.2   High School Drop-outs and College Graduates in Adult Population Aged 25 or Older by Race/Ethnicity, 1990–2015

	1990			2015		
Race/Ethnicity	Number (Thousands)	Percent Total	Percent of Group	Number (Thousands)	Percent Total	Percent of Group
	High School Drop-outs					
Asian	776	2.3	18.5	1,251	5.1	11.5
Black	5,011	15	30.4	3,503	14.4	18.1
Mexican	3,244	9.8	51	6,139	25.3	39.1
Other Hispanic	1,779	5.3	36.7	2,834	11.7	28.9
Non-Hispanic White	22,491	67.5	17.9	10,553	43.5	10.2
Total	33,301	100	21.1	24,281	100	13
	College Graduates					
Asian	1,557	4.9	37.1	4,826	9.9	44.3
Black	1,878	5.9	11.4	3.313	6.8	15.2
Mexican	398	1.3	6.3	1,269	2.6	8.1
Other Hispanic	514	1.6	13.1	1,695	3.5	17.3
Non-Hispanic White	27,643	86.2	22	37,690	77.2	29.2
Total	32,111	100	20.4	48,794	100	26.1

Source: Vernez et al., 1999.

	Share of Group		Share of All Such Children	
Race/Ethnicity	1990	2015	1990	2015
	Native Families			
Asian	19.5	18.2	3.3	1.1
Black	56.9	43.7	30.9	34.6
Hispanics	42.3	38.7	8.7	17
Non-Hispanic White	20.5	15	60.1	47.3
Total	27	22.5	100	100
N (million)	50.3	53.8	13.6	12.1
	Immigrant Families			
Asian	27	20.3	10.1	11.8
Black	54.1	39.6	14.6	11.2
Hispanics	48.9	41.1	56.4	65.8
Non-Hispanic White	25.1	20	18.9	11.3
Total	39.2	33	100	100
N (million)	10.3	19.6	4.1	6.5
	All Families			
Asian	26	19.9	2.6	4.8
Black	56.6	43	27.1	26.4
Hispanics	46.4	40.2	19.7	34
Non-Hispanic White	20.8	15.5	50.6	34.8
Total	29.1	25.3	100	100
N (million)	60.6	73.4	17.6	18.6

Note: Low income families are families with real income below $19,868 in both 1990 and 2015.

Source: Vernez et al., 1999.

24-year-old population to 58 percent of this population. For the Hispanic population (Mexican origin and other Hispanic), 20 to 30 percent will be immigrant. Significantly for Hispanics, the growth of Mexican origin from 1990 to 1995 will be from 8 to 12 percent of the total population at this age range, while the growth of other Hispanics at this age range will increase from 4 to 10 percent during this same period.

The Rand analysis also provides a useful understanding of the "contexts" of Hispanic and immigrant families. On the family income side, the Rand projections suggest that the number of African American children from low-income homes will remain large, while the Hispanic share could nearly double. At the same time, the number of white students from low-income homes is projected to drop substantially. Patterns such as these could lead poverty in the United States to be viewed increasingly as primarily a Latino and black phenomenon.

Importantly, whites and Asians are projected to account for 83 percent of the students who have college-educated parents in 2015, down only modestly from their 89 percent share in 1990. Together, blacks and Hispanics are forecasted to account for 17 percent of this group in 2015, up from about 11 percent in 1990 but far below the 35 to 45 percent of the student-age population that they are expected to constitute in 2015.

Among youngsters from families with parents with little schooling, the percentages of Asians and blacks change very little in the period under Rand's projections, but the white percentage is projected to drop from 37 to 16 percent, while the Latino share is projected to grow from 37 to 59 percent. Looking ahead, these projections suggest that children from educationally disadvantaged families will be increasingly Hispanic, and the absolute number of these Latino youngsters can be expected to grow as well. (The Rand projections show this Hispanic segment growing from 2.8 million youngsters in 1990 to 4.7 million in 2015, four-fifths of whom may be from immigrant families.)

Among children of college graduates, the Rand projections show the number of Asian youngsters tripling between 1990 and 2015 to 2.3 million. They also show the Latino segment tripling to 2.1 million and blacks growing by two-thirds to 1.7 million.

Although these demographic projections are not "certain," they nonetheless suggest several conclusions. First, improving educational outcomes for Hispanic families will remain a very important challenge in 2015. And without significant academic progress for these students, academic achievement parity among racial/ethnic groups will remain an elusive goal. Second, the number of Hispanic students from middle- and professional class homes will probably be much larger in absolute terms in 2015 than 1990, but they will be a relatively smaller pool. Whites and Asian Americans are likely to continue to make up the lion's share of academically achieving students a generation hence—with Asians probably accounting for an ever larger percentage for some time to come. The larger number of achieving students from these two groups will almost certainly mean that competition for admission to selective colleges and universities will remain keen and possibly further intensify.

Experience of Immigrants in U.S. Schools

Two recent large-scale studies are relevant to consider in this analysis (Vernez, Abrahamse, and Quigley, 1996; Rumbaut, 1997), as are several in-depth ethnographies (Valdés, 1996, 1998; Olsen 1997). These quantitative and qualitative studies give relatively new insights with regard to the immigrant student experience in the United States and to the specific Hispanic immigrant experience.

Vernez et al. (1996) used data from "High School and Beyond" (HSB), a national representative sample of more than 21,000 10th- and 12th-graders first interviewed in 1980 and followed over a six-year period through their high school years, graduation, and postsecondary education in U.S. colleges. These data were complemented with data from the 1970, 1980, and 1990 U.S. Census of Population and Housing to analyze participation in U.S. education across all age-groups and over time. Throughout this study, they compare the participation and performance of immigrant children and youths in U.S. educational institutions to that of their native counterparts overall and within each of the four major racial/ethnic groups: Asian, black, Hispanic, and white.

This analysis concludes that immigrant children and youths are as likely as natives to enroll in U.S. primary and middle schools. However, they are somewhat less likely than natives to attend high school: In 1990, participation rates were 87 and 93 percent, respectively. Significantly, all this differential is accounted for by immigrant youths of Hispanic origin, primarily from Mexico. In 1990, one of every four immigrants from Mexico in the 15-to-17 age-group was not in school, a rate nearly 20 percent lower than that for any other immigrant group and 17 percent lower than that for natives of Mexican origin.

Evidence suggests that the relatively low in-school participation rates of Mexican immigrants of high school age is due primarily to their not "dropping in" to the school system in the first place rather than their "dropping out" of school. By age 15, Mexican immigrants have already been out of school in Mexico for two years on average. They do not enroll in U.S. schools either by choice, because of an inability to catch up with others their age or with their native counterparts, or by economic necessity, because they must support themselves and their families.

Conditional on having been enrolled in a U.S. high school by grade 10, immigrant students are more likely than their native counterparts to make choices consistent with eventually pursuing a college education. They are more likely to follow an academic track and take advanced courses in math and sciences. These differences in course-taking patterns hold not only in the aggregate but also in each racial/ethnic group. However, there are variations among immigrants of different racial/ethnic groups, just as there are such variations among natives. Asian immigrants generally performed best on indicators of preparation for college, followed by white and black immigrants. Hispanic immigrants performed the lowest on nearly all indicators of college preparation.

Immigrants in U.S. high schools are also more likely to plan to go to college and to report working hard to achieve their expectations. Similarly, the immigrant parents of immigrant children report higher educational expectations for their children than native parents do. Immigrant children and parents of all racial/ethnic groups studied have higher educational aspirations than their native counterparts. However, this difference in aspirations is three times greater between immigrants and natives of Hispanic origin than it is between immigrants and natives in other groups. This significant decline in the educational aspirations of Hispanics in the United States has also recently been noted by other researchers. Its causes, however, have yet to be thoroughly investigated (Vernez et al., 1996).

High School Graduation

Whatever difficulties immigrant children and youths might face adjusting to their language and to the institutional and cultural norms of this country, their educational attainment has equaled if not exceeded that of native children and youths. Immigrant high school sophomores were just as likely as natives to graduate from high school within four years of their sophomore year, with Asians more likely to graduate than whites, blacks, and Hispanics, in that order.

Immigrant high school graduates were also more likely than their native counterparts to enroll in postsecondary education, attend college, and stay continuously through four years of college. Immigrants' higher rates of participation in higher education hold within each racial/ethnic group. But there are differences between immigrants of different racial/ethnic groups that mirror the well-known differences between natives of different racial/ethnic backgrounds. Asian immigrants and natives scored generally the highest on all indicators of college-going and Hispanic immigrants, and natives scored consistently the lowest on indicators of college-going, with whites and blacks in between. The differences are large. Four out of every five Asian high school graduates go on to college, compared to one out of every two Hispanic high school graduates.

In multivariate analyses, the study reported that the individual and family factors associated with college-going were generally the same for immigrants and natives as well as across racial/ethnic groups. High school graduates whose parents have higher income, higher levels of education, and higher educational expectations for their children are more likely to pursue a college education than others. This confirms the importance of family background and family attitudes toward education in determining children's eventual educational attainment. Also, a student's positive attitude toward working hard in school was found to be positively associated with college-going for all groups. All else equal, immigration status per se was not found to be associated with college-going.

The fact that Hispanics have lower scores than Asians, whites, and blacks on nearly all key family and individual characteristics—income, parental education, and educational aspirations—may explain their lower educational attainment. Rumbaut (1996) reports very similar results in a study of a discrete set of immigrant students conducted in San Diego, California. His five-year study of the educational progress of 2,400 children of immigrants in San Diego found that they quickly embrace English over their parents' native tongues. The study—part of the largest long-range survey of immigrants' children in the United States—also found that these youths had better grades and lower dropout rates than fellow public students whose parents were born in the United States. But the study also found stark disparities in ambition among various immigrant groups and that many resist identifying themselves merely as Americans. San Diego Unified, with 133,000 students, is the eighth-largest school district in the nation. It was chosen for the study in part because white students make up nearly a third of the enrollment, Latinos another third, and blacks and Asians most of the rest. Starting in 1991, the study chose as subjects the 2,420 students in the eighth and ninth grades who had at least one foreign-born parent, then followed them until 1995, when they were near the end of high school. The students represented more than 60 nationalities. About half were born in the United States and half in another country. Mirroring the immigrant pool in California and the nation as a whole, they were about evenly divided among Hispanics (the vast majority from Mexico), Filipinos, and Indochinese and other Asians.

Analyzing district data on grade-point averages (GPAs), Rumbaut (1996) found that the children of immigrants were not driving down achievement but, rather, were outperforming the district as a whole. For example, 29 percent of all ninth-graders in the district had GPAs higher than 3.0, while 50 percent of immigrant children performed that well.

Numerous studies have found that Hispanic students are more likely to drop out than others (Hispanic Dropout Project, 1998). In San Diego Unified, they have a 26.5 percent dropout rate over the four years of high school. But when Rumbaut isolated Hispanic immigrant children, he found a different story: Only 8.5 percent dropped out. The same was true when Rumbaut compared immigrant and U.S.-born Filipinos, Indochinese, and other Asians. In fact, the average dropout rate for all immigrant students was only 5.7 percent. The district's white students dropped out at almost twice that rate (10.5 percent), and the overall district rate was three times as high (16.2 percent). Across the board, the study reported that the immigrant youths placed a high value on schooling, with more than 90 percent agreeing that a good education is essential to upward mobility. Forty-six percent aspired to occupations such as doctor and lawyer, with Filipinos, Vietnamese, and other Asians having the loftiest goals.

But far fewer Mexicans, Cambodians, and Laotians and Hmong set goals that high. Only 22 percent of the Laotians and Cambodians and 24 percent of Mexicans said that they would like to earn an advanced degree, contrasted with 63 percent of Asians, 52 percent of non-Mexican Latinos, and 47 percent of Vietnamese. More than 90 percent of the immigrant students spoke a language other than English at home, yet the proportion who preferred English grew from 66 percent in 1992 to 82 percent in 1995. This shift was pronounced even among the children of California's largest immigrant population, Mexicans. Among youths born in the United States who had at least one native Mexican parent, the rate of English preference grew from 53 to 79 percent over the three years.

Using self-reports as well as test scores, the study also found that 68 percent of the immigrant students read English "very well" and that only 23 percent read another language more fluently. The study's portrait of rapid English fluency mirrors the trajectories of European newcomers to the United States at the turn of the century. Where the findings clash with traditional notions about the lure of mainstream American culture is in the area of self-identity. Students were asked what they called themselves—just American, for example, or some hyphenated American? In 1992, the largest proportion, 43 percent, chose a hyphenated identity (such as "Chinese American"), while 32 percent preferred a national origin label ("Chinese") and 16 percent "pan-ethnic" labels ("Asian," "Hispanic"). Only 3 percent chose the plain American identity. According to conventional wisdom, the longer they live in the United States, the more immigrants and their children prefer American or hyphenated American identities. But the opposite happened in San Diego. By 1995, the percentage preferring to call themselves merely Americans dropped by half, to 1.6 percent, while those favoring hyphenated labels dropped by a quarter, to 30 percent.

The biggest growth was in those identifying with their nation of origin. Among students born in Mexico, the percentage describing themselves as Mexican doubled over the three years, to 67.9 percent. Perceptions, experiences, and expectations of racial discrimination also increased between 1992 and 1995. By 1995, the percentage saying they expect to be discriminated against—despite their educational level—grew from 36 to 40 percent. Such findings both support and contradict other related findings of immigrant student experiences in U.S. schools. Clearly, no one quantitative portrait seems to best represent this experience. This is why recent ethnographic studies of immigrant families and their children are useful. Two studies of this type are addressed in some detail here.

Valdés (1996, 1998) reports the study of Hispanic immigrant families and the schooling of their children. The larger study by Valdés (1996) focused on two males and two females. It took place during a two-year period and involved three middle schools, four newly arrived Latino focal children and their classmates, four different English-language teaching specialists (ESL teachers), and numerous subject matter teachers who had the focal children in class. It also involved interviews with school personnel, with students themselves, and with their parents. A subpart of the study's purpose was to examine how immigrant children who arrive in this country with "zero" English acquire English in schools. To address this issue, Valdés (1998) selected a middle school undergoing rapid population shift and students at the ages of 12, 13, and 14. Two immigrant Hispanic students, one of Mexican origin and one of Honduran origin, participated in this research over a seven-year period.

Lilian, the student of Mexican origin, was 12 years old when she first arrived at her California school. A previous student in Mexico, she had acquired a substantive reading ability in Spanish but had almost no English-language or reading skills. Elisa, a 13-year-old Honduran immigrant, had completed sixth grade in her native country and also had substantial reading and writing experiences in Spanish. Both Lilian and Elisa were eager to go to school and learn English.

For each of these students, mastery of English became the predominant theme in their schooling experience. Valdés (1998) concludes that both students had difficulty in escaping "the ESL ghetto." This phenomenon is a common one for many Hispanic immigrant students: They are placed repeatedly in English-language-emphasis course work and instruction at the expense of access to a grade-level-appropriate curriculum and instruction in subject matter domains. The result for both Lilian and Elisa was predictable, although Lilian dropped out of school at the age of 15, while Elisa finished high school but has only recently begun to attend a community college where her measured lack of English on a required placement test has forced her to enroll in more ESL courses. Valdés (1998) was led to conclude that "the students who had looked forward to schooling the United States were disappointed" (11).

Olsen (1997), in an effort similar to that of Valdés (1996, 1998), followed a cohort of immigrant Hispanic and Asian students through their high school experience at Madison High, a northern California urban school. This study attempted to address the issues of becoming "American" in the world of an immigrant student and the instructors and the curriculum they experienced. In the words of Olsen (1997), "The study illustrates efforts and heartbreaks of those engaged in activity to provide more educational opportunity and equal access to schooling for immigrants, as well as the confusion, blindness, and concerns of those who resist changing their ways for them" (239). Unfortunately, the study of Madison High offered a hard look at the ways in which schools still track and determine very different futures based on race, class, and language. Immigrant students seemed to spend their educational time relegated to classes taught entirely in English in which they were unlikely to thrive or in separate "sheltered" English classes where the emphasis was on English-language development with little or no emphasis on high school content–level curriculum. Immigrant students themselves reported that the key to becoming American was simply to learn English. At the same time, teachers emphasized that the key to educational success was the mastery of basic skills and subject matter content. These teachers reported "seeing" students divided into academic levels that are a result of a student's individual choice and effort. In essence, any student can be successful, achieve at high levels, and be meritorious if he or she chooses to do so and works hard. This view of achievement by teachers contrasted drastically from an immigrant student's experience: "pick your race and take your place" (Olsen, 1997, 241).

More specifically, Olsen concludes that the immigrant student experience is yet another important reflection of race and class negotiations and stratification in U.S. high schools that serve a diverse socioeconomic, racial, ethnic, and immigrant student body. Yet, particularly for immigrant students, taking one's place in the racial and socioeconomic hierarchy seemed coupled with, first, the exclusion and separation of immigrants academically and, second, the extreme pressure to give up national identity and language. Olsen (1997) is quick to point out that these phenomena are not uncontested. Students do try to rise to and overcome this challenge, and, as Rumbaut (1996) indicates, some do. At Madison High, Hispanic immigrants were not likely to do so (Olsen, 1997).

Facing the Challenges

The realities described here are cause for serious concern, and many educators believe that the education system in the United States is poorly prepared to meet the needs of its linguistically and culturally diverse student population, particularly those arriving at its schools as recent immigrants. Gandara (1995) claims that English-language learners were sidelined in the first wave of reform efforts during the 1980s, and a report by the Stanford Working Group (1993) calls the nation's school systems to task for failing to provide these students with equitable educational opportunities. Moss and Puma (1995) found that immigrant students receive lower grades and are judged by their teachers to have lower academic abilities than native-

born students, and they score below their native English-speaking classmates on standardized tests of reading and math. The challenges of educating immigrant students and English-language learners are especially acute
at the secondary school level (Olsen, 1997). If they are newcomers to the
United States, they have much less time than elementary-age students to
learn English and master the academic content required to graduate from
high school. They must pass tests that require English skills they do not
have. They must study subjects such as physical science, chemistry, economics, and geometry that require high levels of English academic language. Most secondary school texts and materials require a high level of
English reading ability. Few schools provide native-language support for
these classes, English-language instruction tied to content, or content
classes taught with adaptations of English appropriate for these students'
level of proficiency. Students learning English often find it difficult to be
accepted in well-established groups of English-speaking students. Finally,
students who hope to attend a college or university after high school face
even greater challenges as they attempt to succeed in classes designated
for college credit and to master the maze of requirements for college acceptance (Romo and Falbo, 1996; Olsen, 1997).

The Courts, Federal Policy, and Immigrant Children

The education of immigrant children has been of some controversy for
decades. In a case that went all the way to the U.S. Supreme Court (*Plyler
v. Doe,* 1982), one Texas school district attempted to exclude Mexican immigrant students from public school altogether. The Supreme Court found
such exclusion unconstitutional. A political initiative in California, Proposition 187, which California voters approved in 1994, attempted to cut off
social services, including public education, to undocumented immigrant
families and children. In March 1998, a federal district judge found Proposition 187 unconstitutional. Proponents of Proposition 187 planned to appeal the judge's decision to the Court of Appeals for the Ninth Circuit. In
the meantime, however, the judge ordered written notice sent to state and
local agencies and education workers telling them that Proposition 187
was invalid and should not be enforced.

The judge ruling that Proposition 187 was invalid relied on the Supreme
Court decision in the *Plyler v. Doe* case. In that case, a Texas school district attempted to deny local school district funds for the education of undocumented children and thus deny free public education to such children.
By a 5-to-4 vote, the Supreme Court struck down the statute as violating
equal protection, arguing that the equal protection clause was intended to
cover any person physically within a state's borders, regardless of the le-
gality of his presence. The Court argued that while public education was

not a right guaranteed by the U.S. Constitution, it was certainly more important than other social welfare benefits. Denying children an education would make them illiterate and would prevent them from advancing on their individual merit and becoming useful members of U.S. society. The Court also rejected the argument of the attorneys for Texas who claimed that undocumented children were less likely than other children to remain within the state and put their education to use there. The Court found nothing in the record to suggest that this was true (Emanuel, 1983).

As mentioned previously, the issue resurfaced in November 1994, when the voters of California passed Proposition 187, the "Illegal Aliens, Ineligibility for Public Services Verification, and Reporting Initiatives Statute." This initiative made undocumented immigrants ineligible for public school education at elementary, secondary, and postsecondary levels. It required various state and local agencies to report persons suspected of being illegal aliens to the Immigration and Naturalization Service. Opponents of this proposition argued that it was not constitutional and that it was contrary to the 1982 Supreme Court ruling in *Plyler v. Doe*. The crafters of Proposition 187 were well aware of the direct conflict between the education provisions of the proposition and *Plyler v. Doe*. Their political goal was to challenge the Supreme Court case (Carter, 1997).

Those in opposition to Proposition 187 argued that the proposition violated parents' due process because families were not given the right to contest being reported as "suspected" illegal aliens. Others argued that the reporting requirement of Proposition 187 might encourage discrimination based on race, color, or national origin. The implementation provisions of Proposition 187 also appeared to violate the restrictions of obtaining personal information about a student without prior consent of the parent. Educators argued that the proposition imposed a law enforcement function on schools that would adversely affect the learning environment for all children. The supporters of Proposition 187 claimed that the ultimate objective of the initiative was to curtail undocumented immigration by making the process of immigration less attractive. However, there is no evidence that depriving immigrant children of education is likely to cause their parents to return to their countries of origin. Instead, it is more likely to cause the second generation to become further marginalized from educational access than they already are. (In a court agreement of September 1999, Proposition 187 was declared unconstitutional.)

Despite the negative climate, increasing numbers of immigrant students—with or without families—have entered the United States in search of the advantages associated with life and work in this country through legal means (McCarthy and Vernez, 1998). Through a general amnesty provision for those able to demonstrate continuous residence in the United States after January 1, 1982, the 1986 Immigration Reform and Control

Act (IRCA) allowed about 1.7 million persons immediately to apply for legalization. Estimates indicate that 87 percent of those applying for the general amnesty were Mexican. Massey, Donato, and Liang (1990) found that as the immigrants obtained legal status, they were more likely to send children to public schools in the United States. Thus, the use of public school services was anticipated to significantly increase as a result of the amnesty provision. Massey and his colleagues estimated that five years after legalization, some 42 percent of all amnesty recipients would enroll children in U.S. public schools. Given that the number of amnesty recipients was in the millions once family members were included and that those qualifying for amnesty were highly concentrated in California (55 percent) and Texas (18 percent), the enrollment of Mexican immigrant children in public schools was expected to increase sharply in those states (Massey et al., 1990, 207).

Several other factors regarding immigration increased the school-age population in the 1990s. Increased legal immigrant quotas added more numbers to the growing school-age population. The family reunification components of immigration legislation also gave priority to children of immigrants already in the United States (Cafferty et al., 1984). The 1990 Immigration Reform Act left virtually intact the family unification provisions of previous law and provided for legalization of sizable numbers of family members of persons previously legalized under IRCA (Bean and Fix, 1992). In addition to legal increases to even higher levels than those preceding the passage of IRCA (Bean et al., 1990), efforts to cut services to immigrants, such as Proposition 187, have actually helped to stimulate an unprecedented boom in naturalization. Once naturalized, the immigrants may claim full social and economic benefits of U.S. citizenship for themselves and their families (Bean et al., 1997).

Since 1990, twice as many people have come to the United States each year than arrived during the "Great Immigration" of European immigrants a century ago. In some cities, the impact of immigration has already been proportionately greater. In Los Angeles, San Francisco, Dallas, Houston, and Miami, foreign-born residents now make up between a fifth and a third of the total population (Valdez et al., 1993). Immigrants' concentration in urban centers and their relatively high fertility rates add to the pressures on American public schools. A contemporary portrait of immigration patterns show that the recent flows of immigrants have relatively low levels of education, which increases the challenge to schools to educate immigrant children who speak little English and arrive with differing levels of sophistication (Portes and Rumbaut, 1990).

The ability of the immigration population to participate in the United States as future citizens depends on the quality of the instruction and training that their children receive and the measures taken to incorporate them into society. Low levels of education command low wages and lead to greater employment instability, which may last over the duration of immigrant working life in the United States (Vernez, 1993). McCarthy and Vernez (1998) showed that Hispanic immigrants and their children are losing ground in educational attainment compared to other immigrant groups and U.S. citizens. Uneven access to preschool programs and low expectations of those Mexican immigrant students who do attend school perpetuate the low educational attainments of large numbers of second- and third-generation Mexican Americans (Chapa, 1990).

Effective Programs: What Works?

At a more general level, the work of Carter and Chatfield (1986), Olsen and Dowell (1989), Lucas, Henze, and Donato (1990), Garcia (1994a), Moran and Hakuta (1995), Rose (1995a), Lucas (1997), and Mace-Matlock et al. (1998) report on the positive characteristics of programs that effectively meet the needs of Hispanic immigrant students. Such characteristics include many that describe good schools in general (e.g., high expectations for academic achievement for all students, strong academic preparation, high levels of parental involvement, opportunities for school engagement through school and extracurricular activities, and strong instructional and organizational leadership). Of particular significance is the best understanding of the immigrant experience by educators. These "uprooted" families are not the norm, and, the more is known about the family and student experience, the more likely educational institutions can be responsive to their circumstances. Weinstein-Shr provides a helpful framework for "getting to know" these families and students:

1. Structure and characteristics of refugee and immigrant communities
   A. Diversity
      - In the communities we wish to serve, in what ways are members diverse?
      - How are divisions expressed in the communities?
      - What are the groups and subgroups?
   B. Community leaders and other key players
      - Who are members of the families we wish to serve? How do they themselves perceive family boundaries?
      - What are kin patterns and social networks that influence how people manage?
      - Who are the caretakers for children in the families we wish to serve?
2. Language, literacy, and education: Community and individual profiles
   A. History
      - What were the educational experiences of target families in their homelands?

- What were the circumstances of flight and the nature of interruptions in schooling?
- What is the history of experience with native language literacy?

B. Language use in the community: Current practices
- What are attitudes toward native language literacy in the target community?
- What are the supports for native language development and use among children and adults?
- What are parents' language and literacy goals for themselves and for their children?
- How can our educational efforts support native language development?

C. Roles of teachers, parents, and children
- What is the traditional relationship of teachers and parents in the country of origin for the community we wish to serve?
- What are the norms for interaction between adults and children in this community?
- How do our program activities fit, or not fit, these norms?
- What are the possible avenues for adjustment or negotiation?

3. Addressing the concerns of adults

A. Surviving trauma
- What were the circumstances of departure from the country of origin?
- What are some of the losses associated with this departure?
- What material and social resources are available for coping with change and loss?

B. Parenting in a dangerous world
- What are the conditions in which newcomers are raising their children?
- What are the key issues for newcomers and old timers alike in the schools and neighborhoods served?
- What are traditional means of disciplining children, and to what extent are they appropriate or possible in the United States?

C. Changing roles, changing relationships
- How are relationships changing among parents, grandparents, and children as a result of resettlement in a new country? Between men and women? Elders and youth?
- What is the role of language and literacy in these changes?
- How can our literacy work play a positive role in families where social conditions challenge even the healthiest of intergenerational relationships?

4. General queries for programming
- How much do we know about the families and communities we serve? How can we learn more both inside and outside our classrooms?
- What is the role of learners' native knowledge and personal experience in our programs and classrooms?
- What are possibilities through our programs for helping adults gather

information about the school system, drugs, discipline, child abuse laws, or any other concerns they may have?
- What are their concerns specifically about their children's schooling?
- What opportunities do our programs provide for adults to discuss their concerns, compare the United States with their homelands, and get support from one another in grappling with complex problems? (Weinstein-Shr, 1995, 129–130.)

What is made clear in these suggestions is that the challenge in serving immigrant students usually transcends the "typical" structures of schooling for immigrant students. Overall, the Hispanic immigrant student is likely to benefit from schools that are characterized by the following attributes:

Valuing the students' home language and cultures. Helping immigrant students maintain a positive link with their culture of origin is the most appropriate way to provide a good education and a strong value for U.S. society. This can include incorporating the home culture into the classroom, including materials on the culture, building on the home-language instruction, and observing the values and norms of the home culture while teaching the majority culture norms. Trying to make sense of a whole new culture, language, and way of life can be very difficult for students who have spent their childhood in other cultures and nations. The home culture and the U.S. culture may have very different expectations of student behaviors, parent involvement, sex role expectations, and what it means to be a mature and responsible person (Olsen, 1997).

Effective programs for immigrant students recognize that individuals cannot change their culture without losing their identity (Lucas, 1997; Olsen, 1997). Immigrant students should not be faced with a choice between assimilating in order to do well at school and rejecting their own culture, which often leads to failure in school (Manaster, 1992). The Manaster study found that successful students were more acculturated, had a clearer sense of themselves, had higher occupational aspirations, and desired stable, responsible jobs. The students' cultures must be incorporated in the learning environment to help them make that positive transition. Results from a survey of immigrant children in San Diego and Miami revealed that, regardless of race/ethnicity, immigrant students who retained strong cultural and family identity tended to outpace others in school, including their native-born American peers, because their immigrant families reinforced the values of hard work and educational achievement (Rumbaut, 1996). Teaching must take into account our increasingly complex understanding of U.S. culture as a multicultural reality (Garcia, 1998). In the Southwest, U.S. culture has evolved in common with Mexican culture, and this multiculturalism provides an interesting and healthy base for school curricula.

Outreach to parents and family. Limited-English-proficient and under-educated parents are often dependent on their children to navigate the schools and learn the language of the host country. A strong factor in the immigrants child's school success is the educational level of the immigrant parents, especially the mother (Rumbaut, 1997). Overall, teachers report the parents of immigrant students are substantially less involved in school functions or as school volunteers than parents of nonimmigrant students. Involvement of parents of immigrant students is highest in elementary schools (Lucas, 1997). A good program will recognize the family's vital role in a child's education and encourage parents to participate. Parents who have high educational expectations for their children and engage them in extensive school-related discussions can help their children overcome other risk factors (Lucas, 1997). Enabling parents to have these discussions will often require providing information in a language that the parent understands and working with a wide range of parental education levels, including those who cannot read or write or even sign their names. It may also involve recognizing that many immigrant youth do not have parents who can become involved in the schooling process. Decisions that parents would normally help youth make become the responsibility of immigrant adolescents when they live with siblings or unrelated adults instead of their biological parents. Parents may have remained in the sending country or may have followed the migrant stream, leaving older children behind to attend school (Soto, 1997). In focus group meetings that the author conducted with immigrant students, one high school student explained that her parents attended activities at the primary school with her younger brothers and sisters, but at the high school level there were no activities they felt comfortable participating in because of their poor English skills. Since she was the oldest child and knew some English, she was expected to resolve her own school problems and help her parents resolve those of her younger siblings. Other adolescents reported that they lived with older brothers and sisters or relatives and had no parents to become involved in their education. School staff must be sensitive to these immigrant family structures and accommodate them in their outreach efforts (Olsen, 1997).

Instruction based on previous educational experience. Studies have shown that certain problems of adaptation of immigrant children are closely related to age of arrival and length of residence in the host country. Language difficulties, interrupted education, the conditions under which immigration has taken place, plus lack of previous school experience all affect immigrant students' school achievement (Garcia, 1998). Knowledge of the English language remains one of the major educational problems of immigrant students in the United States. Although the situation improves with time, this problem particularly affects children who enroll in U.S. schools at older ages (Vernez et al., 1996). Cummins's (1986) work suggests that it takes immigrant students at least six years to get a command of English sufficient to do strong academic work in that language. Pre–high school experience is an essential factor in increasing immigrant students' high school success. Immigrant students who arrive at older ages without previous school experiences are definitely at a disadvantage both socially and academically (Mace-Matlock et al., 1998).

Secondary School and Immigration Students

It is "common wisdom" that immigrant students are typically of the younger variety. Two analyses of demographic trends (Ruiz-de-Velasco and Fix, 2001; Camarota, 2001) provide counter-evidence to this wisdom. In analysis of the U.S. Census Bureau's current policy survey, these reports profile the shift in age of our U.S. immigrant students. Drawing on national data from the U.S. Census and the U.S. Department of Education's Schools and Staffing Survey, Ruiz-de-Velasco and Fix (2001) present a national profile of immigrant secondary school students. Camarota (2001), with a focus on Californians, provides similar evidence of the shift.

According to these reports, immigrant secondary students can be characterized as:

- *Growing as a Significant Part of All K-12 Students.* Children of immigrants (foreign-born or having foreign-born parents) represent a sharply rising share of all students in school, tripling from 6.3 percent in 1970 to nearly 20 percent in 1997.
- *More Attending Secondary School.* Foreign-born children represent a substantially larger share of the total secondary school population (5.7 percent) than of the primary school population (3.5 percent).
- *Limited in English Proficiency (LEP).* As many as a quarter of all foreign-born are not fully fluent in English; about 75 percent of these children are Hispanic and speak Spanish at home.
- *Receiving Limited Instructional Resources.* While more than three-quarters of LEP elementary school students receive special English language development instruction, fewer than half of secondary school LEP students receive such instruction.
- *In Poverty.* Foreign-born children have experienced sharp increases in poverty, from 17 percent in 1970 to almost 44 percent in 1995.
- *Highly Isolated.* Children of immigrants tend to be linguistically isolated in schools as well as economically and ethnically segregated. Almost one-half of all LEP children attend schools in which 30 percent or more of the students are also LEP. Only 2 percent of non-LEP students attend such schools.

- *Becoming a More Significant Reality for California Schools.* Los Angeles and San Francisco have seen twice the number of immigrant secondary students in the 1990s. Together, these metropolitan areas have doubled growth in Hispanic immigrants compared with the other major receiving centers of New York City and Miami.

The challenges facing secondary schools are formidable. In response to these challenges, the Mellon Program for Immigrant Education (PRIME) has made important strides regarding these challenges (Ruiz-de-Velasco and Fix, 2001). PRIME supported secondary school efforts aimed at immigrant students in five U.S. sites. An external review of these efforts resulted in a comprehensive overview of barriers at these sites and suggested improvements:

- *Limited Staff Capacity.* Teachers of mainstream subjects, such as math or history, often lack training to work with LEP students and often maintain that developing students' basic literacy skills is not part of their core task. Principals and counselors frequently lack language skills and cultural understanding to communicate effectively with these students. Suggested remedies include implementing professional development programs for veteran teachers focused on making mainstream subject classes more accessible to students still learning English.
- *Organizational Rigidity.* The division of secondary schools into departments along university lines, the isolation of language development teachers, and the division of the day into 50-minute periods hamper needed individualized instruction for students with special learning needs. For example, the time allotted for learning is too short for students to master both the language and content needed to graduate. Suggested remedies include restructuring the secondary school schedule so that language and subject teachers have the opportunity to collaborate and to reorganize their use of classroom time.
- *Lack of Accountability and Standards.* Curriculum content standards for English language development programs vary widely across states, schools, and even classrooms. Secondary schools also lag behind elementary schools in creating instructional strategies and curricula specially designed to help LEP students meet new grade promotion and graduation standards. Suggested remedies include expanded development of strong curricular and student performance students for ESL (English as a Second Language) and bilingual programs, which serve as gateways to secondary schools' mainstream curriculum.
- *Knowledge Gaps.* Reformers face wide knowledge gaps in how to si-

multaneously build both language and subject matter learning among LEP students. Both types of learning are necessary for immigrant teens to graduate in the short time available to reach that goal. The lack of reliable assessment instruments for LEP students is particularly troubling to teachers. Suggested remedies include more demonstration projects on promising curricular models and more research that addresses four broad areas: needs of understudied subpopulations; optimal ways to teach core subject material to LEP students; educational and social effects of linguistic isolation on students; and development of reliable assessment tools. (Adapted from Ruiz-de-Velasco and Fix, 2001, 81–86.)

The recognition of this new character of Hispanic immigrants will begin to change the nature of schooling at the secondary level. Many teachers trained in the traditional subject areas of math, science, and English will find themselves teaching students that differ with regard to English ability and cultural values. Elementary schools have faced this set of challenges by offering program alternatives inside and outside their classrooms. Secondary schools will now be asked to consider similar accommodations.

Issues of Limited Schooling

In this chapter, I have outlined the characteristics and needs of immigrant students. A particular situation does arise when a school is faced with immigrant students with limited prior schooling. Classification of a student as low schooled varies across districts because this classification is based on criteria established at the local level. Generally, these are students who have led less than age-appropriate formal schooling in their home or adopted country (i.e., they are three or more grades behind their age-level peers) and who demonstrate limited literacy or no proficiency in English. Additionally, a majority of these students are from rural or impoverished backgrounds and may have experienced the trauma of war or violence in their native countries (Mace-Matlock et al., 1998).

Given the wide variation among the students themselves and the lack of uniformity in locally determined classification criteria, a precise profile of these students is problematic. The most important distinction observed is between those students who have had some formal education (and thus have some basic literacy skills) and those who have had no formal education. The latter students, often referred to as "nonliterate," or "literacy" students, present the greatest challenge to schools.

School districts often place students in age-appropriate grade levels regardless of the students' educational histories and skill levels. As a result,

secondary schools that receive immigrant adolescents with limited schooling face an array of new demands and must take the following tasks:

- Teach basic concepts and skills normally taught in the elementary
  grades
- Work effectively with students who have not been socialized into the
  culture of schooling in any country
- Locate, adapt, or develop curricula and instructional materials that are
  age and content appropriate for a diverse group of students
- Connect students and families with appropriate health and human services
- Address the needs of students, many of whom must work at a paying
  job while attending school
- Create a climate of acceptance of diversity throughout the school
- Design program options that allow students to earn a high school diploma or to continue their education in post–high school institutions
- Help teachers, counselors, and other school personnel who may not
  be accustomed to working with this student population

Despite a limited body of research and few successful program models
on which to draw, schools in various parts of the United States are attempting to understand the needs of immigrant adolescents with limited prior
schooling and to design programs to meet their needs. Certain promising
program strategies (Mace-Matlock et al., 1998) include separate or partially separate programs for newcomer students, schedule alternatives, specialized content courses (including native-language instruction, ESL instruction, and sheltered content instruction) that earn graduation credits,
close monitoring of student progress, additional programs that provide
postsecondary options, professional development activities for teachers
and other school staff, and work with families, communities, and organizations outside the school (see table 4.3). Like any program that serves diverse students, one of the most important features of a promising program
is flexibility.

CONCLUSION

Immigration continues to make demands of our public schools at all levels.
The majority of the fiscal responsibility for educating immigrant students
has its greatest impact at the state and local levels, where people have the
most invested interest in their schools. While it is not unreasonable to expect the federal government, the unit of government that makes decisions
about immigration policy, to bear the responsibility to cover some, if not
all, of the costs of educating immigrant children, the implementation of

Table 4.3   Reconceptualizations of Learners, Teachers, and Schools and Their Implications for Immigrant Students

Reconceptualizations of Learners as . . .	*Implications for Immigrant Students*
Active constructs of knowledge	• Supports and values learning through various means, thus acknowledging different learning styles. • Reduces reliance on language as the medium for learning. • Conflicts with the views of many other cultures, which hold that learners take in what teachers deliver. • May require more language use and cultural knowledge than some immigrants have attained.
Collaborators	• Promotes language use in the classroom. • Promotes cross-cultural learning and communication. • Is consistent with learning strategies in cultures with a collective orientation, which traditional U. S. competitive learning is not. • May require more langage use and cultural knowledge than some immigrants have attained. • Requires cross-cultural sensitivity for all involved.
Decision makers	• Draws on strengths of students who play decision-making roles. • Conflicts with collective orientation in emphasizing individual will, action, and responsibility. • May conflict with adolescent roles in other cultures.
Reconceptualizations of Teachers as . . .	*Implications for Immigrant Students*
Learners	• Allows teachers to admit that they need to learn about educating immigrant students. • Provides support for learing about educating immigrant students. • Allows the pooling of expertise from more than one person in working with immigrant students. • Can increase personalization, which benefits immigrant students as nonmaintream learners.
Facilitators	• Increases personalization, which benefits immigrant students as nonmainstream learners. • Conflicts with the views of many other cultures, which hold that teachers should deliver information.
Cultural and linguistic mediators	• Directly addresses the needs and builds on the linguistic, cultural, and personal strengths of immigrant students. • Helps student develop pride in their own backgrounds. • Gives students access to the "culture of power" by developing their academic skills and knowledge.
Reconceptualizations of Schools as . . .	*Implications for Immigrant Students*
Communities	• Encourages everyone to learn about immigrant students and families in order to integrate them into the community. • Requires personalization of schooling.
Learners centered	• Encourages everyone to learn about immigrant students and families in order to design schooling with learnings at the center. • Requires personalization of schooling.
Part of a larger situational and chronological order	• Encourages schools to find ways to engage immigrant families in schooling. • Brings together mulitple providers of service and assistance for immigrant families. • May eventually lead schools to provide assistance for immigrant students as they move beyond high school into work and higher education.
Mediators between home culture and mainstream culture	• Makes information about U. S. culture and schooling accessible to immigrant students. • Shows immigrant students that their cultures and experiences are valued. • Gives immigrant students access to academic knowledge and abilities.

Source: Lucas (1997, 58–59).

adequate programs will remain the responsibility of local school districts. Despite the immediate costs, the education of immigrant youth is an investment in the future of our communities.

California and Texas, as well as the United States, are not alone in struggling with the predicament of how to deal with immigrant youth. Most industrialized nations are dealing with similar issues. What we are experiencing in the United States is part of a global phenomenon. The question of how to educate immigrant students is not one that can be addressed simply with reforms in immigration laws. The immigrant children who will be enrolling in our schools in most urban areas in the next five years are already residing in our communities. Programs must be in place when they arrive in our classrooms.

To make the transition from "outsider" to an integral part of the U.S. workforce and society, immigrant youth must acquire cultural and technical skills through formal education. Portes and Rambaut (cited in Dugger, 1999), Cummins (1986), Ogbu (1987b), and Heath (1989) have suggested that the schooling of immigrant children must be understood within the broader context of society's treatment of these students and their families in and out of schools. No quick fix is likely under present social and schooling conditions. There is no single attribute that is the only variable of importance in the education of immigrant youth. A more comprehensive view, one that includes an understanding of the relationship between home and school and one that integrates students' values, beliefs, histories, and experiences into the educational strategies, is essential for the educational success of Hispanic immigrant students.

A factor that must remain in the forefront of planning for the education of Hispanic students is that Hispanics are not a homogeneous group. Suarez-Orozco (1997) emphasized the stresses and losses experienced by immigrant families that often affect their ability to help their children adjust to life in the United States. The acculturation process also tends to separate immigrant parents from their more acculturated children. When immigrant parents are preoccupied with the economic pressures to make a life for their families in the United States, immigrant youths often to turn to peer groups for support to help them adjust to their difficult surroundings. Issues facing the second generation are very different from those facing the first generation of immigrant education. Many second- and third-generation youth grow disaffected with the school system and, when they experience difficulties in school environments, turn to gangs or drop out of school altogether. Thus, for immigrant children and the children of immigrants, growing up American can be a smooth transition or a traumatic confrontation. In some cases, even when they want very much to become indistinguishable from their American peers, they are viewed as outsiders. In other cases, they may be accepted as American but maintain a strong sense of ethnic identity (Zhou, 1997).

5

Culture and Education:
Seeds of the Individual
and Collective Identity
for Hispanics in Schools

INTRODUCTION

I can remember vividly my first day of school. I was sent off on a large yellow bus by my mother with a Big Chief tablet in one hand and one pencil in the other. It was unclear to me what awaited me at the other end of that five-mile bus ride. Yet I knew that whatever it was, it was important. I recall my mother making very clear that I needed to behave myself, do as I was told, and stay out of trouble. "*Portate bien*" (Be a good boy) were the last words I heard as I boarded that bus. And I did behave, although I did not understand all that my teacher said to me or to the other students.

Unknowingly, I had entered a new "culture" and was asked to make a new set of transitions from where I had been to a new set of futures particularly related to schooling. It was my first contact with a significantly different outside world—a world not dominated by Spanish-speaking adults in the form of parents, uncles, aunts, and extended family members or Spanish- and English-speaking peers in the form of cousins. Based on my own unforgettable fear, I can imagine how most youngsters might feel in a similar situation.

WE LIVE IN A CULTURE OF CULTURES

It has long been characteristic of U.S. schools to perceive of the unique attributes of Hispanic children as a limitation. Likewise, the social attributes of these children's family/home environments have been viewed as detrimental with regard to social, economic, and educational success. In any culture, it is within the context of family/home circumstances that important socialization practices are formed that set the stage for the years to come. This chapter focuses on understanding students' multiple "cultures" and the transitions between them in an effort to provide information that will assist educators and others who work with students to build bridges between their "cultures." The focus will be on describing family, school, and peer cultures; the interrelationships among these; and, in particular, how these combine to affect children's engagement with learning. Of particular interest are features in school environments that aid or impede students in transitioning between home and school.

Similar to Erickson (1987), it is important to distinguish the nature of the lines between cultures, settings, or contexts. Some boundaries are neutral, sociocultural components that are perceived to be equal by the people on each side of the boundary. When such boundaries exist, movement between cultures occurs with relative ease—social and psychological costs are minimal. Alternately, when such borders are not neutral and separate cultures are not perceived as equal, then movement and adaptation is frequently difficult because the knowledge and skills in one culture are more highly valued and esteemed than those in another. Although it is possible for students to navigate borders with apparent success, these transitions can incur personal and psychic costs invisible to teachers and others. Moreover, borders can become impenetrable barriers when the psychosocial consequences of adaptation become too great.

Although the concepts used here are not new, prior research generally has focused on families, peers, and schools as distinct entities. We know that any one of these components can powerfully affect the direction in which students will be pulled. For example, dynamic teachers, vigorous schools, and programs targeted to override the negative effects associated with low socioeconomic status, limited motivation, and language and cultural barriers can produce committed, interested, and academically engaged individuals (Edmonds, 1979a; Rutter et al., 1979; Sharan, 1980; Johnson and Johnson, 1981; Heath, 1982; Walberg, 1986; Vogt, Jordan, and Tharp, 1987; Slavin, 1988, 1989; Joyce et al., 1989; Abi-Nader, 1990b). Likewise, research on peer groups has described the potency and force with which members pull young people toward the norms of groups (Coleman, 1963; Clement and Harding, 1978; Larkin, 1979; Varenne, 1982; Clasen and Brown, 1985; Ueda, 1987; Eckert, 1989). We know too that family indices, such as socioeconomic status and parents' educational levels, are important predictors of students' engagement within educational settings (Jencks, 1972), as are cultural expectations and beliefs (Clark, 1983; Ogbu, 1983, 1987a; Suarez-Orozco, 1985, 1987; Erickson,

1987; Gibson, 1987; McDermott, 1987; Spindler, 1987; Fordham, 1988; Hoffman, 1988; Trueba, 1988a). In other words, we know a great deal about how aspects of families, schools, teachers, and peer groups independently affect educational outcomes. But we need to know how these worlds combine in the day-to-day lives of students to affect their engagement within school and classroom contexts.

As educators attempt to create optimal school environments for Hispanic populations, we need to know how students negotiate borders successfully or, alternatively, how they are impeded by barriers (and borders) that prevent their connection not only within an institutional context but also with peers who are different than themselves. Figure 5.1 attempts to graphically portray this interaction of cultures.

Recent recognition of cultural differences, particularly by the educational establishment, combined with theoretical and empirical interest expressly concerned with extrapolating the cause of such differences (Mead, 1937), has led to a growing body of literature regarding differences in socialization practices. In particular, that literature has attempted to relate familial characteristics to the emergence of particular social organizations that distinguish populations (Tharp, 1989) and how these in turn shape

Figure 5.1.

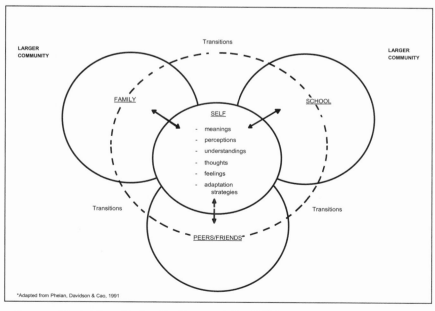

Source: Adapted from Phelan, Davidson, and Cao (1991).

self-identity (Ogbu, 1999) and how these influence participation/nonparticipation.

CULTURAL DIFFERENCE: ROOTS IN THE FAMILY

Although the "Americanization" mentality has predominated, more recent research has begun to perceive ethnic culture as more than a target of elimination. On foundations established by the noted anthropologist Margaret Mead (1937), researchers (notably McClintock, 1974; Kagan, 1983b; Lave, 1988; Tharp and Gallimore, 1988; Valsiner, 1989; Nieto, 1996) have begun to explore socialization as a means by which cultural differences can be understood as opposed to eliminated.

One of the most significant functions of socialization is the transmission of values. By socialization, Mead (1937) and McClintock (1972) refer to the process through which prescriptions and prohibitions are transmitted to members of the social group. The traditional socialization view generally presented in the literature has focused on the family (including siblings and the extended family) as important socialization agents. More recent conceptualizations (e.g., Hetherington and Parke, 1988) have considered socialization agents outside the family as well as the reciprocal roles of the socialization agents and the child. The familial socialization agents include parents, siblings, and the extended family. The nonfamilial socialization agents include teachers, peers, the media (especially television), and other persons with whom the child regularly comes into contact.

Several authors (McClintock, Bayard, and McClintock, 1983; Keefe and Padilla, 1987; Knight, Bernal, and Carlos, 1988; Whiting and Edwards, 1988) have discussed the variables associated with the family background, the family structure, and the broader social ecology that influence the socialization experiences of culturally diverse children. The family structure variables shown to be related to the parents' socialization goals include the strength of familial interdependence, the pattern of status in relationships within the family, and family size (for more details, see McClintock et al., 1983) Strength of familial interdependence consists of feelings of family solidarity as well as attachment and commitment to the family. There is some empirical evidence regarding the presence of close family ties among Mexican American families (Keefe, 1979; Keefe, Padilla, and Carlos, 1979a). For example, research with Hispanic families compared to Anglo American families suggests that there are closer relations and greater loyalty among members, more frequent visitation of relatives, parental encouragement of family-centered orientations in their children, fewer opportunities for children to bring friends over to the house, less freedom for children to play away from home, greater disapproval for children contradicting authority, and fewer decision-making opportunities for the children. Similarly, Johnson, Teigen, and Davila (1983) found parents of Mexican backgrounds to be relatively demanding and restrictive of the children compared to Anglo parents. While caution is advocated regarding the stereotyping of results pointing to stronger interdependence among Hispanic families, McClintock et al. (1983) have speculated about the implications of these characteristics for a child's exposure to nonfamilial peers and in turn for their reward distribution preferences. Thus, less exposure and, therefore, opportunities for social comparisons with nonfamilial peers may make Anglo peers less relevant referents for Hispanic children, thereby reducing the value of competitive (superiority) reward distributions for these children.

Cooper et al. (1991) report a related study of individual and cooperative socialization values. Their study explored the links between individuality and family connectedness in European American, Chinese American, Filipino American, Vietnamese American, and Hispanic American adolescents. The three Asian American groups and the Hispanic American group reported much more concern for familial values as opposed to concern for the individual. In addition, these groups were much more likely to see their siblings and peers as major sources of assistance and advice as opposed to parents. Anglo American adolescents were much more individualistic in their perception of themselves in the family and more likely to seek out parents and adults for critical advice and/or support. Similarly, Seginer's (1989) study of Arab adolescents found that older sisters play a key socialization role. These adolescents see their sisters as important consultants regarding the outside world, future plans, social relations, and education. Mothers are consulted only about pubertal changes, and fathers are consulted about permission, money, and political issues.

Still further evidence of cultural socialization diversity comes from research on Native Alaskan families (Henze et al., 1990). In interviews with Yup'ik families, a non-family-centered socialization pattern was articulated. Keeping in mind that this native group is organized around subsistence functions, a "men's house" provides instruction for boys in all aspects of community life, while the home functions as the place where women transmit information to girls. This gender-separate social structure has evolved over many years as the social functions of each gender have been organized to meet harsh survival challenges. The concept or structure of a core nuclear or extended family is nonexistent. Moreover, like other data regarding American Indian cultures (Tharp, 1989), children are expected to learn by carefully observing adults or older peers and siblings, without asking questions or interrupting activities. These diverse socialization practices have too often been interpreted as deviant instead of diverse. The intent of such examples here is meant to reinforce the overall thesis that the "local" ecology of children outside of school sets the stage for lifelong patterns of social relations, including those that are important in the schooling process.

Besides the family and community ecology, the broader social ecology has also been suggested to be an important determinant of the socialization of children (Kagan, 1983c; Keefe and Padilla, 1987). This broader social ecology includes environmental characteristics such as the urbanization level of the community in which the child lives, the socioeconomic status of the family and the community, and the nature of the minority status of other cultural groups in the community and the prevailing views of the broader society regarding these groups. In many ways, a relatively rural and/or a relatively low socioeconomic environment may lead to socialization experiences that foster interdependency, respect for others, and more sharing of resources. In contrast, a more urban environment may lead to socialization experiences that foster independence, competitiveness, and more reliance on social supports that are external to the family. There has been some empirical demonstration of a relation between the social behaviors of children and urbanization level (e.g., Kagan et al., 1981) and socioeconomic status (Knight and Kagan, 1977). Minority status may lead to considerable variability in socialization experiences simply because the minority child generally has direct contacts with the minority group as well as the dominant Anglo American group (Ogbu, 1982a, 1987a).

ETHNIC IMAGE AND ITS EFFECTS

Ethnic Images in Society

In recent decades, Americans have made considerable progress in the area of race relations. Lynching, de jure segregation, and Jim Crow laws have been abolished. Whites have become more supportive of integration and racial equity (Smith and Sheatsley, 1984; Schuman, Steeh, and Bobo, 1985; Jaynes and Williams, 1989; Smith, 1990). Governments have instituted numerous programs to promote integration and to assist minority groups (e.g., busing, affirmative action, and minority contracting). Recent research has addressed the changes in racial tolerance—changes in the stereotypes or images that people have towards ethnic groups. This research has addressed two questions: What are the images that people have toward several prominent ethnic groups on various dimensions or characteristics, and do the images people have about ethnic groups influence other attitudes and behaviors toward the groups?

In the examination of the ethnic images research, the term "ethnic" is used as a general term to cover six extensively studied groups (whites,

Jews, blacks, Asian Americans, Hispanic Americans, and southern whites) that are defined partly by race, religion, nationality, and region. The term "images" is used here rather than terms like "stereotypes" or "prejudices" to avoid some of the baggage that is frequently associated with these terms. For example, stereotypes and prejudice are often assumed to contain a component of irrationality, including such fallacies as improper generalization, excessive categorization, and rejection of counterevidence (Allport, 1954; Schuman and Harding, 1964; Jackman, 1973). Therefore, ethnic images as utilized here are meant to designate general beliefs that people have about cultural groups, and in particular they are beliefs about group characteristics and attributes.

The belief that Americans are approaching a color-and-creed-blind society is easily disabused by the ethnic image data collected in the *1990 General Social Survey* (see Smith, 1990). First, these data indicate that people are willing and able to rate group members on the basis of their ethnicity. Blacks seem to be the easiest minority group to evaluate, while Asian Americans are more difficult. Second, with one exception, minority groups are evaluated more negatively than whites in general. The one exception is Jews, who are rated more favorably than whites on each characteristic except patriotism. No other group scores above whites on any characteristic. Looking at how everyone rates ethnic and racial groups (including in-group members), Jews are rated most positively overall (first on wealth, industry, nonviolence, intelligence, and self-support and third on patriotism; Asian Americans and white southerners are ranked next (second or third) on almost every dimension. Finally, blacks and Hispanic Americans are ranked last or next to last on almost every characteristic. In summary, Jews are the only positively rated "minority" group.

Ethnic images also are related to the social distance that people wish to maintain between themselves and other groups. As the image scale for each group moves from positive to negative, people are less favorable toward living in a neighborhood where half the neighbors are from particular groups and less favorable to having a close relative marry a group member. While all of the associations are significant, the relationships between images and social distance for Jews and white southerners are modest, while the association for blacks, Asian Americans, and Hispanic Americans are much more substantial.

In sum, images about ethnic groups are significant predictors of support for racial integration and desired social distance. Despite the demonstrable progress in intergroup tolerance over the last several decades, ethnic images are still commonplace in contemporary society. On the whole, these images are neither benign nor trivial. Most Americans see most minority groups in a decidedly negative light on a number of important characteristics. Only images of Jews are generally positive, and even in their case people seem to question their patriotism. All other groups, including the old-stock white southerners, are seen more negatively than whites in general. In particular, Hispanics and African Americans receive very low ratings. These negative ethnic images in turn help shape attitudes toward civil rights and racial integration policies, social distance, ratings of countries, and presumably other group-related issues. Ethnic images remain important determinants of intergroup attitudes. They are crucial components of public opinion on such issues as affirmative action, school desegregation, and many other group-related issues. Contemporary intergroup relations cannot be understood without understanding the images that people have in their minds about the various ethnic groups that make up this country.

Effects on the Individual

How do these images shape an individual's self-identity and behavior? The following discussion is from the work of Smith and Sheatsley (1984) regarding personality formation. Personality formation is shaped by the social categories which the child's sense of ethnic identity is part of. In a world populated by people of many different ethnic backgrounds who often interact and conflict with each other, children's developing sense of their ethnic group identity is an important psychological and social issue. As a consequence, there have been several studies of the development of ethnic identity that focus both on children's ability to identify their own ethnic group and on their attitudes toward their own and other groups (McAdoo and McAdoo, 1985).

Perhaps the most famous research on the development of ethnic identity was carried out by Kenneth and Mamie Clark (1939). The results of their research became evidence that led the U.S. Supreme Court to declare racially segregated education illegal. African American and Anglo children aged three years and older were presented pairs of dolls representing each ethnic group. On successive trials, the children were asked to choose "which boy [doll] you would like to play with" or "which girl you don't like." The Clarks reported that most of the youngest children distinguished between the gender categories of the dolls and that both the African American children displayed a preference for the Anglo dolls. These results were interpreted by the justices of the Supreme Court as evidence that segregation resulted in the development of a negative sense of self among African American children. Studies conducted since the 1950s both confirm the Clarks's original findings (McAdoo and McAdoo, 1985; Spencer, 1988a) and extend them to other minority ethnic groups, including Native Americans (Beauf, 1977). In all these cases, minority group children were more likely to prefer Anglo dolls.

Importantly, these same studies have cast doubt on the notion that minority ethnic group children acquire a generalized negative self-concept. Beauf (1977), for example, reports incident after incident in which Native American children who display a preference for Anglo dolls portray with devastating accuracy their understanding of the economic and social circumstances that make their lives difficult in contrast with the lives of Anglo Americans. Five-year-old Dom, for example, was given several dolls representing Anglos and Native Americans (whose skins were represented as brown) to put into a toy classroom:

> Dom (holding up a white doll): The children's all here and now the teacher's coming in.
> Interviewer: Is that the teacher?
> Dom: Yeah.
> Interviewer (holding up a brown doll): Can she be the teacher?
> Dom: No way! Her's just an aide. (Beauf, 1977)

In Beauf's view, children's choices when presented pairs of dolls are less an expression of their self-concept than of a desire for the power and wealth of the Anglos with whom they have come in contact.

Other recent research has shown that when psychologists attempt to test their social and self-conceptions, young children's expressed ethnic preferences change according to the circumstances. At the level of historical changes, McAdoo and McAdoo (1985) reported that the degree to which African American preschoolers showed a preference for Anglo American dolls had decreased relative to the results obtained in the period prior to the 1960s. They did not speculate on the reasons for these trends, but the end of racial segregation and several decades of political and cultural activism in the African American community are likely candidates. This conclusion was reinforced by Beauf's (1977) finding that young children of parents who were active in promoting Native American cultural awareness and social rights displayed relatively high levels of choice of dolls representing Native Americans compared to children of parents who took little interest in Native American affairs.

Additional evidence of the power of the environment to shape children's ethnic preferences comes from an experimental study that rewarded three- to five-year-old children for choices of black versus white pictures of animals and people (Spencer and Horowitz, 1973). Initially, all the children showed a preference for white stimuli (both animals and people), but after training sessions in which they were rewarded symbolically (by giving them marbles that could be traded for cookies), they displayed a marked preference for black stimuli, which remained intact over a period of several weeks.

In sum, the results of studies on ethnic identity indicate that children are aware of differences by the time they are four years old. At the same time, or not long after, they also become aware of, and form judgments about, their own ethnicity. Their attitudes toward their own and other people's ethnicity seem to depend on both the attitudes of their adult caregivers and the perceived power and wealth of their own ethnic group.

A CULTURAL SYSTEMS ACCOUNT OF
UNDERACHIEVEMENT

The previous discussion of culture and its relationship to the education of Hispanic students in our schools has concentrated on issues of family, home, and the effects of socialization practices on individual children and students. Such a "micro" approach by its very nature concentrates on the individual students' physical/social contract with her or his parents, siblings, peers, and other representatives of social institutions. These interactions are seen as guiding the communicative, cognitive, social, and educational development of the student. In short, these interactions set the stage for either educational success or educational failure.

An alternative to this "micro" understanding has been a "macro" approach proposed by a number of anthropologists and sociologists. This cultural systems approach considers as important the broader social organization of a society (Ogbu, 1982b, 1987a, 1987b; Ogbu and Matute-Bianchi, 1986; Gibson and Ogbu, 1991; Suarez-Orozco and Suarez-Orozco, 1995). Known by various names, including the structural inequality theory (Gollnick and Chinn, 1990), institutional racism (Ovando and Collier, 1985), the perceived labor market explanation (Erickson, 1987), and most notably the secondary cultural systems theory (Ogbu, 1987b), this approach suggests that the specific social placement of a cultural group within the broader social fabric will directly affect the values, perceptions, and social behavior of that group and individuals within that group. Specific to the education of minority groups in the United States, this approach suggests that minority students become convinced by the overall social order that their "place" in society is distinctively disadvantaged. Ogbu (1999) and others (Cummins, 1997; Garcia, 1999) argue that there are two reasons why we should study the relationship between collective identity and schooling. One is that this phenomenon may explain some attitudes and behaviors observed in ethnographic research around the world (Gibson, 1997). For example, while doing fieldwork in Stockton, California (1968–70), some minority groups manifested oppositional attitudes and behaviors toward the schools just at a time when changes to improve their education were being initiated. The minorities organized rallies and conferences to condemn "the system." Some black students in the same community did not want to speak the standard English because it was "white language," and some Mexican American students did not want to learn English because it was "Anglo." The second reason for studying collective identity is to explain differences in behaviors among minority groups themselves. As discussed earlier in this chapter, one major explanation of the school failure of some minorities is that the poor academic performance is caused by cultural and language discontinuities and conflicts because their cultures and languages are different from the culture and language of the school. The problem with this explanation is that, on the contrary, minorities who are academically more successful are those whose cultures and language are more different from the culture and language of white Americans that they encounter in school (Ogbu, 1999). Specifically, immigrant minority students from Asia, Central and South America, the Caribbean, and Africa seem to do better than the nonimmigrant minorities, such as black Americans, Hispanics, Native Americans, and Native Hawaiians. Furthermore, nonimmigrant minorities in other societies appear to experience similar difficulties with the culture and language of the schools (Gibson, 1997). On the basis of ethnographic research in the United States and elsewhere, it seems that the problem is due merely to cultural and language differences, although these are important. But there appears to be something else involved, and that something else might be identity. Gidden (1991, as cited in Gibson, 1995) has argued that people in modern societies no longer share essentialized or ethnic identity because the basis for such an identity no longer exists:

> The idea that each person has a unique character and special potentialities that may or may not be fulfilled is alien to premodern culture. In medieval Europe, lineage, gender, social status, and other attributes relevant to identity were all relatively fixed. Transitions had to be made through the various stages of life, but these were governed by institutionalized processes and the individual's role in them was relatively passive. (Gidden, 1991, 171)

As a result of this breakdown of social groups, each individual is left to "construct" or "negotiate" his or her own unique identity based on personal circumstances and social environment. Identity is no longer fixed; it evolves and is constructed or coconstructed in negotiation between the individual and those continuing his or her social context, including the state in time place. While anthropologists rarely define "identity," the focus of their research is on the way that people, including children, negotiate and construct their identity.

This concept of ethnic identity may be appropriate for a set of the liberated and individualistic white segment of U.S. society. It also fits the identity paths of white ethnic groups in the United States who have more or less the complete option to assimilate into the mainstream. For them, ethnic membership may be unimportant for an individual's sense of who he or she is. As some have pointed out (Gonzalez, 1999), ethnic identity for white Americans has probably become voluntary. White Americans can choose to be Irish on St. Patrick's Day or Italian on Columbus Day (Ogbu, 1999).

This is not the case for nonwhite Americans, like Asian Americans, black Americans, Hispanics, Native Americans, and Native Hawaiians. Nor is it the case for most people in the Third World nations like Indonesia, Mexico, or Nigeria. The present ethnic conflicts and "ethnic cleansing" in many parts of the world do not support the claims that personally "negotiated" identity has displaced collective identity. That is not to say that the two types of identity may not coexist in an appropriate place like the United States. The point of emphasis is that racial and ethnic minorities as persistent peoples in contemporary urban industrial societies still possess collective identity. It seems appropriate to consider this phenomenon to better understand the school experience of these minorities by studying their collective identity.

Ogbu (1987b) has been a powerful spokesperson for this cultural systems explanation of the persistent and disproportionate school failure of some minorities in the United States and throughout the world. He has offered an analysis that distinguishes between immigrant/voluntary minorities and nonimmigrant/involuntary minorities (also termed castelike, outcast, or pariah). The term "minority" suggests a group that is smaller in the numeric sense. In the ethnic context, it means a group that is subordinate to another dominant group and implies a negative power relationship. Numeric majority does not guarantee dominant status. Historically in Latin America, India, and Africa, for example, millions of native peoples were or are in a subordinate position to a minority of "ruling" colonial powers (Gollnick and Chinn, 1990).

Ogbu's (1987b) analysis suggest that immigrant minorities and involuntary minorities may live in the same society and experience the same circumstances: prejudice, discrimination, residential segregation, inferior education for their children, and exclusion from desirable jobs. However, immigrant minorities often do well in school and sometimes are more successful academically, sometimes even more successful than students in the dominant group. East Asians, for example, often test higher on standardized testing than Anglos in the United States. Involuntary minorities like blacks, Hispanics, and American Indians consistently have problems in school, perform below grade level, and have high dropout rates.

Ogbu and Matute-Bianchi (1986) begin to elaborate on a conceptual framework regarding the distinction between voluntary and involuntary minority groups. Ogbu (1987b) proposes that the cultural models of the immigrant and involuntary minorities differ in five key elements:

1. A frame of reference for comparing present status and future possibilities
2. A folk theory of getting ahead, especially through education
3. A sense of collective identity
4. A cultural frame of reference for judging appropriate behavior and affirming group membership and solidarity
5. An assessment of the extent to which one may trust members of the dominant group and the institutions they control

This conceptualization of educational underachievement is worth considering. For example, Suarez-Orozco (1987) proposes that the different Hispanic American groups—Mexican Americans, Puerto Rican Americans, and Americans of Cuban, Central American, and South American decent as well as recent refugees from Central America—are distinct populations and should be understood as such. They face different issues and have different patterns of educational adaptation. Suarez-Orozco and Suarez-Orozco (1995) report that while one-fourth of Mexican Americans nationwide aged 25 years or older had less than five years of schooling, the same was true for only 6 percent of other Hispanics. In the Southwest, only 60 percent of Hispanics were reported to have graduated from high school compared to 86 percent of Anglos. Many Central American refugees, however, are experiencing school success. In an ethnographic study in San Francisco of 200 refugees at two school sites (Suarez-Orozco and Suarez-Orozco 1995), the understanding that these new immigrants have developed on the nature of opportunity in this country have allowed them to succeed academically.

The school success of the Central American refugees was surprising. They "were routinely routed to overcrowded, understaffed, poor inner city schools, into a poisonous atmosphere of drugs and violence," where teachers were afraid of their students (Suarez-Orozco and Suarez-Orozco, 1995). They learned English quickly but were tracked into other low-level classes they had already completed in their own country. Yet many were highly motivated to persevere and succeed in school. The Central American immigrants were perceived as desirable students by their teachers—eager to learn, appreciative, polite, respectful, and hard-working.

According to Suarez-Orozco and Suarez-Orozco (1995), the recent Central American immigrants developed a dual frame of reference in which they compared their situation in the United States with that in their "homeland." Most perceived that in this country they had more and better opportunities for a search for a better tomorrow. The students believed it was self-evident that the future was open to them. Parents overlooked difficulties and emphasized the positive: The United States was fairer, they did not have to pay for schools, there was free hot lunch and libraries, and they felt that teachers were sincerely interested in their students. They developed a folk theory of "making it" in which education became the single most significant factor in getting ahead. This belief was constructed in opposition to the system of getting ahead at home, which was "who you know." In the United States, it is "what you know." The students felt that their parents were doing everything for them and felt a duty to succeed and get other loved ones out of the dangerous situation in their homeland. No matter how bad things were "here" and now, they were not as bad as at "home."

Matute-Bianchi (1990) focused on diversity within a population of Mexican descent in her ethnographic research at Field High School on the central coast of California between 1983 and 1985. She distinguished between five major categories of Mexican-descent students: recent Mexican immigrants, Mexican oriented, Mexican Americans, Chicanos, and Cholos. These categories emerged from interviews with teachers, counselors, aides, administrators, Mexican-descent students, and her own observations. Her emphasis was on the different forms and functions of ethnic labels and identificational consciousness between immigrant "Mexicanos" and nonimmigrant Mexican-descent groups in the United States and their relationships to variations in school performance. Matute-Bianchi (1990) observed a pattern of school success among immigrant Mexican-oriented students and a pattern of school failure among nonimmigrant Chicanos. The two groups were perceived differently by teachers and students. The groups themselves had different perceptions of what their futures held in terms of employment. Specifically, Matute-Bianchi found five distinctive "cultural" groups within her student population:

1. *Recent Mexican immigrants:* Self-identify as "Mexicanos"; arrived in the last three to five years; refer to Mexico as home; came to the United States for economic opportunity; considered "unstylish" by other students; proficiency in Spanish (oral and written) tends to be an indicator of school success
2. *Mexican oriented:* Maintain a strong identity as Mexicano; frequently Mexican born but have lived in the United States most of their lives; parents are immigrants; tend to be bilingual; adept at academic work in English, having received most schooling in the United States; speak English with school personnel, Spanish and English with peers, and Spanish at home; active in *Sociedad Bilingue;* proud of Mexican heritage; many of the Spanish-surname students in college prep are from this group

3. *Mexican American:* U.S.-born English speakers, much more American oriented than previous groups; may not speak Spanish unless it is necessary at home; participate in mainstream activities; tend not to call attention to their ethnicity; some of the most esteemed Mexican descent students in the school; staff described as "totally acculturated"

4. *Chicano:* At least the second generation of their family in the United States; loyal to their own group; avoid school activities; call themselves "homeboys" and "homegirls"; call academically successful students "schoolboys" or "wannabes" ("want to be white"); among the most alienated students in the school

5. *Cholos:* The smallest group in the school; noted for culturally distinct style of dressing that represents an identity that is not Mexican or American; "gang oriented" or "gang sympathizers"; "low riders" perceived to be gang members; feared and held in contempt by Mexican-descent and mainstream Anglo students

According to Matute-Bianchi, the successful Mexican-descent students were achievement and goal oriented. They saw a connection between high school success and adult success. They defined success as having a nice car, a nice house, and a good job and not having to worry about money anymore. They wanted to go to college, although they were not sure of a career choice. They had Anglo and Mexican role models in school. Most stated that their parents' interest and support was essential to their school success. School success was defined as the result of regular attendance, doing homework, asking for help, getting along with teachers, and working "as hard as you can." Some had received support from teachers and counselors.

The Chicanos and Cholos expressed the desire to get good jobs but did not have an idea of how to accomplish that. They did not feel a connection to the future in a positive way, and they lived for the moment or weekend. They doubted that they would graduate, even though they wanted to. They had little exposure to occupations other than the low-status, menial and physically difficult jobs of their parents. They could not think of one successful Mexican-descent adult they knew well. Although they expressed a desire to do well, they exhibited behaviors that resulted in school failure— truancy, poor attendance, disruptive behavior, failure to bring books and homework, poor performance in class, and failure to pass enough classes to maintain academic standing. They were apathetic and defiant of school culture.

Gibson and Ogbu (1991) describe similar findings in fieldwork carried out in St. Croix during the 1970s to study the relationship between ethnic identity, immigrant status, and school performance. Their results were

similar to those found by Matute-Bianchi (1990). In the St. Croix public
school setting, immigrants were more successful than natives, even though
they are similar in class status, color, and cultural background. What about
other ethnic groups? "In the United States, Asian-Americans (Koreans,
Japanese, and Chinese) are the only minority group whose academic
achievement surpasses that of Whites" (Lee, 1991). They exhibit higher
college attendance rates and higher achievement scores than the majority.
But Koreans, who achieve as well as Japanese in the United States, have
much lower achievement rates in Japan than the Japanese. The college attendance rate of Korean high school graduates was less than 60 percent
that of Japanese high school graduates. Lee (1991) suggests that the historical background of the experience of Koreans in their two host societies
provides further insight into the issues of cultural systems and differences
in academic achievement.

Specifically, Lee (1991) argues that Koreans have had an increasingly
positive image in the United States for two reasons. First, Korea has become
of strategic and economic importance to the United States and, second,
most Koreans in the United States are educated people with middle-class
backgrounds. Yet, with the exception of doctors, Koreans have found it
difficult to enter the middle-class mainstream because of language barriers, an inability to transfer skills acquired in Korea, and discrimination
against them in large businesses.

Koreans in Japan, much like those in the United States, have been legally entitled to public education since 1965. By 1981, 80 percent of Koreans were attending Japanese schools rather than Korean, hoping that a Japanese education would contribute to upward mobility and integration.
Korean schools do not have the status of Japanese schools, and their graduates are turned away from qualifying exams for universities and even to
attend barber, beauty, and chef schools. Within Japanese schools, Korean
students are discriminated against by staff, by other students, and even in
textbooks that portray Korea in a negative way and distort its history. Japanese children are brought up to consider Korean culture a "lower" culture.
More than half of Koreans use Japanese names to avoid harassment by
Japanese students. Teachers often treat Korean students with contempt and
feel very negatively toward them. Korean parents must pledge that their
children will not disturb order, and if tuition is required, Koreans must pay
more than Japanese. According to Lee (1991), Koreans are perceived to
hold, and actually do assume, a disadvantaged role in Japanese society.

However, American teachers and American students and their parents
perceive Koreans in a completely different light. American teachers welcome Korean students. They are praised for their qualities that many teachers feel are lacking in Anglo students. They have proven themselves to
be highly successful academically. Educators attribute this to East Asian

parents' high standards, strict discipline, and management of their children's time. They believe that once East Asians overcome the language barrier, they will get jobs. American parents perceive East Asian children as setting a good example for their own children and welcome them as friends (Ogbu, 1987b).

In the United States, Koreans have higher college attendance rates and higher achievement scores than Anglos. Korean parents value education highly and have high expectations of their children, often teaching them at home before they are school age. In Japan, Koreans are a castelike minority with little power in their host society. Koreans in the United States are one of the most successful immigrant minorities.

Although Erickson (1987) claims that Ogbu (1987b) sees "a social revolution" as the only way out of the situation in which involuntary minorities find themselves, Ogbu (1983, 1986, 1987b) does not come to that conclusion. Instead, he points out that many intervention programs are based on the idea that ethnic minorities are "culturally deprived," "culturally deficient," or "socially disadvantaged" and that the school's role is to "redeem" them. Ogbu (1987b) differentiates between "Improvement Research" and "Explanatory Research." He is involved in "Explanatory Research," in particular comparative ethnographic research, "the long range goal of which is to provide knowledge for better and more effective educational policy as well as for preventative and remedial efforts" (Ogbu, 1987a). He cautions against instigating educational change without first understanding both the "micro" and the "macro" aspects of ethnic minority underachievement. This voice is echoed in a volume of the *Anthropology and Education Quarterly* (1997) that provides accounts of immigrant student education in five countries (the United States, Canada, France, Belgium, and Germany). In summarizing these studies, Gibson (1997) concludes,

> A major finding to emerge from the international cases presented here, as well as related studies in the United States, is that minority students do better in school when they feel strongly anchored in the identities of their families, communities and peers and when they feel supported in pursuing a strategy of selective additive acculturation (Gibson, 1997, 445–446)

CONCLUSION

The evidence suggests that characteristics of family background, family structure, and the broader social ecology are important determinants of the socialization content provided by numerous socialization agents and, to a great degree, of the socialization practices to which children are exposed.

Although this understanding of cultural differences is far from complete, such conceptual rethinking of the child, the family, and the development of social motives within particular social organizations is very different from the general conceptualizations that cultural difference is a negative social attribute. Enlightened understanding of diverse student cultures cannot be founded on the "Americanization" prescription: Take all who are not "American" and make them "American." The future for Hispanic students in this country is best understood if "Americanization" issues are set aside and the nature of social variables and their relationship to "cultural differences" and "identity" specific to educational practices and outcomes more clearly examined. The following chapters attempt to do just that.

6

Educational Approaches—
What Works for Hispanics:
General Constructs and the
Early Years

WHAT WORKS: A PERSONAL RENDITION

It is a very common phenomenon. I always know the question is coming when I address an audience regarding the research evidence of effective educational intervention for Hispanic students. It usually comes from a non-Hispanic, but not always. The negative tone of the question is usually one that we are all aware of. It is the "yes, but . . ." question. It is as if these individuals had not been listening to you but instead had been manufacturing a counter to what they think you had been saying.

The question goes something like this: "Yes, but how do you account for your own academic success? You are Hispanic, from a large and poor family, did not speak English, and yet here you are, a product of system you have strongly suggested must change to meet the needs of individuals just like you." Sometimes the question is accompanied by the description of a relative's experience, usually the questioner's grandfather or grand-mother, who came to this country in poverty, did not speak English, and has left a legacy of economic and education success among his or her progeny.

It is a tough question for me—not because the question is a difficult one but because it requires me to think of my own grandfather or grandmother, father, mother, brothers, cousins, nephews, and nieces and to reconstruct for myself the unforgivable lack of educational opportunity that they experienced. It makes me feel as if someone is using my academic success to point the "blame" individually at each of these family members and collectively at my family and other families like ours for their own and their children's lack of academic success. Imbedded in this question is the predominant American perspective that the individual is master of his or her destiny. Success is attributable to individual characteristics, particularly individual intelligence, talent, and motivation. Should I not see this question as applauding my own individual intellect, talent, and motivation? Not at all. Instead, it reflects a superficial understanding of academic success in this country generally and of academic success among Hispanics specifically.

Allow me to examine my own success in response to this proverbial question. My first reaction to the question each time it is asked is to attribute my success to "luck." How else could I react? In a cohort that included nine brothers and sisters and an estimated 60 or so cousins (one of my aunts had 18 children, including three sets of twins), I am the only offspring to have graduated from college. Five attended a college (four of these attended a community college), one graduated, and more than 40 percent of this family cohort never graduated from high school, some never finishing elementary school. All these individuals were born, like their parents and grandparents, in the southwestern United States and attended schools in these areas, some public and some private. Was I so smart and so motivated and so different from my family cohort to have succeeded where they failed? Absolutely not. I have brothers, sisters, and cousins who I know are "smarter" than I am. I grew up with these individuals and saw them comprehend complex intellectual problems, solve them, and succeed in challenging circumstances. I saw firsthand the high motivation, hard work, and kinds of goal setting, analysis, and stick-to-it-ness that is often associated with success in any endeavor. In short, I am about as talented as my cohort is—I am not in the upper 10 percent in this cohort when it comes to native physical or intellectual talent. I am not more motivated or more hard-working than most of my family cohort. Was I just lucky? I believe this is one legitimate conclusion.

I would like to think that it was more than luck. The "raíces" of my success began in a family that valued the importance of education. My father, a poor and humble man who taught himself to read by using the Spanish Bible, said to all of us, "*La educación nunca te la pueden quitar*" (No one can take away what you have learned). This was a profound insight from a family head of household who had been asked to move his family when he could not pay the rent. He had lost much of what he owned during the Great Depression and had worked primarily as a farm laborer in work-related situations that were for the most part completely out of his control—sometimes there was work, and sometimes there was no work.

He understood, as did my mother, aunts, and uncles, that it was what we learned—our education—that was the critical key to our future economic and social well-being. There was no question of that. But given that constant for my extended family, that was not enough to ensure educational success.

For my family and me, this was a very sound foundation. But it was not an academic foundation. My parents did not lap-read to me—my mother never learned to read or write. I did not have the opportunity to "see the world"—no vacations, no travel, no museum visits, and limited access to the news media and mass media, as we had a radio that worked on and off and never was attended to by my parents since there was no Spanish-language programming. My playmates for the most part were my many cousins, each of us socialized in the same linguistic and cultural environments until we went to school. Even after attendance at school, the social and economic dependence on the family minimized our interactions with other students and their families. We were insulated, but we were safe and secure. We knew who our friends were, and we knew where to go for help—to our nuclear and extended family. But even under such safe and nurturing circumstances, academic success was not a common occurrence. Having experienced this in my own life, it is difficult for me to accept arguments that the blame for Hispanic school failure today resides only in family circumstances that place children at risk. Children in my family were not placed at risk in that way, yet we did not succeed educationally.

What was important about this upbringing, then, was not the specific education preparation "raíces" but, rather, the broader understanding that education was important, that hard work was important, and that respect for adults who could show you the way, particularly the respect for our own elders and school teachers, who we could look to for future learning. My uncles were wonderful storytellers who could weave wonderful lessons about life from real experiences in their own lives or from handed-down proverbs (*dichos/consejos*) and religious teachings. Young children found themselves gathered around these individuals as they shared these stories among themselves, knowing full well that we were all listening. It never seemed like a directed lesson in life, ethics, or the literacy of the oral tradition, but we all learned so much. In addition, we learned by watching and doing. When you are poor, every able hand is a resource. We all had chores from the earliest age I can remember. We were asked to "watch, then do." We were never provided a verbal or written description for doing assigned tasks or chores, and we were never rewarded socially or economically for accomplishing those tasks. The clear expectation was that you would do those things assigned to you; you would work hard while doing them with the understanding that the task would be done well, or you would do it again. All this seems to set the stage for being a good student.

My "luck" for academic success came from several important factors. The critical "barrier" that my older family cohort members confronted and that proved to be significant was the absence of their language and culture in the schools they attended. When we all went to school, we met the English-speaking world in its harshest terms. My brothers and sisters lost their names and could not engage in an English curriculum or for the most part could not communicate with the teacher, someone whom we were told repeatedly to trust implicitly for her wisdom and role as a mentor. I recall very clearly that my previous learning opportunities in a language and culture rich with learning and teaching opportunities were not even a consideration in the schooling enterprise. My older brothers, my sisters, and many of our cousins came to the conclusion that school was not for them, even when our family elders continued to press hard that they attend and be successful in school. It was the younger members of our family who succeeded to some extent in such an environment. Very directly, we benefited from our older brothers and sisters, who learned enough English in school to help us learn rudimentary communication in that second language. Younger family members arrived at school bilingual in Spanish and English—we could communicate with the teacher and at least preliminarily engage the curriculum. Before you conclude that English-language ability was the critical variable, allow me to remind you that my own brothers' and sisters' children were either bilingual or predominantly English-language speakers at the time they entered school. Yet the educational success of that cohort is not significantly different than that of their parents. It is much more than knowing English.

For me it was a critical set of teachers—teachers who did recognize my talents but challenged me to higher standards. Most teachers did not expect much of me. I was quiet, spoke enough English to get by, but was not articulate in English, and it was evident that I was poor and came from a background of "educational disadvantages." It seems that this should have signaled to educators that I might need "more" than the average student might. *Instead, it seems to signal to them that they should expect less than what they expected of the average student and clearly substantially less than they expected of their "gifted" students.* And I obliged them in my elementary and junior high school years. I met their expectations perfectly. I learned not to work very hard in my studies, to get by, and to do as many of my Hispanic peers did, namely, to look elsewhere for opportunities to achieve—in sports, in gangs, or in work but not in academic aspects of schooling. It was several Spanish teachers and several athletic coaches who were the exception. They were truly my lucky charms.

My junior high Spanish teacher wondered why I took her class since I spoke Spanish fluently, but she never seemed worried about it. I got easy C's in the class without even opening a book or doing any homework. I do recall my English-speaking classmates recognizing me as a resource and asking for my help. I recall that it made me feel good. It was probably the only positive feeling I had in school, except for sports. It was not the case that I had negative feelings toward school, I just did not have many positive ones.

As for sports in those elementary and junior high years, there, like in my Spanish class, I did have some talents, thanks to my brothers and cousins, who had me playing basketball and baseball at an early age. In school, my forte was sports. I could run, jump, shoot baskets, and hit home runs with the best of them. My shyness, quietness, and Spanish-dominant background were not factors here. Coaches and students alike recognized my talents—I was captain of my elementary basketball and baseball teams and of my junior high basketball teams. I worked hard and met the high expectations of the coaches and the competition—it was a place for me to achieve and to be respected and a place where my athletic "background" was actually an appreciated asset.

This was not the experience for many of my Spanish-speaking or bilingual peers, children of the same neighborhood who did not have the athletic ability or training. For them, school was "a real drag." For them, defending our turf and assuring respect for our "barrio" and making money usually through illegal means (that was all that was available to us) led to the formation of and participation in gangs. Of some 50 Hispanic sixth-grade classmates in my elementary school, I can count on my fingers the number of those who graduated from high school. Twice as many, mostly males, had serious brushes with the law, serving time in *"la reforma"* (reform school) and in prison. Most left school prior to high school to assist their own large families with another source of income or started their own families early. When I visit my hometown, I often run into them and ask about them, their families, and our school colleagues. Most are surviving well, but none report positive educational experience for themselves or for their offspring. Education in general is still highly regarded, but schooling success is the exception.

My own "track" of athletic achievement continued in high school, thanks to a demanding baseball coach, one who expected to field the state championship team every year and who searched for, recognized, and developed athletic talent. He was demanding and nurturing at the same time. He went out of his way to respect individual and team performance. He looked after his players as if they were his own children. He cared, possibly because I could help him achieve his goals, but he cared. He made sure I went on to a community college on a baseball scholarship. That was my partial ticket to a higher education.

The other part of that ticket came from similarly dedicated educators. My 10th-grade Spanish teacher seemed very strange to me at first. I was there for an easy grade. Why would she not cooperate? Instead, she made it very clear that because I already knew most of what she would be teaching my classmates, her expectations, should I choose to remain in her course, were going to be much higher. "You have a gift," she said. "I had to work very hard to speak a language that I love but comes so natural and easy for you, a language you almost refuse to respect—I want you to use that gift." I read *Don Quixote* while I helped my classmates with "*buenos dias, como estas*" (good morning, how are you?). In addition, this teacher made it very clear that to participate in high school sports, I had to have a C average, and she was not above flunking me if I did not meet her high standards. I later learned that she was in close communication with my basketball and baseball coaches and my geometry and English teachers, who went out of their way to remind me that I needed to stay academically eligible to continue my sports participation. It was a conspiracy that led for the first time to academic achievement and a feeling of academic worth. My study habits improved, my participation in class improved, and my grades improved.

It started with someone who cared, who saw the resources that I brought with me, and who set about to utilize those resources to take me further—in my mother's words, "to provide the wings of an eagle." My 11th-grade Spanish teacher kept the pressure on, and soon academic success became its own reward. Access to that success opened new worlds, created new visions and goals, and offered me resources that were not available to many of my family members.

I graduated in the top 15 percent of my class and went on to the community college on a baseball scholarship (which covered tuition and books; I lived at home and worked part time). An interest in a particular topic in a community college led to some good grades and a particularly solid relationship with a professor who encouraged me to move on to a four-year institution. Another professor at that institution encouraged me to go to graduate school—something my parents, family, and I did not even know existed as a professional opportunity.

I received some excellent counseling and summer research experience in those undergraduate years. I decided that I was deeply interested in the emerging human science of psychology and particularly interested in the development of young children—it was fascinating to learn that children acquire as much knowledge in their first five years as they will during the remainder of their lives. Moreover, I had a younger brother who, I learned while in college, had Down's syndrome. Growing up with him and having the responsibility to care for him as our family worked in the fields, I could not understand why he just never "learned" like I did and why he did not enjoy the same games my brothers and I enjoyed. I can trace my first interest in psychology to a personal need to understand one of my brothers who was institutionalized at the age of eight because a social worker and a court of law determined that my aging mother and father could not "handle" him. Poverty, I learned, has its legal and personal consequences. Those were the days when institutionalization was an answer to this instance of diversity and long before the days of special education and the Individuals with Disabilities Education Act. (Years later, with the help of my family and my own professional understanding of the psychology of mental disabilities, my brother was removed from the institution and now lives in a group home working to earn his own living.)

These personal circumstances and educational opportunities led me to a graduate from a program in human development where professors and other student colleagues encouraged me to take on the responsibilities of research, scholarship, and teaching. I was recruited to my first academic position, thanks to the consciousness created in the early days of affirmative action and a specific affirmative action program at the University of Utah. From there, I began the slow but sure academic socialization process related to procuring extramural support for my research, publishing that research, teaching undergraduates, preparing graduate professionals, and moving up the academic ladder.

With this senior status comes the opportunity and responsibility to do things right—to ensure that my research and teaching and that of my professional colleagues is of the utmost integrity and that it challenges and forwards an important domain of intellectual inquiry, while at the same time doing the right thing, and engages us in the important theoretical, empirical, and broader professional preparation pursuits that ensure equity and excellence in education for all learners.

As you might conclude, it was not all good luck or individual talent and motivation that allowed me to "achieve" educationally or all bad luck and lack of talent and motivation that led many of my family and friends to "fail" educationally. It was a strong family infrastructure, combined with school personnel who saw potential and resources in me and who adapted their pedagogy, curricula, and expectations to address my own circumstances and, of course, a little bit of luck. As educators, we cannot do much about luck, and only remotely can we influence family infrastructure, even though it is important. But we can adapt our pedagogy, curricula, and expectation so that *all* students can in fact succeed educationally. The remainder of this chapter and the chapters that follow emphasize the reality of this conclusion with a focus on those educational endeavors that have demonstrated these attributes of academic success for Hispanic students in this country. Some I have had the personal honor to know and study, while others I have admired only from a distance. All make evident that our Hispanic students need not experience academic failure.

A HISTORICAL SURVEY OF AMERICAN EDUCATIONAL TREATMENT OF HISPANIC STUDENTS, 1965 TO 2000

Beyond my own set of stories, the foundations related to the schooling initiatives targeted at Hispanic students in the United States will be the focus of this chapter and the next two. In doing so, this effort will include an expanded discussion of the issues that bring together guiding frameworks and educational policy and practice of significance to these students. Within the last few decades, educational approaches related to culture and education have shifted from a focus on "Americanization" (San Miguel and Valencia, 1998; Gonzalez, 1999), educational equity (Ramirez and Castaneda, 1974), to multicultural education (Banks, 1981; Grant and Sleeter, 1988), and more recently to the research documentation of "effective" instruction of children from diverse cultural and linguistic groups (Purkey and Smith, 1983; Tharp, 1989; Garcia, 1994b, 1999). The following discussion introduces the conceptual underpinnings and empirical knowledge bases related to an understanding of Hispanics and education and the broader understanding of cultural diversity as it relates to schooling. In doing so, teaching and learning will be addressed with regard to linguistic, cognitive, social, and educational activity that has developed over the last two decades. Such actions have reshaped in a dramatic way our view of cultural and linguistic "difference" in education for Hispanic students.

Educational Equity

No one argues about the significance of education in this country. We are all quite convinced that an educated society is beneficial for sustaining and enhancing individual well-being and our standard of living and for maintaining a democratic society (Dewey, 1921). Moreover, education is perceived as a vehicle for achieving the "American Dream." Therefore, it is not surprising that numerous social institutions have attempted to initiate and maintain their educational endeavors in conjunction with efforts in the public schools. In fact, today's adult will have been exposed to more formal educational experiences (courses, workshops, seminars, conferences, and so on) outside the usual kindergarten–high school process than within it. Education in this society, from cradle to grave, is important to our citizens.

If so, then equal access to educational opportunities is a corollary to this basic assumption. This was clearly brought home by the 1954 U.S. Supreme Court decision in *Brown v. Board of Education*. Montgomery and Rossi (1994) remind us that the lesser-known victory of Hispanics in the *Lemon Grove* case in the 1940s might be regarded as the first successful desegregation case in the United States. This landmark case concluded that separate or segregated education for black Americans was unequal to the education provided for white Americans. In essence, the Court argued that every effort must be made to address equal access to education regardless of race. This decision was reinforced for Hispanic Americans, Asian Americans, Native Americans, and women during U.S. congressional activity during the 1960s and 1970s "War on Poverty" era. The major legislative piece, Title IV of the 1964 Civil Rights Act, banned discrimination on the grounds of race, color, or national origin in any program receiving federal financial assistance. (Title VII of that act addresses educational equity across gender.) Not coincidentally, the Elementary and Secondary Act of 1965 began to provide millions of federal dollars in assistance to state and local school systems. Therefore, if these school systems were to make use of federal funds, they would have to be held accountable to the standard of nondiscrimination.

Directly, this legislation banned recipients of federal resources from "restricting an individual in any way in the enjoyment of any advantage or privilege enjoyed by others receiving any service, financial aide or benefit under the (federally) funded program." Moreover, the recipient of federal funds was prohibited from utilizing criteria or methods that would have the effect of impairing accomplishments of the objectives of the federally funded program with respect to individuals of a particular race, color, or national origin. Significantly, other provisions of this legislation provided the possibility of a private cause of action (a lawsuit) against the federally funded institution to rectify issues of discrimination. Students and their parents need not wait for the federal government to find funded programs out of compliance. They could independently move the courts to seek relief. And they did. A barrage of legal action aimed at addressing education inequities soon followed.

In addition to legal action, further administrative and legislative activity also was a consequence of this initial legislative attention to equal educational opportunity. In 1970, the Department of Health, Education and Welfare issued a memorandum, later referred to as the "May 25 Memorandum," which clarified the mandate of the 1964 Civil Rights Act with respect to the non-English-speaking populations of students: "Where a liability to speak and understand the English language excludes national origin minority group children from effective participation in the educational program offered by a school district, the district must take affirmative steps to rectify the language deficiency in order to open instructional programs to these students." The 1974 Equal Educational Opportunities and Transportation Act placed this administrative protection for language diverse students into formal law. The act makes "the failure by an educational agency to make appropriate action to overcome language barriers that impede equal participation by its students in its educational programs" an unlawful denial of equal educational opportunities.

Taken together, these legal and legislative initiatives placed the societal values regarding the importance of education into a form of direct relevance to culturally diverse populations. In essence, any child, regardless of race, color, national origin, and language, is entitled, equally, to the benefits of educational endeavors. This equal education approach to the growing number of culturally diverse students pervaded our schools for over a decade and is still a part of what drives many educational initiatives for these students. In 1998, the U.S. Department of Education released a detailed report regarding those concerns still presently confronted by efforts of school equal educational opportunity by Hispanics (U.S. Department of Education, 1998). But equal access has not been the only stimulus driving our educational interest in Hispanic students.

Intelligence, Testing, Culture, Cognition, and Equity

Over the last five to seven decades, the educational establishment has been guided by theories that hold the construct of "intelligence" as the central factor in learning. And equality of treatment has often been determined in educational institutions by using this "intelligence" construct to the detriment of Hispanics. This central construct implied the existence of mostly inherited ability of an individual's mind to perceive, organize/store, and utilize symbolic information. To its credit, this ambiguous construct of intelligence attempted to reconcile the distinction between the physical aspects and the abstract/symbolic nature of our existence. To its discredit, the construct depended extensively on biological determination (we "inherited" our intelligence) and on the assumption that intelligence could be validly and reliably assessed through a simple set of standardized items placed together in an intelligence test. Culturally diverse children have historically been negatively affected by this enduring construct (Laosa, 1996a).

The use of intelligence tests with culturally diverse students and adults has generated much interest in the differences found between this population and normative groups. Careful examination of the testing literature has revealed several problems that are basic to this area of understanding the mind. The problems focus on personal, social, and cultural differences. Furthermore, psychometric assessments of the mind (intelligence tests in particular) have failed to assess adequately the "intelligence" of this diverse population owing to language problems (inappropriate linguistic understanding), inappropriate test content, and failure to include these groups in the normative samples. Because of its devastating effects to culturally diverse student populations, it is appropriate to discuss this issue here. Inherent in this discussion is the theme that constructs of the "mind" built on intelligence and intelligence testing have been educationally misinformed.

The publication of *The Bell Curve* (Herrnstein and Murray, 1994) has reinvigorated a bitter public debate on significant scientific and societal issues, including a set of interrelated theories of conceptual frameworks regarding the influences of and different roles played by genetic and environmental factors in the development of human intelligence; arguments regarding racial, ethnic, and group differences in intelligence; concerns about possible bias in the tests; and questions concerning the implication of scientific research on these issues for education and public policy. Essentially the same issues have been addressed over a long period of time, often with the same attributes of negativity (Wigdor and Garner, 1982). Laosa (1995) suggests that, like a refractory strain of retrovirus, the issues tend to remain latent and from time to time resurge brusquely to the fore of public consciousness.

Because intelligence level is typically measured by means of standardized IQ tests, the available scientific evidence bearing on questions regarding the influences of genetic versus environmental factors on the development of intellectual ability rests largely on scores derived from such tests and similar measures of general intelligence. Conceptions of this construct—which specifically denotes general cognitive functioning as assessed in the psychometric tradition of a general factor derived from a battery of diverse cognitive ability tests—and how to measure it have changed remarkably little in the past 50 years (Terman and Merrill, 1973; Carroll, 1982, 1993; Lubin, Larsen, and Matarazzo, 1984; Kaufman, 1994). At the heart of the heated controversy rekindled by the publication of *The Bell Curve* is the view—espoused by many of the book's critics—that, because of the lower average scores by members of particular racial, ethnic, and socioeconomic groups, incorrect inferences will be made as to the abilities of persons from these groups, and hence their educational, occupational, and employment opportunities will be limited or even denied. Moreover, the use of standardized tests scores as a basis for making judgments regarding racial, ethnic, and socioeconomic group differences in abilities— and, more significantly, in the capability to develop these abilities—is seen by many as indefensible in light of strong allegations that there are biases inherent in standardized ability tests, which unfairly penalized persons from backgrounds different from those of white, middle-class, native speakers of English. Thus, the question of test bias and the relevancy and use of standardized ability measures remain central concerns for Hispanics with regard to issues of civil rights; equity and fairness in educational, occupational, and employment opportunity; and social justice.

Explanations of Differences in Measured Intelligence

Questions of how to assess and interpret individual differences in human intellectual abilities have long been of central concern to psychologists and educators. Some violent polemics have centered on the issue of interpretation data on intelligence tests. Two traditional views on intelligence have persisted since before the turn of the 20th century: assumptions of *fixed intelligence* and *predetermined development* (for historical overviews, see Hunt, 1961; Laosa, 1977). These two assumptions often underlie the ideas that intelligence is an innate dimension of personal capacity and that it increases at a relatively fixed rate to a level in a range predetermined at birth. The motions of fixed intelligence and predetermined development clearly have potentially adverse effects on education, employment, and occupational policies and practices since they encourage neglect of intellectual development. The argument is often made that because intelligence is predetermined, no amount of cultivation can significantly increase it. The assumption that intelligence and other personal characteristics are fixed can easily lead to an unwarranted emphasis on the matter of personal selection and corresponding underemphasis in the areas of training and personal growth (Hunt, 1961; Laosa, 1977, 1984). Moreover, if an overemphasis on innate ability as a determinant of performance is a societal belief, it can function as a self-fulfilling prophecy (Bjork, 1994).

That there exist differences in IQ test scores across ethnic groups generates no disagreement. The disagreements center on the explanations (i.e., interpretations) of the causes of the observed between-group mean differences. It is generally agreed that the observed within-group individual differences in general intelligence reflect both genetic and environmental influences. Disagreements exist, however, regarding the relative importance of these two influences and the degree and changeability of inherited intellectual characteristics.

Is there a plausible alternative to the explanatory hypothesis that the observed group differences in mean intelligence test scores are the result of genetic differences in intelligence? Laosa (1995) answers this question affirmatively, proposing that between-group environmental differences are large enough to explain group differences in mean IQ. To illustrate the argument, Laosa (1995) considers the acquisition of vocabulary, which is an omnipresent component of widely used tests of intelligence. Vocabulary is learned, and the resulting individual differences in vocabulary can be considered a major result of the learning environment and innate differences in learning ability. Hence, the average differences in environments between Hispanics and white American children in opportunity to learn the particular vocabulary (and the other component subjects, i.e., knowledge and skill domains) employed in intelligence tests are such that they are adequate to explain Hispanic–white differences in IQ tests scores without the need for positing genetic differences development effort—that we try to measure the opportunities to learn as precisely as we do the individual's cognitive performance. And for adequate communication about group differences to our fellow professionals and the public, "it would seem imperative that when we provide information on group differences on IQ, we accompany it by equally detailed data on 'EIPQ,' an Environmental Intelligence Producing Quotient" (Campbell and Frey, 1970, 456–457). In other words, looking at each component subject of intelligence and achievement measures, one should score the environment for the degree to which it has produced similar experiences. Only when we can assess the "opportunity to learn" along with some test score can we be sure that we are more robustly understanding the meaning of that test score. Under such circumstances, we are likely to minimize both false positives and false negatives in high-stake decisions based on those test scores.

Recent conceptual contributions to these issues surrounding test fairness have also questioned today's use of IQ and standardized assessment tests. As Messick (1989, 1995) argues, test use needs to have both an *evidential* basis and a *consequential* basis. This need to analyze the consequences of the uses to which tests are put poses serious challenges for test users and test producers. Whereas analysis of the likelihood of some consequences (e.g., short-term adverse impact) can be accomplished with relative ease—even though there may be differences in perspectives on the manner of analysis—it is far more difficult to evaluate consequences of a longer-term or more global nature. Linn (1989) offers as example the challenges involved in evaluating the consequences of the decisions taken by the National Collegiate Athletic Association to require that the combination of grade-point average in core subjects and scores on college admissions tests exceeds a specified minimum in order for the athlete to be eligible to compete during the freshman year of college. Studies were undertaken to investigate a variety of issues related to the policy as it was initially proposed as well as to several alternative policies. These analyses addressed issues of likely adverse impact, differential prediction of grades, academic progress, and graduation. As Linn observes, however, many other issues considered relevant by supporters and opponents of the policy were not, and possibly could not have been, addressed—including, for example, the effects of the policy on the decisions of minority student athletes to take different courses in high school, on the guidance and support services (including test preparation courses) provided by high schools, on the likelihood that students who are not eligible their freshman year will still attend college, on the actions of colleges to support athletes who are not eligible their freshman year, and the long-term effects on the education and employment of racial and ethnic minorities. The point of this case illustration "is not . . . to suggest that all these consequences should have been investigated before any action was taken, or even to suggest that they are all part of a complete analysis of bias in test use and interpretation. Rather, it is intended to show that judgments about what is a desirable and fair use of a test depend on a host of considerations and on the values that are attached to various effects" (Linn, 1989, 6). A measurement specialist could appropriately define the absence of predictive bias in accord with the *Standards for Educational and Psychological Testing* (American Educational Research Association [AERA], American Psychological Association [APA], and National Council on Measurement in Education [NCME], 1985, 12) by finding that "the predictive relationship of two groups being compared can be adequately described by a common algorithm (e.g., regression line)." It should be recognized, however, as Linn again enjoins, that "this definition neither corresponds to the meaning of the critic who charges test bias nor resolves the issue of how the scores of minority test takers should be used or interpreted" (Linn, 1989, 6). This point is recognized also in the *Standards,* which acknowledges that its definition of predictive—or selection—bias is adopted "with the understanding that it does not resolve the larger issue of fairness" (3). There is no doubt that concerns about the fair uses of tests for ethnic and racial minorities will continue to be a major theme in years to come.

Clearly, scholars familiar with the literature on U.S. social policies know that the authors of *The Bell Curve* did not need the scientific literature on individual and group differences in intelligence and achievement to propose the public policies they espouse in the book. Even the authors of *The Bell Curve* do not unequivocally suggest that their public policy proposals arise necessarily from the scientific data. Scarr (1994–95) points out that Murray had proposed—sans scientific data—essentially the same policies many years ago to a skeptical Congress. As Laosa (1995) reminds us, the view that antipoverty programs are ineffective, indeed counterproductive, is not a new theme for Murray. Moreover, it is ironic that in his earlier book *Losing Ground* (1984), Murray's critique emphasized the rationality, or reasoning ability, of the poor, unwed parents, school dropouts, and criminals:

> Specifically, I will suggest that changes in incentives that occurred between 1960 and 1970 may be used to explain many of the trends we have been discussing. It is not necessary to invoke the *Zeitgeist* of the 1960s, or changes in the work ethnic, or racial differences, or the complexities of postindustrial

economies, in order to explain increasing unemployment among the young, increased dropout from the labor force, or higher rates of illegitimacy and welfare dependency. All were results that could have been predicted (indeed in some instances were predicted) from the changes that social policy made in the rewards and penalties, carrots and sticks, that govern human behavior. All were rational responses to changes in the rules of the game of surviving and getting ahead . . .

I begin with the proposition that all, poor and not-poor alike, use the same general calculus in arriving at decisions; only the exigencies are different. (Murray, 1984, 154–155).

In contrast, part 3 of *The Bell Curve* concludes as follows:

The lesson of this chapter is that large proportions of the people who exhibit the behaviors and problems that dominate the nation's social policy agenda have limited cognitive ability. Often they are near the definition for mental retardation. . . . When the nation seeks to lower unemployment or lower the crime rate or induce welfare mothers to get jobs, the solutions must be judged by their effectiveness with the people most likely to exhibit the problem: the least intelligent people. And with that, we reach the practical questions of policy that will occupy us for the rest of the book. (Herrnstein and Murray, 1994, 386)

This change in the rationale used to support essentially the same policy directions is a fitting illustration of the proposition that it is values, attitudes, and beliefs, not rigorous rules of evidence and logic, that typically govern the process of drawing policy implications from scientific data. This conclusion strikes home to this author in a direct way. A low standardized test score kept me out of the Naval Academy in 1964. If a similar standardized test or IQ test had been used to lock me out of postsecondary educational opportunities, I am sure that I would not be where I am today. As long as we hold on to outdated theories of intelligence and allow them to guide public policy or individual educational decisions, other Hispanics will be placed at an unfair disadvantage.

Cognition and Multilingualism

For Hispanics, particularly those who live in bilingual circumstances, a separate but significant theoretical approach to the understanding of multilingualism and its effects has focused on the cognitive (intellectual) character of the student. Based on correlational studies indicating a negative relationship between childhood bilingualism and performance on standardized tests of intelligence, a causal statement linking bilingualism to "depressed" intelligence was tempting, and this negative conclusion characterized much earlier work (Darcy, 1953). Because of the myriad of methodological problems of studies investigating this type of relationship, any conclusions concerning multilingualism and intellectual functioning (as measured by standardized individual or group intelligence tests) are extremely tentative in nature (Darcy, 1963; Diaz, 1983).

Leopold (1939), in one of the first investigations of bilingual, German/English acquisition, reported a general cognitive plasticity for his young bilingual daughter. He suggested that linguistic flexibility (in the form of bilingualism) is related to a number of nonlinguistic, cognitive tasks, such as categorization, verbal signal discrimination, and creativity. Peal and Lambert (1962), in a summarization of their work with French/English bilinguals and English monolinguals, suggested that the intellectual experience of acquiring two languages contributed to advantageous mental flexibility, superior concept formation, and a generally diversified set of mental abilities.

Related bilingualism research (Feldman and Shen, 1971) reports differential responding between Chicano Spanish/English bilinguals and English monolinguals across three separate tasks reflecting Piagetian-like problem solving and metalinguistic awareness. Results indicated significantly increased cognitive flexibility for Chicano bilinguals. Others have compared matched bilinguals (Afrikaans/English) and monolinguals (either Afrikaans or English) on metalinguistic tasks requiring separation of word sounds and word meanings. Comparison of scores on these tasks indicated that bilingual concentrated more on attaching meaning to words rather than sounds. Ben-Zeev's (1977) work with Hebrew/English bilingual children is also related to the metalinguistic abilities of these children. Subjects in these studies showed superiority in symbol substitution and verbal transformational tasks. Ben-Zeev summarizes "two strategies characterized by thinking patterns of the bilingual in relation to verbal material: readiness to impute structure and readiness to reorganize" (1017). Even more research specifically with Chicano bilingual students (Kessler and Quinn, 1986, 1987) supplies additional empirical support for the emerging understanding that all things being equal, bilingual children outperform monolingual children on specific measures of cognitive and metalinguistic awareness. Kessler and Quinn (1987) had bilingual and monolingual children engage in a variety of symbolic categorization tasks that required their attention to abstract, verbal features of concrete objects. Spanish/English, Chicano bilinguals from low-socioeconomic backgrounds outperformed low-socioeconomic English monolinguals and high-socioeconomic English monolinguals on these tasks. Such findings are particularly significant given the criticism by McNab (1979) that many bilingual "cognitive advantage" studies utilized only high-socioeconomic subjects of non-U.S. minority backgrounds. It is important to note that findings of metalinguistic advantages have been reported for low-socioeconomic Puerto Rican students as well (see Galambos and Hakuta, 1988).

Theoretical attempts linking multilingualism to cognitive attributes have emerged. In an attempt to identify more specifically the relationship between cognition and bilingualism, Cummins (1979, 1981, 1984b) has proposed an interactive theoretical proposition: that children who do achieve balanced proficiency in two languages may be cognitively "advantaged," while those that do not achieve balanced proficiency in two languages may be cognitively "disadvantaged." Interestingly, Diaz (1985) has proposed an alternative hypothesis and supportive data that suggest that cognitive "flexibility" of the multilingual is at its maximum during early stages of multilingual development, before balanced proficiency is attained.

Therefore, it is not quite clear how bilingualism with Hispanic students directly influences cognitive development. Is it always an advantage? Can it be a disadvantage? Is early (and balanced) proficiency advantageous and late (and unbalanced) proficiency disadvantageous? These questions are not yes answerable (Hakuta, 1986; Garcia, 1991b; August and Hakuta, 1997). However, it is the case, first, that Hispanic bilingual children have been found to score both higher and lower than monolingual children on standardized measures of cognitive development, intelligence, and school achievement and, second, that Hispanic bilingual children have been found to score higher on specific Piagetian, metalinguistic, concept-formation, and creative cognitive tasks.

An emphasis an educational equity has led educators to focus on the intellectual, linguistic, and socioeconomic attributes of Hispanic students (San Miguel and Valencia, 1998). The concern has been specifically to assess the intellectual and linguistic needs of the students and to do so equitably. Having done so, the concomitant approach has been to construct equal opportunities for these students to succeed. Their emphasis on assessments and opportunities has assumed that the role of education is to bridge the gap between students' needs and general academic success as defined for all U.S. students. No particular attention to the cultural attributes, individually or collectively, is called into play. Therefore, educational equity interventions attempt to deal with educational disadvantage: These students come from impoverished academic backgrounds, speak a language other than English, are immigrants and poor, and so on. The "equity" approach has become superseded by a more comprehensive concern related to the multicultural character of this and other U.S. student populations.

BEYOND EQUITY TO MULTICULTURAL EDUCATION

From the educational establishment and minority groups themselves came another important educational thrust of particular consequence to Hispanic students. Mostly aimed at curriculum reform, this initiative suggested that the curriculum in this country should reflect the diverse character of the cultural and linguistic groups of the country. A *multicultural education* was recommended for several reasons. First and foremost, the curriculum should better represent the actual contributions by various cultural groups to this country's society. The curriculum in schools was criticized for its unbalanced perspectives that emphasized Western European values, history, literature, and general worldview (Banks and Banks, 1995). The United States was not one monolithic culture, and, the curriculum should reflect that cultural diversity. Second, a multicultural curriculum would inform "majority" group children of "minority" group contributions and would at the same time reaffirm the "minority" group significance to the society—helping in the development of positive self-esteem. Third, multicultural education was perceived as a school reform movement aimed at changing the content and process within schools. Its goal was not only to provide equal educational opportunity but also to enhance the schooling experience for all students.

The multicultural education concept took on several distinct approaches to the instruction of students in general and of Hispanic students in particular. However, the major impact of this reform movement has been in the area of the curriculum, that is, the area of schooling that addresses the content of instruction. In essence, this major reform attempted to address *what* students should be learning. This reform made it quite clear that we needed to know more about this country's diverse cultural groups and that after we had uncovered such knowledge we needed to dispense it in our everyday schooling endeavors. This overall agreement about the importance of including curriculum that addressed diversity was significant, as there was some disagreement with regard to the goals of such activity.

Sleeter and Grant (1987) have provided an excellent review of these discrepant goals and the overall limited consequences of the multicultural education reform movement on American education. Within a model described as "Teaching the Multiculturally Different," the goal was to help educators assist culturally different students succeed in mainstream schooling. Although not directly implicating the need to "change" or "assimilate" children of different backgrounds into the mainstream, this goal seemed to serve as a foundation for this form of multicultural education. This prescription was usually subtractive in nature. That is, children with different cultures and languages were asked to leave these attributes behind through the assistance of bridgelike educational programs that promised access and success in academic and then, later, other societal domains. Multicultural education, in this view, was seen as a temporary, highly directed educational endeavor that would lead to a melting pot of a successful and more homogeneous student population.

Early vestiges of Head Start can been seen to reflect this multicultural approach. For preschool children ages three to four, Head Start, and its extension for the early elementary student, Follow Through, were perceived as bridges to the mainstream academic environment. Other compensatory education programs, like Federal Title I programs, which provide resources to address underachievement directly, are in this same category of educational programs that are meant to bridge nonachieving students with achievement. They are temporary in nature and have the goal of transitioning unsuccessful students to success through a process likened to natural cultural assimilation. In such assimilation, Hispanics and others with diverse cultures and languages come to embrace mainstream American values and acquire English as their main mode of communication. Schools are asked to serve as an organized vehicle to hasten this natural form of assimilation.

It is important to note that these multicultural educational efforts did consider as important the cultural diversity of the students, families, and communities they served. In this way, they were distinct from earlier "Americanization" educational strategies. The best example of this drastic "Americanization" approach came from the history of American Indian education. Recall that one education effort aimed at America's natives centered around taking youngsters from their families and placing them in boarding schools hundreds and sometimes thousands of miles from their homes. In such boarding schools, these students were not schooled in their native language or acquainted with their cultural heritage. These efforts were meant to serve not as bridges to American society but as direct breaks with their native and negatively perceived language and culture (Hornberger, 1997).

The bridging goal of some multicultural education efforts was also combined with another goal: enhancing human relations (Perry, 1975; Colangelo, Foxley, and Dustin, 1982). Such a goal was seen as best achieved by learning about and with each other. In so doing, diverse populations would be able to understand each other, and the corollary of this better understanding would be enhanced communication and social relations. Distinct from the assimilation and bridging goals and procedures, educational programs reflecting this approach to multicultural education asked students to add knowledge about other groups not like their own and to utilize it in ways that would enhance social accommodation of diversity—"let's learn to get along better by knowing more about one another." The most dramatic example of such a large-scale program of this type can be found in Canada, where, in the province of Quebec, French-speaking populations (Francophones) were in constant social and economic dispute with English-speaking populations (Anglophones). The solution to this social relations problem was Bilingual–Bicultural Immersion Education (August and

Garcia, 1988). Anglophone children were placed in French-only schooling programs for the first three years of their educational experience. Over time, the goal of the program was for children to acquire knowledge of both the language and the culture of Francophones with the expected product of better human relations. Evaluation of these programs indicates that these expectations were achieved without any academic achievement cost of children learning academic content in a language other than their own home language.

Yet another approach to multicultural education has been much more "activist" in nature. Its goals serve to promote respect for diversity. Beyond just acquiring and disseminating information regarding cultural diversity, this approach is aimed at developing intellectual and societal acceptance of cultural diversity as a goal in and of itself (Gay, 1975; Grant, 1977b; 1999; Garcia, 1979; Banks, 1981, 1984; Gollnick and Chinn, 1986; Fishman, 1990). Since the 1990s, this approach has been popular and influential and has attempted to bring together issues of race, ethnicity, gender, and social class. The thrust of such initiatives has been to permeate the curriculum with issues of diversity—diversity in literature, social thought, scientific approaches, historical construction, and so on—while at the same time serving up criticism of "standardized" curricula, particularly those that reflect Western European contributions as the standard. A corollary of this approach is the overall multicultural and social reconstructionist perspective that is also espoused (Appleton, 1983; Suzuki, 1984). In essence, students are asked to become social critics, particularly as it relates to issues of social injustice. Adoption of this multicultural educational approach would help rid society of pervasive social injustices inflicted on the basis of race, ethnicity, and gender.

An example of a proactive stance with regard to multicultural education has emerged from the bilingual education community in this country. In the last five years, double-immersion programs have begun to be introduced into large Hispanic school districts in California, New York, Texas, Illinois, and Florida. In these programs, the goal is to produce a student population that is bilingual and bicultural. For Anglo, English-speaking students, the goal is English- and Spanish-language literacy with the program beginning in kindergarten. These students are exposed to Spanish-language instruction in classrooms with Hispanic Spanish-speaking students and to a curriculum that address bicultural concerns. For Hispanic students in the programs, the goals are the same. These goals are in concert with the notion of actively promoting cultural diversity, with a healthy academic respect for the linguistic and cultural attributes of the diverse students involved (Lindholm and Christiansen, 1990). Similar programs in the public schools of San Francisco, San Diego, Detroit, New York, and Chicago are housed in "magnet" schools. The intent is to have a highly cultural, diverse set of students come together around a thematically designated curriculum that is multilingual and multicultural. Such programs attempt to integrate African American, Latino, Asian, and other culturally diverse student populations by recognizing diversity as a potential positive in addressing equal educational opportunity and multicultural education agendas (Garcia and Stein, 1996).

It seems appropriate to conclude that attention to multicultural education in this country over the last two decades has produced a set of debates and substantive "multicultural movement" in education. New curriculum efforts by publishing companies have been launched to address concerns of "bias" raised by proponents of multicultural education. Teacher training programs have been required to provide specific training at the preservice level. School-based programs, such as the "magnet" and double-immersion bilingual education programs described here, find their roots, at least partially, in the values and goals of multicultural education. The previous discussion has attempted to place multicultural education into three broad categories based on the goals of distinct but not necessarily exclusive goal agendas. These goals range from those related to bridging/assimilation for culturally diverse students to enhancing human relations to actively promoting cultural diversity as a societal goal. Keep in mind that these goals build on the previous historical and ongoing initiatives dealing with equal educational opportunity—no child should be denied the benefits of education. These two educational initiatives have individually and collectively changed the nature of educational response to the growing presence of cultural diversity in our schools.

BEYOND MULTICULTURAL EDUCATION
TO WHAT WORKS

Since the time of Socrates, educators and philosophers have argued for a kind of teaching that does more than impart knowledge and teach skills. Knowledge and skills are important enough, the argument goes, but true education and real teaching involve far more. They involve, fundamentally, helping students understand, appreciate, and grapple with important ideas while developing a depth of understanding for a wide range of issues.

Yet teaching aimed at these important goals is presently most notable for its absence from U.S. classrooms. Goodlad (1984), for example, reports,

A great deal of what goes on in the classroom is like painting-by-numbers—filling in the colors called for by numbers on the page . . . [teachers] ask for specific questions calling essentially for students to fill in the blanks: "What is the capital city of Canada?" "What are the principal exports of Japan?"

Students rarely turn things around by asking questions. Nor do teachers often give students a chance to romp with an open-ended question such as "What are your views on the quality of television?" (108)

If this portrait is true in mainstream American classrooms, it is even more true in classrooms with low-income Hispanic children. Because of the perception that these students fundamentally require drill, review, and redundancy in order to progress academically (Brophy and Good, 1986), their learning opportunities are likely to be excessively weighted toward low-level factual and skills-oriented instruction. As important as skills and knowledge undoubtedly are, no less important are more cognitively demanding learning opportunities that promote, as philosopher Mortimer Adler (1982) has written, the "enlarged understanding of ideas and values" (23). To that end, the following discussion will attempt to move beyond the more "conceptual" issues addressed earlier in this chapter to a body of knowledge that emphasizes "what works."

Equal educational opportunity and multicultural education efforts have failed to address a number of important educational concerns. For the most part, they have lacked strong research foundations, addressed only curricula (not instructional methods or pedagogy), produced many single case studies of ethnic groups, and produced little empirical data to substantiate the positive effects of implementation. As described earlier in this book, academic achievement for Hispanic populations has not been enhanced significantly over the past decades. Equal educational opportunity activity has and continues to generate legislative and legal policy along with concomitant resources to address this core societal value. But such action has not addressed, in any comprehensive manner, how educational equity should be achieved. Moreover, educational inertia in and around multicultural education has similarly espoused important societal values and has led to advances on a number of educational fronts. But it has also not produced a set of comprehensive strategies that address the educational concerns it has raised (Sleeter and Grant, 1987; Grant, 1999). Therefore, the result of these educational equity and multicultural reform initiatives has been to raise issues and to create awareness and even a diverse "zeitgeist." These initiatives have accomplished that outcome, and they have been assisted by the demographic reality of a changing, culturally diverse society.

An important legacy of the last three decades of educational activity centered on culturally diverse populations, particularly the result of multicultural education endeavors, has been the extended case study approach to cultural diversity. The educational community has produced an extensive literature of the characteristics of different racial, ethnic, and ethnolinguistic groups. The goal of this work has been to document the cultural and linguistic attributes of different groups in this country such that these attributes could be understood and utilized to better serve these populations. It was not uncommon to learn that American Indian children were nonverbal (Appleton, 1983), Asian American children were shy (Sue and Okazaki, 1990), Mexican American children were cooperative (Garcia, 1983b), African American children were aggressive (Boykin, 1983) and Anglo children were competitive (Kagan, 1983a). Although this case study work was meant to further advance our understanding of culturally diverse students, it often had the effect of promoting stereotypes. Moreover, it did not recognize the broader, well-understood axiom of social scientists who study culture: There is as much heterogeneity within any cultural group as there is between cultural groups (for an extended discussion of this issue, see chapters 2 and 3). Unfortunately, descriptively useful indicators took on explanatory values: If that student is Mexican American, she must be cooperative and speak Spanish. Educational programs that were developed to address these cultural attributes soon discovered that many Mexican American children were not cooperative and did not speak Spanish. If all Mexican Americans are not alike, if all African Americans are not alike, if all American Indians are not alike, and so on, then what set of knowledge about those groups is important educationally?

EFFECTIVE INSTRUCTIONAL PRACTICES
IN THE EARLY GRADES

The importance of guaranteeing excellence for Hispanic children is becoming increasingly salient as America moves into the 21st century with numbers of these students increasing (California Department of Education, 1997; U.S. Department of Education, 1998). What factors may promote Hispanic students' academic achievement? Though few researchers or educational program developers have established coherent models or programs that address the question specifically, there is literature that may shed light on the question. First, some studies focus on individual characteristics of students, such as resilience and identification and engagement with school, and on the social supports from peers, families, and communities that may promote these behaviors. Second, recent research identifies classroom characteristics and practices that hold promise for engaging Hispanic students and for advancing their achievements. Third, school variables, such as resources and climate, may be important predictors of students' outcomes. I will address some educational programs that promote Hispanic students' academic achievement.

Researchers consistently find that Hispanic students are represented disproportionately among those who are economically disadvantaged (Miller, 1995). Children living in poverty have less access to formal learning opportunities, fewer resources, greater health problems, and developmental delays, all of which can negatively impact educational outcomes (Garcia, 1999). Although being a minority student is not a risk factor in and of itself, as Montgomery and Rossi (1994) note, experiencing adverse treatment inside or outside the classroom because of one's race or ethnicity is a risk factor. Such variables or "risk factors" obviously impede the achievement of Hispanic children.

As I have discussed at some length, cultural differences also contribute to the academic challenges for Hispanic children. Schools attempt to assimilate minority students to mainstream values without considering the potential ramifications of doing so. When the values of the home and community are incongruent with the values of the school, minority children may experience confusion, stress, and adjustment problems that ultimately result in low self-esteem and poor academic performance (Ford and Harris, 1996). Hispanic students who do achieve may be viewed as assimilating and run the risk of being accused of "selling out" or "becoming a coconut" by their Hispanic peers (Ogbu and Matute-Bianchi, 1986). Peer rejection can be very damaging for racial and ethnic minority youth for whom the need for peer affiliation is very strong (Gandara, 1995; Ford and Harris, 1996).

Despite these and other obstacles that Hispanic youth may face, there are those who achieve academic success through their resilience. Resilience is defined as the ability to succeed regardless of challenging or threatening circumstances. Resilient children are able to do well in school despite family, community, or social circumstances that are not congruent with academic success. What enables these children to achieve despite the obstacles to their success? The following characteristics have been found to foster resilience: an internal locus of control and high self-esteem (Fin and Rock, 1997), strong interpersonal skills, a capacity to be responsive to others, a high level of activity, good problem-solving skills, flexibility, independence, a clear sense of purpose, and a good parent–child relationship (Wong, Haertal, and Walberg, 1993). Wong and her colleagues suggested that schools may foster students' resilience by defining clear educational goals, encouraging students to take responsibility for helping each other, having adequate learning resources, and keeping parents actively engaged and informed.

Closely related to research on the factors associated with resiliency, a few studies have identified the characteristics of high-achieving minority students, including Hispanics. For example, Lee, Winfield, and Wilson (1991) reported that high achievers (defined as scoring above the national average in reading achievement) tend to come from families of higher social class with a higher proportion of working mothers. Lee and her colleagues found that the schools attended by high-achieving African American students were comprised of families of higher socioeconomic status, had higher student commitment, offered enriched curricula more often, and had a lower proportion of students in remedial reading. A positive attitude toward achievers and toward school, strong belief in the tenets of the achievement ideology, and a low incidence of psychological issues, such as fears and anxieties, also characterize high-achieving minority students (Ford and Harris, 1996).

In contrast to resilience, researchers increasingly conceptualize poor educational performance as the outcome of a process of academic disengagement, which may begin as early as a child's entry into school. In a comparison of the relationship between self-esteem and achievement for a national sample of white, African American, and Latino students, Osborne (1997) found that self-esteem was correlated with achievement at all grades but decreased most dramatically between 8th and 12th grade. This result suggests that as students progress through school, their sense of self becomes less and less tied to their academic performances and achievements. To improve student achievement and engagement, schools must foster investment behaviors, such as encouraging students' involvement and interest in school-related activities (Montgomery and Rossi, 1994).

In addition to the importance of individual factors to students' patterns of engagement and achievement, certain cultural and social factors play key roles. Ogbu (1986) contends that minority students, including Hispanics, "do not believe as strongly as Whites that school credentials are sufficient" (127) for attaining success in society. According to Ogbu, minority students' low achievement is due to how they are treated educationally, socially, politically, and economically. Therefore, if students perceive low incentives and rewards for academic engagement and achievement, as Ogbu's theory postulates, they are likely to be discouraged from persisting and engaging in school. Montgomery and Rossi (1994) state that successful students often have parents, teachers, and peers who "push" them to do their best academically. These students know that if they fail to engage and persist, they may experience undesirable outcomes, such as reproaches from teachers, loss of privileges at home, or criticism from their friends. Similarly, Ford and Harris (1996) state that the high expectations of parents and affiliations with peers who share a strong achievement orientation are important social factors that prevent underachievement among gifted African American students.

Researchers have consistently found the troubling fact that many social risk factors may reside within the confines of the student's classroom. Specifically, researchers have found evidence that minority students in general are exposed to teacher behaviors that, in some cases intentionally and in other cases unintentionally, reflect prejudiced or discriminatory attitudes.

First, in predicting eight indicators of second-generation discrimination, Meier, Stewart, and England (1989) found that the greatest single predictor was the racial distribution of the teaching faculty. In 43 of 44 statistical models, the researchers found that higher percentages of African American teachers were associated with lower levels of second-generation discrimination. Second, in a review of the literature on teacher expectancy, Irvine (1990) concluded that teachers, white teachers in particular, held more negative expectations for African American students than for white students. Furthermore, teachers held more negative views regarding the personality characteristics, traits, abilities, behaviors, and potentials of African American students. Similarly, Dusek and Joseph (1986) reported that African American and Mexican American students were not expected to perform as well as white students by their teachers.

All teachers tend to communicate their expectations to students in either subtle or overt ways. Some of the classroom experiences of students for whom teachers hold low expectations include being called on less frequently; when called on, providing less time to respond; giving the answer rather than helping to solve the problem themselves; criticizing more often; praising less; and paying less positive attention but disciplining more strictly (Brophy, 1983). Research shows that African American students are aware of social injustices and believe that they have to work harder than their white classmates to succeed (Ford and Harris, 1996). In response to racism, Hispanic youth may react in anger and rebellion. They may deliberately excuse themselves from the academic achievement, making reasonable decisions to "drop out" (U.S. Department of Education, 1998).

WHAT WORKS: OPTIMAL LEARNING AND EXCELLENCE

August and Hakuta (1997) provide a comprehensive review of optimal learning conditions that serve linguistically and culturally diverse Hispanic populations—conditions leading to high academic performance. Their reviews of some 33 studies indicate that the following attributes were identified by this case study research strategy:

> A supportive school-wide climate, school leadership, a customized learning environment, articulation and coordination within and between schools, use of native language and culture in instruction, a balanced curriculum that includes both basic and higher-order skills, explicit skill instruction, opportunities for student-directed instruction, use of instructional strategies that enhance understanding, opportunities for practice, systematic student assessment, staff development, and home and parent involvement. (August and Hakuta, 1997, 171)

A more recent report by the National Research Council in March 1999, *Starting Out Right: A Guide to Promoting Children's Success in Reading,* summarizes a large body of research over the last two decades regarding reading and effective reading instruction for students who come to school speaking Spanish as their primary language. That report makes clear that both phonetic analysis and the making of meaning are important in the beginning stages of reading development. Of significance, the report makes very clear that the body of research available regarding the reading development of English by nonnative English speakers whose first language is Spanish is most effective by providing reading instruction in the child's native language.

These features resonate with other recent studies of effectiveness for programs specifically designed for linguistically and culturally diverse populations (Lockwood and Secada, 1999). California Tomorrow (1995), in a study of early childhood care in California, concluded that a set of principles guided quality child care across a variety of care settings that serve a growing community of linguistically and culturally diverse families:

1. Support the development of ethnic identity and anti-racist attitudes among children.
2. Build upon the cultures of families and promote cross-cultural understanding among children.
3. Foster the preservation of children's home language and encourage bilingualism among all children.
4. Engage in on-going reflection and dialogue. (California Tomorrow, 1995, 8)

In a state-mandated study of exemplary schools serving the state's linguistically and culturally diverse students (mostly Hispanics), several key attributes were common in those schools serving these students (Berman, 1992a). These features included flexibility—adapting to the diversity of languages, mobility, and special nonschool needs of these students and their families; coordination—utilizing sometimes scarce and diverse resources, such as federal and state monies and local community organizations in highly coordinated ways to achieve academic goals; cultural validation—schools validating their students' cultures by incorporating materials and discussions that built on the linguistic and cultural aspects of the community; and a shared vision—a coherent sense of who the students were and what they hoped to accomplish led by a school's principal, staff, instructional aides, parents, and community (Berman, 1992a).

Three more recent "effective-exemplary" analyses of schools that serve high percentages of linguistically and culturally diverse students nationally are worthy of mention (Thomas and Collier, 1995b). In studies of five urban and suburban school districts in various regions of the United States, three key factors are reported as significant in producing academic success for students. The studies focus on the length of time needed to be academically successful in English and consider factors influencing academic success, such as the student, program, and instructional variables. These studies include some 42,000 student records per school year and from 8 to 12 years of data from each school district:

1. Cognitively complex academic instruction through students' home language for as long as possible and through second language for part of the school day
2. Use of current approaches to teaching academic curricula using both students' home language and English through active, discovery, and cognitively complex learning
3. Changes in the sociocultural context of schooling, such as integrating English speakers, implementation of additive bilingual instructional goals, and transformation of minority/majority relations to a positive plane (Thomas and Collier, 1995a)

A series of case studies of exemplary schools throughout the United States serving highly diverse and poor student and mainly Hispanic student populations also illustrates what can be done to promote academic excellence (McLeod, 1996). In these studies, selected schools with demonstrated academic success records were subjected to intensive site-by-site study with the goal of identifying specific attributes at each site related to the functioning of the school as well as a more ambitious effort to identify common attributes across the sites. Schools in four states (Texas, Illinois, California, and Massachusetts) were particularly successful in achieving high academic outcomes with a diverse set of students and utilized the following common goals for ensuring high-quality teaching:

Foster English acquisition and the development of mature literacy. Schools utilized native-language abilities to develop literacy that promoted English literacy development. Programs in these schools were more interested in this mature development than transitioning students quickly into English-language instruction. This approach paid off in English-language development at levels that allowed students to be successful in English instruction.

Deliver grade-level content. Challenging work in the academic disciplines was perceived and acted on simultaneously with the goals of English-language learning. Teachers organized lessons to deliver grade-level instruction through a variety of native-language, sheltered English, and ESL activities.

Organize instruction in innovative ways. Examples of innovations included "schools-within-schools" to more responsively deal with diverse language needs of the students; "families" of students who stayed together for major parts of the school day; "continuum classes" in which teachers remained with their students for two to three years, helping teachers become more familiar with and respond to the diversity in the students; and a more flexible grouping of students on a continuous basis so as to respond to the developmental differences between their native language and second language.

Protect and extend instructional time. Schools utilized after-school programs, supportive computer-based instruction, and voluntary Saturday schools and summer academies. These school activities multiplied the opportunities for students to engage in academic learning. Regular teachers or trained tutors were utilized to extend this learning time. Not surprisingly, a majority of students took advantage of these voluntary extensions. Care was taken not to erode the daily instructional time that was available—erosion often related to auxiliary responsibilities by teachers that take valuable time away from instruction.

Expand teachers' roles and responsibilities. Teachers were given much greater roles in curricular and instructional decision making. This decision making was much more collective in nature to ensure cross-grade articulation and coordination. Teachers in these schools became full copartners. They devised more "authentic" assessments that could inform instruction, developing assessment tools and scoring rubrics in reading and mathematics.

Address students' social and emotional needs. Schools were located in low-income neighborhoods serving poor families. Therefore, a proactive stance with regard to issues in these communities was adopted. An after-school activity that was aimed at families, particularly dealing with issues of alcohol and drug abuse, family violence, health care, and related social service needs, brought the school staff together with social service agencies at one school site. Similar examples of actual family counseling and direct medical care were arranged at other sites.

Involve parents in their children's education. Some of the schools were magnet schools to which parents had chosen to send their children. In such schools, parent involvement was part of the magnet school contract. This included involvement in school committees, school festivals and celebrations, student field trips, and other activities. In nonmagnet schools, parent outreach services were an integral part of the school operation. In all cases, communication was accomplished on a regular basis in various home languages. Parent participation in governance of the school was a common attribute, although levels of parent participation were highly variable (adapted from McLeod, 1996, 13–33).

In a more intensive case study of two elementary schools and one middle school, Miramontes, Nadeau, and Commins (1997) describe in detail the development of exemplary school attributes with an emphasis on linking decision making to effective programs (see table 6.1). These schools,

Table 6.1   Exemplary School Attributes/Premises for Effective Elementary Schools

Premise 1—Active Learning. Knowledge is best acquired when learners actively participate in meaningful activities that are constructive in nature and appropriate to their level of development.

Premise 2—The primary language foundation. The more comprehensive the use of the primary language, the greater the potential for linguistically diverse students to be academically successful. There are always ways to nurture the primary language regardless of school resources.

Premise 3—The quality of primary language use. There is a difference between a token use of the primary language in instruction and its full development as a foundation for thinking and learning.

Premise 4—Strategies for second language development. Second language development creates an added dimension to instructional decision making. Instruction must reflect specific strategies designed to meet the needs of second language learners.

Premise 5—Contexts for second language development. Second language instruction must be organized to provide student the time, experiences and opportunities they need to fully develop language proficiency. This requires a range of social and academic contexts in which both language and content are emphasized.

Premise 6—First and second language environments. Bilingual academic proficiency requires that clear, distinct, and meaning enriched contexts for each language be created during instructional time.

Premise 7—Transitions and redesignations. Decisions regarding transition to formal second language reading and redesignations that exit students from programs cannot be made arbitrarily.

Premise 8—Instructional assessment. Instructional assessment must be based on students' first and second language development, rather than on grade level or predetermined criteria. An appropriate assessment plan should address language and literacy development, as well as content knowledge.

Premise 9—Parents and community. Parents and community need to play a major role in the learning and schooling of their children.

Premise 10—Planning for cross-cultural interactions. Instruction must be organized to help students understand and respect themselves and their own culture as well as the cultures of the broader society. Planned cross-cultural interactions are an essential component of programs for all students.

Premise 11—Socio-cultural and political implications. Socio-cultural factors and political context must be considered in making decisions regarding every aspect of program planning.

Premise 12—Teachers as decision makers. Teachers are decision makers. As part of a learning community they are all equally responsible for decisions regarding the instructional program for linguistically diverse students.

Source: C. B. Miramontes, A. Nadeau, & N. L. Commins (1997, 37–38)

serving a majority of Hispanic students, over a period of several years developed local, state, and national recognition for their academic success with very linguistically and culturally diverse student bodies—schools with as many as five languages represented in significant proportion. These authors concluded that a set of premises were key in guiding the development and reform of the schools' effective programs.

Recent articulations regarding these challenges reinforce this charge. In their enunciation of standards for English-language arts, the National Council of Teachers of English and the International Reading Association (1996) recognize the following:

- Students develop an understanding of and respect for diversity in language use, patterns, and dialects across cultures, ethnic groups, geographic regions, and social roles.
- Students whose first language is not English make use of their first language to develop competency in the English language arts and to develop understanding of content across the curriculum.
- Celebrating our shared beliefs and traditions are not enough; we also need to honor that which is distinctive in the many groups that make up our nation. (3)

The National Association for the Education of Young Children (1996) echoes these same concerns in its position statement related to educational practices regarding linguistic and cultural diversity in early childhood:

Early childhood educators can best help linguistically and culturally diverse children and their families by acknowledging and responding to the importance of the child's home language and culture. Administrative support for bilingualism as a goal is necessary within the educational setting. Educational practices should focus on educating children toward the "school culture" while preserving and respecting the diversity of the home language and culture that each child brings to the early learning setting. (12)

In conclusion, information derived from recent research indicates that Hispanic students can be served effectively (Lockwood and Secada, 1999; Romo, 1999; Tashakkori and Ochoa, 1999). These students can achieve academically at levels at or above the national norm. Instructional strategies that serve these students best acknowledge, respect, and build on the language and culture of the home. Teachers play the most critical role in students' academic success, and students become important partners with teachers in the teaching and learning enterprise. Although much more research is required, we are not without a knowledge base that can make a difference.

7

Educational Approaches—
What Works for Hispanics:
The Adolescent Years

It was in the later elementary grades that I became directly aware of gangs. My immediate family had been reduced by the marriage of my elder brothers and sisters to just four—my father, my mother, my younger brother, and myself. We could no longer meet the demands of working a farm. We moved into an abandoned basement next to my elder brother's home in the "city"—actually a small town of some 30,000 residents. Here, for the first time, I attended an "inner-city" school, a highly segregated Hispanic elementary where children from three distinct neighborhoods or "barrios" (Riverside, El Paso, and Connected Lakes—my barrio) came together at school. There was no doubt about the Hispanic presence at the school as was the case in several other schools in the city—at least three other schools were highly segregated with Hispanic students. I learned years later that this segregation was not just happenstance but very clearly orchestrated by the school board as they drew and redrew boundaries for school attendance. Like many other small communities in the Southwest, this segregation was primarily a Hispanic-versus-white phenomenon (San Miguel and Valencia, 1998). Very few African American families lived in my own community. I was in high school before I met my first African American student.

In that segregated and poor school, I learned quickly that it was in my best interest to associate myself with a gang. Having grown up in a highly rural context where such affiliations were not common (I had heard my older brothers speak of rival Hispanic gangs in nearby towns), it was difficult for me to understand the significance of these associations. After losing three or four fights after joining the school, I began to realize that such affiliations might be useful since each time I was challenged physically I had no one to help me either resolve the challenge or assist me should the challenge move to a physical level. I just got tired of getting the snot knocked out of me. There was a history of gang formation in this community among Hispanics and others because there were indeed white gangs ("Cowboys" and "Okies") that I later learned were tied to protection of geographical territory, particularly by young men in an effort to keep the girls in their territory from "unwanted" exposure to boys from other territories. But all I wanted was someone to help me from getting the snot knocked out of me. It was, at the most primary level, a decision having to do with self-defense. Yet I knew enough about some affiliations from my family that I should avoid: *"Cuídate de los pachucos"* (Watch out for those Pachucos). In my community, Pachucos were the bad guys—they did not wear *facuchis* (long, dressy coats and baggy pants) as depicted in accounts of Pachucos in Los Angeles in the 1940s and 1950s. In my community, they were Spanish speaking, wore black leather jackets, and wore their hair combed back with plenty of grease—and they had no compunctions about throwing a punch, striking out with bicycle chains, or using a switchblade. They even took pride in having spent time in *La Reforma* (reform school). It was a sixth-grade Pachuco at my school who had decided to make my life miserable.

For me and many like me, at an age when group affiliation for defense or for other reasons becomes important, a choice had to be made. I knew I could avoid the lickings I was receiving by joining the Pachuco gang—others were doing just that. Then as today, this was not an easy task. Various rituals would need to be performed, most having to do with physically harming others or subjecting oneself to physical abuse. As luck would have it, another Hispanic student had joined this school community at the same time I had and was receiving the same treatment. We decided, for reasons of self-defense, to form our own "gang." With him and several others who were continually finding themselves at the mercy of the Pachucos, we came to an uneasy but sustained compact that held for the remainder of the school year. In short, we decided to avoid conflicts with each other, to respect each other's turf. Unfortunately for the Pachucos, but fortunately for us, they began to find their way into La Reforma much like the older members of their gang. Our gang became more involved in athletics and, in today's nomenclature of adolescent associations, became "jocks"—a group that served to bring us together around common interests that included the nurturing and protection of the membership.

The next year, most of the Pachucos went on to one junior high and us jocks to another. Both those junior highs were much more integrated, yet we retained our gang affiliations in those new sites for exactly the same reasons that we had formed them. We hung together as each gang and member faced new challenges of affiliations within the schooling confines. We came to be known in our respective schools as gang members. White students would go out of their way to avoid us, and the Cowboys and the Okies would challenge us. Whether we were Pachucos or jocks, we were perceived the same—as Hispanic gang members. It was this perception by others that actually brought the Pachucos and the jocks together on several occasions to address the challenge of either police authorities or other non-Hispanic gangs. We became allies with the Pachucos, and some members actually became my friends. Being Hispanic in this community became an overriding variable, given that we were both treated the same even though our "gang cultures" varied.

As I visit this community today, I run into both the Pachucos and the jocks of my youth. They are not much different today, even though their pasts may have been different for a period of time during adolescence. The Pachucos are indistinguishable in dress and behavior from the jocks. They have families and work hard, most at physical labor. The backgrounds of these two distinguishable gangs in my own life did not lead to different social or economic outcomes. This is not to say that the scars of adolescence weigh more on some than on others. Serving in La Reforma and continuing brushes with the law have taken a toll. Yet in the broader community of this same small city, these adults are still perceived as "outsiders," as Hispanics, and all are readily associated with gangs—with all the negative connotations that go with that association. Much like in my day, they are all thrown together on the basis of their ethnicity.

It has not changed much today for a group of adolescents who are finding their way to adulthood. Their own search for identity, group affiliation, nurturing, and safety is still with us. It is particularly the case for our Hispanic youth on the farms, towns, and cities of the United States. Findings from the National Institute of Justice survey (Conley, Kelly, Mahanna, and Warner, 1997) reported that gang membership was predominantly African American (47.8 percent) and Hispanics (47.7 percent), with an increase in gang participation of 13 and 18 percent, respectively. Significantly, the number of white and Asian gang members increased by over 50 percent. Hispanic adolescents in particular continue to be challenged to identify and affiliate, and too many are forced into choosing an antisocial, anti-schooling, antiacademic affiliation mainly because it is the most reasonable option and because too many in society expect them to do so (U.S. Department of Education, 1998).

HISPANIC ADOLESCENCE: A TIME OF SIGNIFICANT SOCIAL/ACADEMIC RISK

Researchers, educators, and parents have long known the challenges of adolescence in the United States (Dryfoos, 1998). Telltale signs of academic underachievement are reported particularly for African American and Hispanic adolescents during early adolescence (Larson and Rumberger, 1995a; Mahiri, 1998). Yet problems with academic work account for only half the reasons that these students are unsuccessful in school (Wehlage et al., 1989). Rumberger (1998) indicates that a high proportion of Hispanic school dropouts, as much as 40 percent, are associated with nonacademic variables. These students are likely to have poor attendance (Rumberger, 1993) and much less of a bonding to school (Ekstrom et al., 1986). The National High School and Beyond database indicates that twice as many Hispanics admit to cutting classes in middle schools than the general population (Rumberger, 1998; U.S. Department of Education, 1998). Larson (1989) reports that Hispanic middle school students did not significantly differ in truancy or absence rates at the beginning of the seventh grade, averaging about 12 percent truancy/absence. However, this rate more than doubled by the end of the year, to 27 percent, and continued to increase at later grades for those student who did not dropout. And, significantly, Whelage et. al. (1989) indicate that each young Hispanic and African American adolescent dropout who they interviewed expressed the feeling that schools and teachers did not care about them and that they had no adult at school to turn to for assistance. Rumberger's (1998) sobering conclusions should ring very loud to all of us:

- 17 percent of Hispanic students have dropped out by ninth grade.
- Less than 50 percent of Hispanics in ninth grade have earned enough credits to be on track for graduation.
- By the end of 10th grade, 31 percent of Hispanic students have dropped out, and less than 21 percent have earned enough credits to be on the track to graduation.

Given these dire statistics of school failure for Hispanic adolescents, the prognosis for school success is not optimistic. However, very specific educational endeavors, some reaching outside the classroom, have been well documented as making a difference. The remainder of this chapter will attempt to specifically address these and other positive developments in the field of education that raise hope for turning around the "destiny" of adolescent Hispanic students in our schools.

ACHIEVEMENT FOR LATINOS THROUGH
ACADEMIC SUCCESS (ALAS)

The ALAS (*alas* means "wings" in Spanish) project targeted middle school Hispanic students who have been identified as particularly at high risk for school failure. This includes indices of social and academic well-being, such as limited motivation for school attendance, an extended record of very low school achievement, and a continuous record of disciplinary actions by school and police authorities. In my day, they might be identified as the Pachucos. The ALAS program is founded on the premise that child behavior and development is an interaction between multiple contexts of influence and the individual characteristics of the child (Jessor, 1993; Garcia, 1999). Such an approach recognizes the significance of the adolescent's family (e.g., culture, language, and income), community (e.g., social services, juvenile justice system, and peer-related social activity), and finally the school (e.g., teachers, school organization, administration, and peers). The intervention strategies of ALAS are designed to enhance the effectiveness of each of these entities as well as to increase their collaborations.

Specifically, ALAS organized itself into four components: (1) the student-centered component, focusing on social problem solving training and counseling, recognizing positive student performance, and efforts to enhance positive school affiliation; (2) the school component, focusing on frequent teacher feedback to the students and parents on academic progress and school attendance; (3) the family component, focusing the use of community resources and parent training in student monitoring of broader student activity and school participation; and (4) the community component, focusing on enhancing collaboration between nonprofit types of community service agencies (like those supported by the United Way or those housed in churches) and the juvenile justice system, ensuring that students interacting with the police and courts had advocacy representatives.

More specifically, the ALAS project had on its "intervention" team a full-time bilingual/bicultural social worker with extensive experience working in the communities of the students as well as teachers and school administrators and counselors. Team members knew many of the families, community organizations, and school personnel. They could communicate with representatives of these entities in either language and knew the "cultural" conditions of those with whom they were communicating—parents, teachers, counselors, social workers, policemen/women, and judges.

The ALAS project was implemented in a middle school with approximately 2,000 students, 96 percent Hispanic. The data reported by evaluators (Rumberger, 1998) is specifically focused on some 50 students participating in ALAS and a randomly selected group of students, matched to the ALAS participants, grades 7 to 9. The results are impressive. By the end of the ninth grade, close to 100 percent of the ALAS students were still enrolled in school compared to 80 percent of the non-ALAS students. Some 80 percent of the ALAS students were on track to graduation, having attained the prerequisite credits during middle school. Less than 50 percent of the non-ALAS students were at the same point. School attendance, truancy, and grades were also significantly enhanced for the ALAS students as compared with the non-ALAS students. More telling are the longer-term differences between these two student cohorts though the 12th grade, even though the ALAS program did not extend beyond the ninth grade: At each grade level, ALAS students significantly outperformed non-ALAS students.

The ALAS project is unique it that it took the most high risk Hispanic students and made a significant difference in their lives. These were the hard-core students, those moving very directly into antisocial perceptions of themselves and into peer organizations that would serve them well within gang organizations. Schooling was moving directly out of their lives, and the judicial system was looming directly ahead. Through a comprehensive treatment, these students' futures were redirected within the context of our definition of academic success. The ALAS model viewed the family, the school, and the community as important contexts of influence that interacted with each individual student to either support or hinder development. Rather than passing on students from one institutional context to another like a baton in a relay race (Rumberger, 1998), family members, school personnel, and community agencies worked together to monitor and support students while building the capacity themselves to be more responsive and effective. As a result, each institutional representative, singularly as well as collectively, increased its ability to positively influence youth behavior. At the roots of the ALAS program was a clear understanding of these adolescent students' cultural and social circumstances.

Project Theme

It was immediately following a presentation of the previous ALAS findings at a state conference that a local middle school principal issued the following public challenge: "Well, that's all very interesting. But I'm not sure we can *help* our students. We are a 90 percent Latino school and are not doing well and we want to do better. How do we change? Maybe you ought to come out and help us become a responsive school rather than telling us about those that have already attained their goal?" I could not answer his first question. But how could I refuse his challenge? Here was a principal who had an interest in responsive change. And he was giving me an opportunity to answer that important question: How does one move from a "bad" school to a "good" school in a Hispanic student context? We immediately called a meeting to discuss this.

And we went beyond that meeting and several others. The principal, Mr. Carlos Garcia, invited me and a group of university colleagues to his school to speak to teachers. (Carlos is now superintendent of the Fresno California Unified School District.) On the scheduled day, an announcement was read over the PA regarding our visit: "Dr. Garcia and a group of his colleagues will be in the library after school today to discuss a possible intervention that will help our students and community." I learned later that he had also put notices in each of the 30 or so teachers' mailboxes. Mr. Garcia could not attend the meeting because he had a student crisis develop, and we had some nine teachers who joined us in the library. I lectured to the group a bit about the research we had done, and we discussed the possibilities of working in the school. Two teachers politely indicated that they were not interested and left while the remaining group decided to meet one more time to discuss the possibilities. The teachers said that they would ask around to see whether other teachers were interested. Some two weeks later, we arranged another meeting that I attended along with eight teachers, six from the first group and two recruits. Mr. Garcia had a conflicting engagement and never had time to come to subsequent meetings. (In fact, he left the school to work in another district a few months later.) We decided at that meeting to give it a try.

Overall Strategy

The project's approach was guided by a set of agreed-on principles (or cornerstones), extracted from our review of research literature, that had been demonstrated as effective in promoting Hispanic student's literacy, mathematics, and English-language development in school. The following are principles that the team (eight teachers, four university faculty members, and two graduate students) developed:

- Any curriculum, especially one for "diverse" children, must address all categories of learning goals. We should not expect "less" for this student population.
- The more linguistically and culturally diverse the children we teach are, the more the content must be related to the child's own environment and experience.
- The more diverse the children are, the more integrated the curriculum should be. Children should have opportunities to study a topic in depth and to apply all kinds of skills they have acquired in a variety of home and school contexts.

- The more diverse the children are, the more the curriculum should address learning through active endeavors rather than passive ones, particularly informal social activities such as group projects in which students are allowed flexibility in participating with the teacher and other students in engaging academic material.
- The more diverse the children are, the more important it is for the curriculum to offer opportunities to apply what they are learning in a meaningful context.

Because the proposed project was ultimately concerned with "students learning how to learn," particular significance was assigned to strategies drawn from effective schooling research that support the achievement of basic skills and the acquisition of higher-order linguistic and cognitive processes and that use linguistic, analytical, cognitive, and metacognitive processing to maximize academic learning:

Strategy 1: Use of thematic, integrated curriculum, such that academic objectives are achieved through content-integrated instruction

Strategy 2: Emphasis on small-group activities incorporating heterogeneous language grouping and peer tutoring and emphasizing higher-order linguistic and cognitive processes (in which learning proceeds from the concrete to the presentational and then to the symbolic)

Strategy 3: Emphasis on literacy activities: interactive journals, silent reading followed by small-group discussion, interactive literature study, individual and group-authored literature, and mathematic learning logs

Strategy 4: Use of cooperative learning strategies, emphasizing the systematic participation of each student in processing curriculum materials

Strategy 5: Documentation and discussion of interpersonal inequities related to gender, ethnic, and linguistic differences among middle school Mexican-descent students with a focus on strategies that would foster equal status interactions and support effective learning in general

The project reorganized the seventh-grade instructional environment at the middle school for 54 students. Specifically, an instructional intervention was implemented for two heterogeneous groups of approximately 30 students each. One group was made up of English Only (EO) and reclassified bilingual (Spanish and English) students in the seventh grade, while the second group included EO and Fluent English Proficiency (FEP) with higher-level LEP students who are near the transition level or are already in transition English reading. These students were with the same classmates in four of the six periods.

Eight teachers worked collaboratively with university faculty to implement an interdisciplinary, collaborative curriculum for these two groups (Theme students). The content area subjects taught were reading, English, science, mathematics, and social studies (science was taught for one semester and social studies for the other). The two groups of students were integrated with other students from the rest of the school for two periods a day, during which time they participated in physical education classes and an elective class.

A comparison group (Comparison students) was established consisting of 48 students in the regular middle school program. They changed classes throughout the day and experienced six different combinations of students from six different nonintegrated content area subjects.

Recall that the Theme students were heterogeneously grouped into two strands, one bilingual and one English only, in which they remained through math, reading, language arts, and social studies/science (these flip-flop midyear). Within the first week of school, the Theme group's instruction began using the Olympics as the first thematic unit. Using that theme as a springboard, the four content areas were taught. The teachers met to share their individual areas of curriculum focus with the Olympic theme and to integrate lessons across the curriculum.

At the end of the project's second theme, the Arts, a parent potluck with student presentations took place. This provided an opportunity to involve and further inform parents about the project. The staff were available to present rationale and answer questions. Students presented a description of their Theme classes and shared completed projects.

Specific Activities

Professional Enhancement of Teachers

- Project teachers participated in preservice and in-service training activities specific to LEP-effective instructional strategies particularly related to cooperative learning, peer tutoring, literacy as a sociopsycholinguistic phenomenon, and the cognitive foundations of literacy, mathematics, and science. This was accomplished at a weeklong institute held at the university, also in two preservice workshops.
- Project teachers met monthly to network regarding the implementation of instructional strategies.
- Project teachers observed each others' classrooms and participated in discussions regarding their observations.

Assessment of Classroom Practices

- Project teachers and research team members collaborated in the development and implementation of specific academic assessment strategies.

- Previous effective schooling measures were reviewed, assessed, and used to develop a specific assessment of the instructional character of the program.
- Members of the team participated in training relevant to assessment techniques, including student, parent, and teacher interview techniques and conducted interviews with students, teachers, and parents.

Enhancement of Students' Academic Learning

- Theme project students were pretested in September–October using equivalent English and Spanish achievement tests (CTBS and SABE, respectively), and a comparison group of 48 students in the same school matched on academic achievement were identified, pretested, and posttested.
- Target students were placed in heterogeneously structured learning groups that maximized effective communication and learning. Comparison group students followed the present curriculum and scheduling program.
- Target students participated in a core integrated curriculum that promoted increased opportunities for language and literacy development and integrated content-related instruction. The integrated instruction was organized around eight themes: the Olympics, the Fine Arts (Popular Music, Art, and Fashion), the Ocean, Crime and Nonviolence, Careers, Gender, AIDS, and Ethnic Identity. Students and teachers selected these themes together.
- Students worked in collaborative learning groups characterized by academic heterogeneity and an orientation to positive interdependence.

Improvement of Students' Self-Esteem

- Students were recognized for both their individual achievements and their contributions to group products.
- Students worked in cooperative learning structures—particularly the Tribes process—to develop skills in leadership and cooperation.
- Students in cooperative groups discussed specific situational conflicts and utilized problem-solving skills to determine solutions.
- Teachers implemented programs that recognized student improvement and success for students across a range of abilities.
- Teachers integrated lessons that promoted understanding and appreciation of individual and cultural differences.

Results. Recall that pre- and posttests in areas of language, reading, writing, and mathematics were given to Theme students and the Comparison group of students in the same schools. In addition, survey data regarding the students' academic self-concept and social identity were gathered, as were interviews from students' data on the same domains. This last set of data was gathered at the end of the students' sophomore year in high school. Moreover, parents were interviewed regarding their social identities and their perceptions of schooling. What follows is a brief overview of results that were obtained in these specific domains:

1. Academic achievement in language, reading, and writing
2. Ethnographic data related to academic self-concept
3. Social identity of students and parents
4. Long-term effects of participation in the program

Language, Reading, and Writing

Academic achievement measures in English and Spanish were obtained for the various groups of the study during the spring semester of the academic year. For English-only and bilingual students in the Theme group and the Comparison group, six subsets of the English version of the California Test of Basic Skill (CTBS) along with seven subsets of the English version of the Language Assessment Scales Reading/Writing (LAS) were used for this analysis.

On each subtest, the English-only Theme group performed higher on these measures of academic achievement. Moreover, the bilingual Theme group did not differ significantly from the English-only Comparison group on any of these measures. The bilingual Theme group had been identified by their need for further academic development and was made up of English-dominant students who participated in bilingual classrooms with their Spanish-dominant peers. It was academically significant that this group did not differ from a group of English-only curriculum students.

Other results indicate that the Theme group consistently performed higher on other measures than their appropriate Comparison group cohorts. This is particularly the case for bilingual students. On six of the seven subsets, bilingual Theme students scored significantly higher than bilingual Comparison students. Of particular interest were the significant differences found between these groups on the measure of written language ability.

In short, the results of the this analysis indicate a consistent pattern of achievement outcomes that favor the Theme group students. This consistent pattern was evident for bilingual as well as English-only Theme group students.

Ethnic Data on Student Self-Concept

Recall that a part of this intervention attempted to address issues of ethnicity as opposed to ignore it, as is the case in general. An analysis from the participant classroom observations, student interviews, and teacher interviews produced several findings. These findings were categorized into four separate domains:

1. ETHNIC IDENTITY

Mexican-origin and Anglo students did not use a wide range of ethnic labels when referring to themselves and other students at the school. When we asked students to identify the different types of students at the school in terms of specific ethnic labels commonly heard in the community, they used only a few terms: usually "Mexican," "Mexican American" and "American." Very few students were familiar with the term "Chicano." When asked what distinguished individuals within a generic category of "Mexican," such features were expressed in terms of language ability, physical appearance, and country of birth. One Anglo girl discussed differences among Theme students in terms of those "who are bilingual and those who are straight." Most of the Mexican-origin students were familiar with other ethnic labels, (e.g., Cholo and Pocho) but did not feel that they applied to the Mexican-origin student population at the school. When asked to categorize themselves students of Mexican origin, they most frequently chose "Mexican" or "Mexican American." The most commonly used ethnic labels for the Anglo students among both groups were "white," "American," and occasionally "Anglo."

Despite an awareness of differences with the Mexican student population, most of these students emphasized commonalities across people, especially the groups in the school. They gave responses such as "It doesn't matter if you're Mexican or American, people are people." This is not to say that students do not perceive differences among students at their school or even categories of students. However, distinguishing features did not necessarily reflect differences in ethnic identification. When asked to identify different groups in school without any prompts for ethnicity, all but two students distinguished students in other ways (e.g., "athletes" versus "nerds," "popular" versus "not popular," and "good students" versus "bad students").

We observed that a handful of students, girls in particular, appeared to exhibit a certain amount of tension in discussing specific ethnic labels carrying a negative connotation (e.g., "Cholo"), especially if these labels indicated behaviors that could be linked to ethnic identity. One girl in the Theme stand discussed how she had changed in the last year. She described how just a year before she was an "angel," someone who did her homework regularly, listened to her mother, and did what her older brother told her to do. "Now, my friends have changed me: I now dress differently, I don't do my school work, I get into fights with family members, things like that." She concluded that this was both "good" and "bad." It is "good" that she no longer lets her overbearing brother boss her around but "bad" that she talks back to her mother and that her work is lagging. I use this example here to expand on the notion of the importance of peer influence and "identity."

2. POSITIVE SENSE OF SELF-ESTEEM

Mexican-decent students exhibit a positive sense of self and express pride in their Mexican heritage. In a variety of different contexts, students expressed pride in being Mexican, giving examples of different holidays and special occasions when they felt particularly proud. It is not clear in what specific ways, if any, this positive sense of self is linked to ethnic pride; whether it is in any way connected to a particular ethnic label or to their positive attitudes toward Spanish–English bilingualism; and/or in what ways it is linked to other social experiences in the school, family, and community. With regard to the positive sense of self and ethnic pride, of particular interest was finding out whether any of the Mexican-descent students wanted to change places with any of the Anglo students in the class or in the school, especially those who were identified as popular, attractive, and/ or high academic achievers. Very few of the students we interviewed expressed any desire to change places with anyone else, frequently responding with surprise that such a question would even be asked: "Why would I want to do that? I like being me." We also asked the students to identify which aspects of their physical appearance they would change, if any. There were some important gender differences here, especially among some of the darker-skinned Mexican-descent girls. While the boys, with several exceptions, did not identify any changes they would make in their physical appearance, many of the girls said they would change the shape of their nose, remove freckles, or lighten the color of their hair or skin.

3. FUTURE ASPIRATIONS

All students, regardless of ethnicity, aspire to professional careers. All students were interested in pursuing a profession. In the case of the survey data, the most commonly chosen categories were law (45.7 percent), medicine (40.6 percent), and careers in the arts (over 30 percent). When presented with a choice of careers, students often chose a range of possibilities that included professions as well as service-related jobs. For example, one student responded to being interested in becoming a scientist, mechanic, doctor, waitress, photographer, or beautician.

Among the Mexican-descent students, there was no interest in becoming a farm worker or cannery worker, the jobs that were commonly held by their parents. They were aware of the difficulties of these occupations, as revealed in the following comments:

"A mí no me gusta trabajar en el campo porque así aprende uno como se cansan los padres para mantenernos y comprarnos lo que queremos."

If I played professional football, I wouldn't have to work as hard as my parents. They sweat for hours working in the fields. I wouldn't like that.

Finishing high school and/or college is in everyone's future plans. Students link schooling to future success. Students indicated that getting a good job in a profession necessitates a college career, although they believed they could get adequate jobs (mechanic, beautician, and so on) with four years of high school. Moreover, everyone reported a similar attitude among their parents. With very few exceptions, all students said that their parents would be moderately to greatly upset if they quit school before high school graduation. Some talked about how their parents set forth in very realistic terms their options: the farm fields or something better. For them, the "something better" meant an occupation that could be attained by staying in school and, they hoped, going on to college. The survey data revealed one distinction between Anglos and Mexican-descent students: Mexican-descent students were evenly divided in terms of pursuing two years of college and four years, while Anglo students overwhelmingly favored finishing four years of college.

Mexican-descent students lacked specific instrumental knowledge on how to prepare for the careers they wanted to pursue. This finding emerged from student interviews. Though Mexican-descent students knew college was a prerequisite to many of the professions they expressed interest in, they lacked specific knowledge about the different types of postsecondary education, the different credentials and opportunities each offered, and the number of years required to complete particular levels of training. This is in marked contrast to many of the Anglo students interviewed who had a much clearer, although sometimes inaccurate, picture of the differences between a community college and a four-year institution of higher education. Most of the Anglo students understood the connection between higher-status occupations (e.g., teaching, nursing, and architecture) and the need to complete at least four years of college. In contrast, many of the Mexican-descent students felt that a two-year education at the local community college would be sufficient to enter these occupations. One girl said that to be a doctor "you have to have five years of something before you can get out of the university." Very few of these students knew the names of colleges other than one or two of the local community colleges, and none knew where to obtain this information. Many assumed that this information would be presented to them later in their educational career. A point observed in these discussions is the extent to which these students conceptualized the pursuit of a college education as something one sets out to acquire in much the same way one purchases, for example, an expensive car. What is lacking in their comments is any substantive knowledge of the instrumental behaviors, orientations, and scholastic achievements required.

Among those Mexican-origin students who did have some idea about the demands of a college education, the pursuit was seen as potentially very difficult, as a struggle. One girl described the obstacles in her way: "getting pregnant and poor grades." Money was also frequently reported as a major obstacle. As one girl noted, "You need lots of money to learn in college." This is not to say that these students felt that college was an impossible dream, just that it entails a great deal of hard work and struggle, above and beyond the rigors of the academic requirements. Several explicitly stated that if they worked hard enough, they would make it to and through college, noting the experiences of a cousin, aunt, older sibling, or close family friend.

Mexican-descent students feel that being bilingual and biliterate will contribute to their future success. These students frequently expressed very positive attitudes toward bilingual ability. They feel that knowing Spanish and English will benefit them later in the various job opportunities, citing the advantages of being able to communicate with monolingual speakers of each language. Frequently, students gave examples of specific job situations, possibly derived from their own actual experiences, in which a bilingual employee was able to assist a monolingual speaker. According to the survey data, this perceived advantage was also true for half of the non-Mexican-descent students. On the whole, Mexican-descent students in the study were eager to maintain or improve on their Spanish-language skills by continuing to take classes in Spanish.

4. ACADEMIC STRATEGIES AND PERCEPTIONS ABOUT SCHOOLING

Doing homework and listening/behaving in class were the features most often linked to doing well in school. Doing homework and behaving are the hallmark of a good student, as reflected in both the interviews and the survey data. When students were asked to describe what it takes to be a good student, they responded with "by doing my homework and listening in class," "by paying attention to the teacher and doing all the work," and "by not messing around and getting your work in on time." They felt that

being quiet in class was also important. Responses to survey items revealed that 50 percent felt that completing schoolwork was the single most
important attribute of a successful student (as a choice among the following attributes: asks lots of questions, does all his or her work and does not
talk much, talks a lot but gets the work finished, and is smart). When asked
to identify a successful student in their class or describe someone they
considered to be a good student, they invariably described or named someone who did their homework and was well behaved. When asked how they
thought they could improve their own academic performance, nearly
everyone said that they should do their work, listen in class, and pay attention to the teacher.

Students are not challenged by their schoolwork. In interviews, as well
as in many but not all observations of actual classroom sessions, students
exhibited little enthusiasm or genuine engagement in their classes. In
many ways, this assessment is connected to the data substantiating the preceding findings. Two-thirds of students in the EO strand felt that classes
were boring, while just under half in the B/L strand shared this view. Only
15 percent of the students felt that schoolwork was too hard. Moreover,
the majority students in both strands (but particularly the EO students)
wished that their classes were more interesting.

Social Identity of Students and Parents

Social identity is an intriguing and complex construct. It is simultaneously
a *social product,* for it emerges out of a complex set of biological, social,
and cultural influences, and a *social force* that emanates from the created
product to direct a number of social activities, including the processing of
personally relevant information, the shaping of political attitudes (Hurtado
and Gurin, 1987), and intergroup behavior (Tajfel, 1978; Hurtado and Garcia, 1994).

Identity research with Mexican-descent persons has focused almost exclusively on ethnic identity—the sense of oneself as a member of an ethnic
group. While ethnicity is undeniably significant, it is not the only critical
dimension of the social identities of Mexican descendants. Few studies,
however, have investigated such potentially important nonethnic dimensions as occupation, race, family, religion, or language. Yet when asked to
select from a series of social labels, the one label they felt best described
them, a sample of Detroit Hispanics was as likely to choose a nonethnic
category as an ethnic social one.

This aspect of the study examined the social identities of the school's
seventh-graders and their parents by administering a multiple-dimension
measure of social identity that includes race, class, family, and ethnicity.
By comparing the differences and similarities in the social identification

of parents and their offspring, an empirical basis can be formed for how social identity, including ethnic identity, is transmitted from one generation to another.

The sample consisted of 110 seventh-graders and one of their parents. Of the 110 students, 23 were white and 87 of Mexican origin. Of the 87 Mexican-origin students, 31 chose to take the interview in Spanish and 56 in English. Of the 100 parents interviewed, 77 chose to take the interview in Spanish and 23 in English (only seven Mexican-origin parents chose English for the interview). Over half the sample (53 percent) had family incomes between $11,000 and $24,999; 21 percent had incomes between $2,000 and $10,999, 12 percent had incomes between $25,000 and $39,999, and 14 percent had incomes of $40,000 and above. On the average, parents had a junior high education (6.5 years). Most of the parents were presently married (88 percent).

As might be expected, results indicate that in comparing the social identities of parents and their children, there emerged some similarities as well as some differences. Both parents and children have a familial dimension (which includes gender) to their social identities (sibling, daughter/son, gender, parent, spouse, or *compadre* [companion]). For parents, there is a strong religious dimension (Catholic, Christian, or religious person) that is not present in their offspring. As might be expected, while parents identify with their occupations (family breadwinner and farmworker), children still have not developed social identification with occupations. The greatest divergence between parents and children is the manifestation of their ethnicity. While the ethnic dimension of social identity for parents includes such labels as Mexican and Hispanic, for children they include Mexican American, American of Mexican descent, U.S. citizen, Mexican, and American.

This multidimensional character of social identity is not surprising. From these data, it seems that ethnic identity in adolescent years is just emerging, while in later years it becomes more static. During early adolescence, such identity does not seem linked to academic achievement, as in "Mexicans are not supposed to do good in school." Such links have been found in high school (Ogbu and Matute-Bianchi, 1986).

Long-Term Effects of the Theme Project

Three years later, we conducted a follow-up study to measure both the Theme and the non-Theme project students' future aspirations, academic performance as measured by course grades, and perceptions of middle school. The method in executing the follow-up project was a self-administered survey. Questions in the survey included the following:

- What is your grade-point average?
- Was your middle school a good institution?

- Did you receive excellent grades in middle school?
- Did you find the subjects in middle school to be very interesting?
- Did middle school teachers help you develop interest?
- Did middle school teachers help you plan for future goals?
- Did middle school teachers like you?
- Did you hate your middle school?
- What are your future plans?
- Do high school teachers help plan for the future?
- Do high school teachers like you?
- Do you feel comfortable at your high school?
- Do you get along well with other students in high school?

Sample population. In the follow-up study, the questionnaire was submitted to the students who were enrolled at the local high school receiving these students. Thirty-eight students were found to participate in the study, with 17 in the Comparison group and 21 in the Theme group. Students completing the survey were never told that the purpose of the survey was directly related to assessing the effects of any particular program.

The implementation of the Theme project has had a significant effect on grades, with the Theme group having approximately 70 percent of their grades above average and the Comparison group 75 percent below average. Although this is a self-report indicator, confidence in this indicator is enhanced since students were clear about the confidentiality of their responses. Also, 65 percent of the Theme students perceived their middle school as a good institution, while only 40 percent of the Comparison group reported such a perception. Moreover, 80 percent of Theme students reported middle school subjects as interesting as opposed to 30 percent of the Comparison students.

In addition, teachers were perceived by the Theme students as providing greater inspiration. Some 85 percent of Theme students agreed that teachers helped develop interest. Only 47 percent of the Comparison students agreed that teachers helped develop interest. Also, 57 percent of Theme students indicated that teachers helped them plan for the future as opposed to 40 percent of the Comparison students. The implementation of this project also created a significant difference with the students' future aspirations. Some 85 percent of Theme students indicated a strong desire to go on to college, while only 69 percent of Comparison students expressed this desire.

In summary, four years later, the same Theme students who attended the middle school project are now in high school. The results of the previous analysis indicate a consistent pattern of outcomes related to grades, perceptions of middle school, and future aspirations, each dramatically favoring the Theme students.

Conclusion

The ALAS and Theme project efforts brought together middle school teachers with other university faculty for a specific intervention aimed at Hispanic students. These redesigns were founded on recent empirical work that has identified responsive collaborative and curriculum interventions with Hispanic students along with recent theoretical formulations that are of general relevance to enhancing academic success. ALAS students received a comprehensive treatment aimed at various contexts of their lives. Theme students participated in an educational experience that kept them together for the majority of their school day. This experience included participation in small, heterogeneously structured learning groups through which instruction was delivered around jointly determined themes that integrated reading, language arts, math, science, and social studies. The academic outcomes of these ALAS and Theme students were compared to a group of students who participated in the same school and received the standard treatment.

The implementation of the project required extensive rethinking of the existent middle school organization by teachers, administrators, and participating nonschool personnel. Moreover, the restructuring that took place required extensive collaboration. The results of the projects are clearly positive. That is, consistent positive comparative academic outcome data favor the student participants of the ALAS and Theme interventions over the conventional program implemented at the middle school. Specifically, comparative analyses in the areas of school attendance, academic preparation, and academic achievement favored the ALAS and Theme students.

Although these empirical results are promising, it is important to identify a number of constraints of these "controlled" studies. With the inability of the present project implementation and data procedures to specify specific causal links between the intervention subcomponents and the dependent variables, the results of the study are difficult to specifically interpret. It does seem appropriate, however, to conclude that the results suggest a set of school, classroom, and community restructuring alternatives that may provide enhanced educational successes for a population of educationally vulnerable students.

RETHINKING, REBUILDING, AND ENGAGING CHANGE FOR HISPANIC HIGH SCHOOL STUDENTS

California is a microcosm of the peculiar state of affairs concerning the education of Hispanic students in the United States. A recent study of California high schools indicated "that California is generating 50,000–75,000 non-completers (students who go to high school but never finish), just about the same number as students who become eligible for the University of California system" (Minicucci and Olsen, 1993). The number of graduating high school Hispanic students in 1995 was reported to be 60,000, but only 4 percent, or 2,000, actually found their way to the University of California system. The figures produced by the high school system of the state are simply a sign of the complicated and often neglected educational circumstances of minority high school students. Recently, researchers, educators, and some sectors of society have begun to voice a concern about the students whose language and diversity should be viewed as an advantage for the future and not a liability for the present (University of California, 1993).

This concern can be summed up by the echo of former Secretary of Education Lauro Cavazos when he concluded that populations that are culturally and linguistically diverse have been perceived by the larger society as linguistically, cognitively, socially, and educationally vulnerable because of their nonmainstream culture and their lack of English proficiency at the critical age for schooling (Cavasos, 1990). In California high schools, this perception has become a grim reality for Hispanic students. Forty percent of Hispanics leave school prior to high school, 35 percent of are held back at least one grade, and 70 percent attend segregated schools (up 56 percent from 1956).

A study by Minicucci and Olsen (1993) has directed our attention to four areas that directly affect the education of Hispanic high school students:

- Overt levels of conflict, violence, and tension
- The status quo of separation (both social and institutional)
- The conflict students feel when caught between two worlds—when a world around them insists on assimilation as the bottom line for acceptance
- The ability of secondary schools to address these issues and design appropriate interventions

Although these findings undeniably require additional study, research on the effective instruction of minority populations—and Hispanic students in particular—has yielded conceptual understandings and empirical findings that could be included in a practical, multifaceted instructional plan to enhance the academic learning of Hispanic students at the high school level (Lucas, Henze, and Donato, 1990).

A substantive impediment of many Hispanic students is tracking, a practice that can be initiated in the elementary school but most often is initiated at the junior high school and is vividly established in high school. In tracking, class assignments often are driven by perceptions (accurate or inaccurate) of the student's level of academic achievement. Oakes's (1985) analysis of low-income and minority populations in middle school, junior high, and high school settings demonstrates the practice of tracking minority students in terms of their access to higher-order cognitive experiences; once minority students enter a track identified for low achievers, their opportunities for academic success are significantly limited. A student placed in a remedial class automatically increases his or her chances of being enrolled in another remedial class. Such a student receives an abated education. Remedial courses do not challenge or expose the student to knowledge. In most cases, teachers with no expertise in language acquisition and development or in cultural sensitivity are placed in classrooms that are remedial and with low-income and linguistically diverse students who are most in need of the high-quality instruction that might better be provided by experienced teachers (Finley, 1984; Gamoran and Berends, 1987a; Haycock and Navarro, 1988).

Teaching has traditionally been equated with knowledge transmission in Western society (Garcia, 1999). In most instances, language-minority students find a style of teaching that transmits limited knowledge that is linguistically and culturally biased. School curricula tend to emphasize lower-level skills and knowledge that fail to promote peer interaction and knowledge, and "most American high schools still have a long way to go to substantially improve the engagement and achievement of their students" (National Center of Effective Secondary Schools, 1991, 19). In their efforts to "improve" the quality of education of their larger populations, high schools seem to forget the most vulnerable groups in their ranks.

While serving in the U.S. Department of Education from 1993 to 1995, I became particularly concerned about Hispanic high school students. That concern led to the specific support of several recently issued reports that address the issues: *Improving Schooling for Language-Minority Children: A Research, Policy, and Practice* (August and Hakuta, 1997), *The Hispanic Dropout Project Report* (U.S. Department of Education, 1998), and *The Report of Secondary Schools Serving Limited English Proficient Students* (DevTech Systems, 1996). I drew from these reports particularly to highlight case studies of high schools serving Hispanic students well, academically and socially.

San Diego Union School District: Project "Write"

The San Diego Union School District is located in Encinitos, California, some 50 miles from the U.S.–Mexico border on the Pacific coastline. It is a suburban district, just outside San Diego, and is perceived by many as an affluent district. Yet 10 percent of its high school students are Hispanic, poor, and speak Spanish as their primary language. I have chosen to use this district and its Project "Write" here as an example of a program serving Hispanic students outside the confines of the inner city and not in a predominantly rural context. Recent demographic data suggest that more Hispanic students are finding themselves in the suburbs (Garcia, 1999).

In the late 1980s, San Diego was implementing an English-as-a-second-language (ESL) program that utilized a traditional grammar-based approach. Though students were attaining success in oral proficiency, many experienced academic difficulty when they made the transition to the regular English class. Using research by Cummins, which suggests that proficiency in language has two dimensions—basic interpersonal communication and cognitive academic language proficiency—the staff deduced that their current approach was not developing student proficiency in cognitive language. To do so would require new ESL instructional approaches and materials. Students would need more reading of literature and more writing that was comparable to that offered in the regular English class. More authentic assessments were also essential to enable staff as well as students to monitor language acquisition. To accomplish these ends, staff training and new curricula would be needed.

As the board of education and teachers began revamping the entire bilingual program, California was in the midst of education standards reform. The Statewide English Framework of California was being developed, and research on portfolio assessment was under way. Many of the district staff were directly involved in professional networks and university projects at the heart of curriculum and assessment reform in the state. Thus, district staff had firsthand knowledge of state standards, authentic assessments, and restructuring strategies. At the same time, certification to teach bilingual students was being encouraged throughout California, given the shortage of certified personnel and the burgeoning numbers of LEP students. The district offered training toward certification, which was sought by many of the English teachers at the junior and senior high schools. According to one administrator, "Everything was coming together to support reform. Staff were receiving training in new pedagogy, involved in statewide reform efforts, and were applying their new learning as they revised the bilingual program."

District staff wanted to make sure that the program offered to students with limited English proficiency met the same high standards as that offered to the other students. Thus, bilingual programs were aligned to the regular program through curriculum themes and assessment strategies. Recommendations of national (e.g., Goals 2000) and state groups (e.g., the California English Framework and Second to None) were also used to align the program with both national and state standards to ensure that their approach reflected the latest research on secondary students.

According to one teacher, "Project 'Write' put ideas and words in context." Under the old program, student learning was fragmented since so much of the instruction focused on isolated word lists. With Project "Write," students were reading different forms of literature and creating different forms of writing. They were discussing and analyzing literature with their peers, which gave them more authentic opportunities for using language. Work samples rather than worksheets were being maintained in a portfolio and then evaluated by the teacher as well as the student. A common scoring rubric was used that enabled comparability in scoring across teachers and communicated to students the standards in language that need to be achieved. In a sense, Project "Write" offered a new approach to teaching language and assessing student progress that was dynamic, interactive, and reflective of more authentic teaching and learning.

Project "Write" has been unusually successful in improving student outcomes. Over 200 students were served during the project's implementation. Results indicated the following:

- Participant scores on standardized literacy tests and on the district rubric were consistently higher than those of a district comparison group.
- Participant scores on the district rubric when compared to their grade-level peers (English-dominant students) were higher and were statistically significant.
- Participant scores on the district Basic Skills Assessment, which is required by the district for graduation, showed a steady increase from 52 to 92 percent of the participants meeting the required minimum standard for graduation.
- Dropout rates for participants consistently decreased and were about half the total of the district (e.g., district rates were 13 percent in 1992, 11 percent in 1993, and 7 percent in 1994, while participant rates were 6 percent in 1992, 3 percent in 1993, and 3 percent in 1994).
- The percentage of participants taking the SAT doubled.
- Participant enrollment in challenging academic courses increased.

While the quantitative data clearly show that Project "Write" is making a difference in the achievement of students, staff testimony suggests that there is other evidence of impact. For instance, more former Hispanic students who participated in Project "Write" are now attending college, and 15 received scholarships in the 1996 graduating class. Students are also avoiding disciplinary problems and are generally avoiding involvement in the local gangs (DevTech Systems, 1996).

Project PRISM: The International High School, New York City

I have chosen this case study because it highlights the challenge of working with Hispanic immigrant students in the context of a highly diverse inner-city setting. The International High School (IHS) serves 460 students from 60 different countries. The majority of students are from Central American and Latin American countries and speak Spanish as the primary language.

The IHS works with the community and social services. For example, project staff have brought doctors and dentists into the school. The Parent Fair is a valuable vehicle for imparting information and services and building bridges with the community and social service agencies. Counseling to deal with family issues is also provided. The IHS brings in people from outside the school to assist in dealing with students and guardians and to provide support in languages the school does not have. These services are folded into the program. For example, social service organizations from different ethnic groups help where needed, a local hospital provides teen pregnancy classes, and the Sunnyside civic organization provides staff for creative clubs and college advisers.

The IHS program is schoolwide, with a learner-centered, interdisciplinary curriculum. The primary mode of learning is in heterogeneous, collaborative groups. Assessment throughout the school is focusing on portfolios and exhibitions incorporating self, peer, and instructor evaluations. School and instruction are designed to capitalize on diversity.

At the heart of IHS approach is content-based language instruction using language as an outgrowth of content; by experiencing and learning new concepts, students extend their language base. The IHS believes that comprehension precedes language. It concentrates on the substance of disciplines and sees language as a means of defining, explaining, and elaborating on this substance instead of seeing content as something that gets in the way of language development. When linguistic points arise that require explanation or elaboration, they are dealt with. This exegesis of grammar and language does not become an end in itself.

The school philosophy is that there is no such thing as homogeneity. Specific goals include the following:

- To graduate students from high school with sufficient skills to attend college
- To produce students who function at a high academic level in English
- To develop an academic level of English enabling students to succeed at a college level
- To provide counseling and support to help families work
- To assist with immigration issues and medical care

Students take four classes each 13-week cycle, while teachers teach three courses each cycle, enabling them to focus their attention on a smaller number of students while extending and deepening the curricula for their courses. Each faculty member serves as an adviser to a group of 15 students who meet for 70 minutes each week to address a variety of student needs, including school-related issues; personal, social, or developmental concerns; and establishing peer-support networks and mentoring relationships. The structure provides for a balance of exposure by focusing on four subject areas, such as literature, global studies, mathematics, science, and so on.

On a typical school day, students spend much of their time working on individual and group activities. Teachers design these activities frequently with student input and serve as facilitators of learning. They offer guidance during instruction rather than lecturing. The school schedule consists of a five-period day. Class periods are 70 minutes long, thus allowing time for students to become engaged in their activities. Underlying these instructional practices is the idea that students will benefit from the individual attention of the teacher as well as from collaboration with other students. Hence, students are taught to rely on themselves and on one another for revision of written assignments, study and development of vocabulary, and mastery of content.

Progress within the program is measured by graduation rate, dropout rate, attendance rate, the course pass rate, and portfolio assessments in academic courses. Further, there is a role for student self-evaluation and peer/cluster evaluation, and students use progress sheets to chart progress six times per year on high school credits necessary to graduate. In the past, New York State Regents competencies in the subject areas were used. Currently, in order to graduate, each student must present a summary statement and a graduation portfolio to a panel that includes staff. The IHS scored over the New York City norm in math, reading, writing, and history. Their success rate in City University of New York (CUNY) is higher than the average student at CUNY and higher than the average LEP student. The 1995–96 retention rate was 96.8 percent, the promotion rate was 89.1 percent, the school attendance rate was 93.5 percent, and 95 percent met graduation criteria. In addition, over 90 percent of IHS's graduates plan to attend postsecondary institutions.

¡Español Aumentivo!: Houston, Texas

The 1992, the Houston Spring Branch Independent School District implemented a program for Hispanic students known as ¡Español Aumentivo! The program focused on three areas: instructional intervention, parental involvement, and staff development. Four middle schools and two high schools were selected for project implementation since these schools had the largest numbers of Hispanic students with limited proficiency in English and the highest poverty levels. The student population targeted for services were preliterate Hispanic secondary school students with little or no previous education in their native language and who were limited in English proficiency. Students were considered preliterate if they scored between the first and ninth percentile on the Iowa Test of Basic Skills and if they demonstrated weak literacy skills on the district-developed Spanish test. Approximately 200 students and 400 parents were targeted for services each year.

The curriculum of the intervention focused on the development of functional Spanish. Functional Spanish was based around relevant themes and situations that students encounter in their everyday living. The six themes were Humor, Mystery, Fantasy/Imagination, Love, Multicultural Tolerance, and Success. While schools had flexibility in how thematic instruction was presented, each unit was to be tied to the one overarching theme of "choices," and the content was correlated with the curricular objectives of the state. Each unit was designed to integrate grammar and usage vocabulary, thinking strategies, listening skills, speaking skills, reading competencies, and computer usage. Literature materials are broad based so that students can expand their interests, knowledge of literary forms, and skill in reading. Computers, along with other forms of technology, are used for writing, publication, and research. Portfolios of student work are maintained and are used by both students and instructors to monitor progress and improvement. In addition to the refinement and expansion of the functional Spanish course, guides for sheltered mathematics, ESL social studies, music, and parent education classes were prepared by staff in the Title VII project. Using techniques for teaching ESL, instructional strategies were developed that content teachers could use to support LEP students. According to one administrator, "By providing support to the content teachers, this ensured that all students, even those with limited English proficiency, were receiving the same content." The involvement of parents was seen as key to the success of ¡Español Aumentivo! Since most parents did not speak English and many lacked experience with how schools operate in the United States, there was very little communication between secondary schools and parents, and thus parental involvement was low.

¡Español Aumentivo! was highly successful in enhancing staff skills, increasing student achievement, and involving parents. Over the course of three years, data showed that staff were able to acquire new instructional strategies that enabled teachers to provide more student interaction with other students as well as with teachers. Using an instrument designed by the University of Houston, the project classes outperformed control classes on many variables such as teacher–student interaction, instruction in small groups, and communicating tasks and work plans. Student achievement also climbed. In portfolios, the project group exceeded the control group in written expression. Reading and language arts scores on the Iowa Test of Basic Skills were also higher for the project than for the control group, as were oral skills on the IDEA Oral Proficiency Test and scores of the functional Spanish test. In terms of attendance and school promotion, project students maintained better grades, attendance, and completion of grades than the control group.

Parental involvement improved in both the number of parents participating and the nature of their interaction with the school. At the beginning of the project, few parents were attending meetings on a regular basis. This increased by 30 percent during the last year of data collection. Increased parental involvement has led to activities throughout the community, with more health fairs, parenting programs for prevention of drug and alcohol abuse, and so on being offered on a regular basis.

Project AVANCE

AVANCE was based on theoretical and cognitive foundations of the Theme project, a middle school intervention for Hispanic students discussed earlier in this chapter. That project suggested that typically underserved students can succeed academically if instructional strategies that emphasize cooperative learning, student-generated themes, and close staff networking are woven into the existing academic framework of the institution with relatively minor changes. Modifications that challenge "seldom-questioned regularities of school culture" (Oakes, 1992a, 5) and that on the surface seem quite simple are very difficult to fulfill, and at times their outcomes are difficult to predict. The AVANCE intervention was not immune to the obstacles mentioned previously. A large portion of the discussion that follows will detail AVANCE's intervention.

The reorganization intervention at the high school benefited 60 students. Specifically, the instructional intervention called for two heterogeneous groups of approximately 30 students each. Both groups were made up of EO, reclassified bilingual (Spanish and English), and ESL students. Students were selected only if teachers, counselors, or students considered themselves "high motivation" students.

The team of seven teachers, one counselor, and university researchers worked collaboratively to plan and implement the curriculum. The content area subjects were English, science, mathematics, and social science (world civics was taught for one semester and health studies for the other). The two groups of students integrated with the rest of the student body for two periods during physical education and an elective class.

A comparison group was established consisting of 60 students in the regular high school curriculum. These students changed classes through-out the day and experienced six different combinations of students from six different nonintegrated content area subjects; they were randomly se-lected. Within the first week of school, teachers initiated implementation of the theme of "Community" as their first thematic unit. To prepare, the teacher attended a summer conference to share and plan their individual areas of curriculum focus within the Community theme and to integrate lessons across the curriculum.

An office at the high school was established to hold weekly meetings. Teachers and research team met to discuss, share, update, and relate perti-nent information. The agenda for the meeting included discussions on the theme's progress, classroom visitations, budget, meetings, and data collec-tion.

The organization of meetings and related on-site businesses were dele-gated to the project's two-period coordinator; this individual also taught four classes. The coordinator's main responsibilities were to arrange meet-ings, order materials, arrange instructional support, and deal with any lo-gistical problems.

Project teachers participated in workshops specifically related to cultur-ally and linguistically diverse children. The workshops were created by the National Center for Research on Cultural Diversity and Second Language Learning at the University of California, Santa Cruz, campus. The work-shops and classes included prominent researchers in the field who shared their research findings as well as demonstrations, classroom videos, and hands-on activities. Other events the teachers attended included the fol-lowing:

- Teachers and principals visited the site of the Theme project. The teachers visited classrooms and afterward met with Theme teachers to ask questions concerning their program.
- A private workshop conducted by two leading educators addressed specific concerns and field questions about thematic teaching.
- Teachers planned a series of five monthly meetings to address and plan the curriculum and structure of the program.
- Teachers attended a three-day summer conference to select a theme and to finalize the curriculum and structure of the program.
- Students and teachers participated in a one-day tour/workshop at the University of California, Santa Cruz, dealing with science and tech-nology.

Results

To illustrate AVANCE's passage from vision to reality, teachers were inter-viewed and classrooms observed to assess the implemented reform. In one sense, teachers were the judges and jury as to the effectiveness of challenging the traditional delivery of education and the actual outcomes of such venture. The teachers' perspective in one sense "magnifies one dimension of a particular practice while temporarily filtering out the others" (Oakes, 1992b, 5) and at times brings to the forefront dimensions never discussed while planning the intervention.

Course Standards and Evaluation

A major point of discussion among the teachers centered on a desire to uphold the standards required to enter college preparatory courses while meeting the needs of those students slightly below those academic levels. This discussion reached to the level of course content and assessment of students. While the majority of teachers stayed with the student-centered content of AVANCE, one teacher felt a need to sometimes alter content to allow the less academically prepared students to understand. A major commitment voiced by the teachers was their unwillingness to "water down" the curriculum.

During the course of the project, teachers generally agreed that their Hispanic students who understood enough English benefited the most because they could participate in an academic environment that was unlike a mainstream classroom.

A major change was the attitude toward real assessment of the students' academic performance. One teacher stated,

> When you say evaluation, I say grade. I have what I hope to be a wide variety of activities. I evaluate their "portfolio," their lab binder or lab notebook; exams, unit test, quiz, lab work and their self evaluation. I grade on a participate/not-participate basis. If I have an exam which is in English (all exams are in English), I would allow students to do other things to make up for points they missed in the test.

This attitude carried over to the manner in which teachers viewed their own performance as teachers,

> Not only do I have to cover what I'm required and they'll be tested on, but I have to cover the themes.

It also affected how their curriculum shifted from an exclusive book academics to an everyday-life academics and their impact on real-life issues:

> Tests reflect what people do in real life. For example, in my ESL class Library Skills, I phrase all questions in a way, for example, What would be the first

thing you would do if you were in interested in electronics at the library? The test mimics a real-life process of being able to get a book.

One condition that was expected to have an impact on the AVANCE project was the scarcity of Hispanic language-minority students who could, based on the teachers' expectations, meet the academic challenge. Considering the current state of education, some teachers felt that AVANCE recruited and received students who were willing to face the academic rigors but who were not fully prepared to deal with the academic consequences. However, the English I teacher made clear how he felt about the students once he had worked with them:

> I would be willing to say that I would put my English I class against any other group at [this school] against the CORE pieces of work, pick any other English teacher. Give a multiple choice test. They'd do O.K. Those who have English will come out stronger.

During the process, teachers appeared enthusiastic about the manner in which academics could be used to communicate with parents. There was an air of optimism when teachers realized that their academic curriculum could also serve to establish a dialogue between parents, students, and teachers.

Student-Generated Themes

A major challenge teachers encountered was the notion of allowing students to actively participate in defining the curriculum. The first challenge arose when teachers questioned how to make a comprehensive academic partnership between teachers and students while simultaneously embracing the community, in other words, how to effectively continue delivering the mandated districtwide curriculum and weave into it the new theme-centered agenda. Particular attention was given to the composition of the student body: The students participating in this program came from low-socioeconomic-status groups or were recent immigrants who were given the least amount of academic support and were perceived as unwilling to work academically. With hesitation, the teachers accepted the notion of allowing the students' input. But once the first theme was selected, the teachers welcomed the partnership. As one teacher said,

> Having student-generated themes formalized student input for curriculum because they create the theme, we [teachers] let them imagine what they want to study. They write the curriculum at the start of the six-week unit. From assignment to assessment, they are more involved.

The formation of this partnership became one of the more successful aspect of the program. It allowed students to nominate their top three theme interests. The three themes were analyzed to determine which one was the top vote getter, they used the available resources, and they could be woven into the mandated school curriculum. In some instances, themes were discussed and then expanded to include a broader range of issues and provide more leeway to include their mandated curriculum in support of the theme.

One theme that required little expansion was the Gangs theme, into which the English teacher incorporated *Romeo and Juliet.* In mathematics, the curriculum centered on the number of Hispanics in prisons and drew the connections between Hispanics, gangs, and prison. From a science perspective, students observed and studied gangs using animal behavior, including social grouping and territoriality.

As the program progressed, teachers realized that the partnership, envisioned as problematic and difficult to implement, became one of the best inclusionary exercises to promote student participation, input, and academic responsibility.

Staff Networking

At the onset of the project, teachers were made aware of the existence of open lines of communication to inquire, suggest, or constructively criticize the program as it moved forward. This unique opportunity to discuss students and the curriculum and to make decisions that impacted their own academic environments gave the teachers a sense of professional growth and camaraderie:

> I've gotten to know some of the teachers in the program very well. You don't really get to know people in other departments. It's affected us as teachers. *We* can share things in the future around campus.

To most teachers, the opportunity to interact with teachers from other departments enhanced their sense of the collective consciousness that provides information and mutual cooperation to assess students' needs and suggestions on how to address intellectual needs appropriately:

> And another thing that has been an issue on the positive side is that we've been able to communicate between the teachers on a daily or weekly basis. It's pretty evident if a student is not him- or herself. We work together on understanding some of that behavior.

Effective Strategies and Practices

A major aim of the project was to promote effective instructional strategies. Teachers were challenged to actively promote and implement strategies that promoted an integrated curriculum as well as students' interaction. Classes were shifted to deliver the same English, math, and science content using a different approach. The alternative method required more hands-on activities, language proficiency grouping, and the use of more gestures and drama:

> [I] put notes on the board or the overhead; explaining or rephrasing of texts; doing symbols or pictures of concepts; I did more close activities; I tried to work in a tutorial second period.

Another teacher said,

> I use the same palette of tools . . . in different combinations . . . prior knowledge, saying you are the content of the course, telling them my job will change [the text] rather than look at text as school, looking at their experience as the source of knowledge.

In this new format, teachers experienced a different style of teaching speakers with limited English proficiency. In particular, ESL and sheltered English were replaced by more student interaction, use of gestures and body movements to increase communication between Hispanic students with limited English proficiency, and Hispanic and Anglo English-proficient students.

Student Outcomes

In the beginning of the third and final year of the project, several data resources were gathered and analyzed. These included a math group of 23 non-AVANCE students in order to gain insights into the impact of the project on students' orientation toward school and academic subject matter. That original matched group and the AVANCE group of 23 were expanded to 30 because data on seven of the AVANCE students were lost. Hence, the original AVANCE group consisted of 30 students. The subject poor was augmented by including two other matched comparison groups of 30 students per group, thus bringing the total number of groups to four and the total number of students to 120.

Grade-point average. Students selected for these groups were matched on measures of grade-point average (GPA) on entering high school and credits earned toward graduation as of the middle of grade 11. With regard to incoming GPA for all four groups, the Anglo group had the highest GPA (3.20) on entering high school with the AVANCE (2.96) and non-AVANCE (2.92) groups closely following at second and third highest, respectively. The mid–grade 11 GPA results follow a slightly different order. The high

GPA of the Anglo group endured at 2.75 with the non-AVANCE group falling in with a 2.5, followed by the AVANCE group with 2.18. The shift in GPA of the AVANCE group in particular is probably due to the course-taking-patterns data that revealed that many more students in this group were taking college preparatory courses than students in the non-AVANCE group.

Course-taking patterns. Hispanic students of the non-AVANCE group were taking many more non–college preparatory courses than the matched LEP Latino students of the AVANCE group. Of particular interest is the high number of non-AVANCE versus AVANCE students enrolled in industrial arts and English Language Development (ELD) courses. This is not surprising when one considers the tracking problem of Hispanic students (Harklau, 1994). Hence, while non-AVANCE students remained in the language development track and in vocational courses, the matched Hispanic students of the AVANCE group were taking more college preparatory courses and, interestingly, were taking these courses earlier in their high school careers. Their early enrollment could be a contributing factor to the fact that more AVANCE students failed advanced-level courses the first time taking them. Twenty students took geometry in 10th grade, and five failed the first time. Interestingly, however, three of those students reenrolled and passed the course with grades of B and C.

Further, more than 50 percent more AVANCE students as compared to non-AVANCE students took chemistry. The large imbalance of AVANCE versus non-AVANCE students enrolled in college preparatory courses provides evidence of fulfillment of one of the goals of the project that aimed at improving student access to academic material. Student enrollment data illustrate that AVANCE students were motivated toward academic success, whereas their matched counterparts of the non-AVANCE group were not influenced toward academic course material.

Academic Intrinsic Motivation Inventory: Expanded Version

After the first year of participation in the AVANCE program, the Children's Academic Intrinsic Motivation Inventory (CAIMI) was administered. Results showed overwhelmingly that the AVANCE group scored significantly higher on achievement motivation in all categories of the inventory—reading, mathematics, social studies, and science—as well as on the general measure. The AVANCE students scored particularly high on intrinsic motivation in science, mathematics, and overall general achievement motivation.

The same inventory was administered to the additional AVANCE and non-AVANCE students and to the Anglo groups during the third academic year of the project. Hence, scores were obtained for 30 students in each group. Scores were compared using analysis of variance (ANOVA) and the Tukey HSD test. Results of this analysis indicate significant differences between groups, with the AVANCE group scoring much higher on all measures of the inventory. As was the case in the earlier AVANCE versus non-AVANCE administration of the inventory, differences appear to be particularly acute in mathematics, science, and the overall general category. The mean scores of all students were submitted to an ANOVA to ascertain whether the differences in variance in scores are greater than would be expected by chance. The significant F value at the $p < .0001$ level indicates that, indeed, the differences between treatments are substantially greater than would be expected by chance, suggesting that a treatment effect exists. Hence, it appears that involvement in the AVANCE program may have an effect on student academic intrinsic motivation. In order to pinpoint the significance and to ascertain the minimum difference between treatment means that is necessary for significance, the Tukey HSD was computed. An HSD value of .69 confirms the significance by demonstrating that the AVANCE group is significantly different from all other groups on all measures of the CAIMI.

Teacher-Change Follow-Up Interviews

The impact of the philosophical and instructional orientation toward the education of LEP students on the teachers involved in the AVANCE project was a concern from the outset and was monitored during the course of the project. Previous reports have expressed varying degrees of impact on various features of "AVANCE pedagogy" for different teachers in the project. In general, teacher data have consistently illustrated that the program appears to have been successful. More specifically, the following findings evidence that success:

- The use of student-generated themes was a categorical success for attracting students to and engaging them in academic materials.
- Teachers had some degree of difficulty adhering to the proposed integrated thematic curriculum designed to promote student collaboration. Teachers tended to adapt rather than to radically change their instructional practices.
- An evident tension existed between maintaining the curriculum and accommodating LEP students. Teachers' refusal to "water down" the curriculum increased the demands on their time and patience, but in the end their shift in practices positively affected their overall approach to instruction.
- Teachers who entered the project with a cultural deficit view exited

the program willing to match their AVANCE students to any across the school population.

- During the project, teachers established and maintained a collegial discourse with regard to student needs. Maintaining open dialogue was seen as one of the highlights for teachers.

CONCLUSION

The vision to create a program specifically designated to students access to the content curriculum of their high schools and to expand their language skills was strategically addressed in the AVANCE project and others discussed in this chapter. The application of the principles developed by researchers and theoretical frameworks of "what works" when addressing the needs of Hispanic students were closely examined and translated into specific practice.

The fact that these specific programs were implemented allows me to offer some thoughts about process and outcomes:

1. School personnel can organize, create, and "reorganize" within the school's framework to improve the educational environment of diverse Hispanic students.
2. Allowing new teaching techniques and organizational methods combined with nonschool collaboration can enhance the learning of students.
3. Educational change at the high school level must take into account volatile issues (e.g., plans after high school and intergroup and within-group relations) that can affect the students on a daily basis.
4. Regardless of language (English) knowledge, when a student is academically challenged, that student will respond positively.
5. There is a need to drastically update the means by which families and school and nonschool institutions meet, communicate, and discuss their students.
6. Hispanic students at the high school level must be provided with a challenging and integrated curriculum to optimize the opportunities to succeed in life.

Table 7.1 summarizes intervention components for the case studies reviewed.

This chapter has traveled a route from an individual assessment of "what works" for Hispanic students to case studies of specific research that document effective instruction in effective interventions at the middle and high school levels. This route, and the stops along the way, provides a

Table 7.1   Instructional Interventions Used by Case Study Projects

Instructional Interventions	Project PRISM	Project Theme	¡Español Amentivo!	Project AVANCE	Project "Write"	ALAS
ESL		√	√	√	√	√
ESL embedded in content	√			√		√
Sheltered science			√	√	√	
Sheltered social studies			√	√	√	
Tutoring			√	√	√	
Mentoring	√	√	√	√		√
Enrichment	√	√		√		√
Use of technology such as computers	√	√	√	√		
Performance assessment	√	√	√	√	√	√
Portfolio assessment	√		√	√	√	
Functional Spanish (instructional in native language)	√	√	√	√	√	√
Community/parent focus	√	√	√	√	√	√

detailed account of Hispanic student success. Such information at the personal or research level gives particular insights regarding the existence of and the development and implementation of educational interventions in real schools that serve Hispanic students academically and otherwise. These are particular instances that my own experiences and collaborative research endeavors offer in an attempt to address the issues of underachievement so often experienced by this population of students.

It is important here to offer my thanks to the teachers, administrators, students, and parents of the sites in which these studies took place. Without them, these studies would not have been possible or as significant in their contribution to our understanding of effective schooling for Hispanics. In particular, teachers in these studies seem to play a major role in making educational programs work. I cannot say enough about the dedication, hard work, specific instructional skills, and personal commitment these people showed in serving as advocates for these students. It was as if these students were their own children. Such commitment to advocacy is very difficult to measure and quite impossible to teach. Yet in each of the exposés in this chapter, this aspect of the teacher is there in major proportions. In reminds me, as it did my colleagues, that effective schooling is a social enterprise, conducted by individuals who care about one another and respect what they bring to the enterprise and then go forward together. The following chapter presents more evidence for this conclusion and the fact that Hispanic student academic success can be a reality for postsecondary education.

8

Educational Approaches—
What Works for Hispanics'
Preparation for Admission to
Postsecondary Education

WORK OR EDUCATION: TOO OFTEN THE CHOICE

When I graduated from high school, my parents held a picnic in my honor.
I did not realize until then how prized a high school graduation was for
them and for my extended family—they were all there to celebrate the
occasion and wish me well in the future. But I do think that the graduation
was perceived more as a prize to have won than as a step into the future. I
particularly recall that my mother and aunts were happy that high school
was over—they made it clear that this was a culminating event. Many of
them had never even attended school. Graduating from high school was a
good thing to have done. But now the real world of work should be a priority. My mother was concerned that I was considering going to the local
community college on a baseball scholarship. I recall very clearly that she
understood this opportunity as one related to continuing my "playing" as
opposed to continuing my education while at the same time avoiding work.
She was very clear about discouraging this opportunity on those grounds,
while my father was more neutral on this issue.

In a family with few resources, the opportunity to be fully and gainfully
employed is of the highest priority. I had finished my senior year during a
time when my father could no longer work in the fields; he had taken a
part-time dishwashing job at a local restaurant, a job my mother would
help him do on at least two evenings a week. The family, then consisting

193

of my parents and myself, was on the welfare rolls. This meant that we had access to rice, beans, sugar, and cheese on an "availability" basis and that we had access to health care benefits offered by the state. It was during this period that I first visited the dentist and learned that I had over a dozen cavities. Our social worker, a kind and gentle lady, arranged to have them filled. It is not hard to imagine that full-time employment for me was judged as important not only for me but also for the family. My mother made that very clear. Even though I worked part time after school and continued to work during summer harvests, it was my time to work—time to contribute in a substantive way to the family's economic well-being.

At the high school graduation picnic, my elder sister sent a different message to my family and me by providing me with the spectacular gift of a portable typewriter. Now, why would I need a typewriter if I was to go into the world of work as my family and I knew it? My sister and my older brothers took advantage of this gift to lend their support for continuing my education. They indicated to my mother that I could continue my job as shoeshine boy and janitor at the local country club (a summer job my cousin had obtained for me) while I went to college. That job had become important in providing a small but significant amount of income to the family, particularly as long as "welfare" provided the basic foodstuff for us. With that little money, which I dutifully turned over to my mother without keeping a cent, and help from my brothers and sisters, we were in "acceptable" economic circumstances. My mother relented to my attending the community college, and my father, brothers, and sisters seemed happy to have the situation resolved.

This now interesting conflict between work and education arose again at the time I graduated from the community college. It was exacerbated by an offer of employment at the time of graduation brokered by my baseball coach. My town was growing, as was airline service to the town. The new airline that had emerged to serve growing communities like ours turned to the community college for future employees. I had played baseball and had also distinguished myself academically, thanks to several professors who supported my academic studies—an English professor, a math professor, and a psychology professor. I had made the "dean's list" each quarter and graduated with honors. Each of these professors encouraged me to transfer to a four-year institution and actually made sure that I applied for scholarships, several of which I won. My baseball coach, knowing my personal situation better than the professors did, found me a job.

By all standards, the job was a good one. It paid $200 per week to start—more money than I had ever earned and plenty of money to get our family off welfare. Being on welfare was a stigma to my parents, as they were proud of having raised a large family without "assistance." The choice for me was clear: take the job. It is at this time that my older brothers and sisters had been able to negotiate social security benefits for my elderly parents. Such benefits were not perceived by them in the same way as welfare benefits. These benefits were seen by my parents as earned since they were based on previous work that they had done, not on the generosity of the state. Even though my parents had not paid into the social security system because of their status primarily as farm laborers, the social security system's dependence on work history was considered very different than the welfare system. The meager social security checks began to meet the basic economic needs of my parents—in fact, they even saved some pennies. My role as primary economic provider was significantly lessened.

For this reason, I felt that I could make the following proposal: I could go to Salt Lake City, attend the University of Utah, pay for that education with the scholarships I had won (including a tuition scholarship offered to me by the baseball coach), and live with my sister and brother-in-law. Both of them worked full time, and I could help them with their younger elementary-school-aged children—baby sit and help around the house— and, of course, pay them as much rent as I could muster. It turned to be about $10 per month. Their eldest son was leaving to join the U.S. Army, so room was available in their home, and my help would be welcomed. My sister supported the proposal, which became a reality. Resolved again was this conflict between work and education. I turned down the job but was not very confident that doing so was the right thing. In retrospect, it was the right thing to do.

Unfortunately, the experience of many Hispanics today is not much different than my own. And, unfortunately, their choice of work versus education often does not have the same result as it did for me. When adolescents are making choices about their future, it is the availability of supports and opportunities, most often outside the home, coupled with access to "instrumental" knowledge about the pathways to a higher education, that are paramount. Previously, I have made a strong case for knowing one's own "roots" and the role those cultural, linguistic, and social roots play in individual and academic success. When determining one's future in higher education, it is the knowledge of alternative "routes" that becomes just as important. My mother and father, particularly my mother, placed the highest priority on work as opposed to education after high school. Anyone knowing their personal circumstances can see why— neither had any experience with higher education. They had no personal knowledge of alternative routes that could lead to even better work opportunities. No one in my family had such opportunities.

I was the first of my family, central and extended, to go on to college. My family had no instrumental, practical knowledge about the route to college, although my brothers and sisters supported my decision to go, and my elder sister offered me a place to live. It is this family support, coupled with the resources and instrumental knowledge outside the family, that was important in my situation. This included the existence of a welfare system that provided the opportunity for me to stay in high school, a social security system for my parents that provided a basic safety net for their continued economic security, and supportive professors who promoted, encouraged, and assisted in ensuring my continued education. It is this combination of internal family and external forms of support that made a substantial difference in my route to a higher education. For the large majority of Hispanic students today, not much has changed, even though more Hispanics today are finding these routes. Allow me to turn to a more formal analysis of Hispanics and their participation in institutions of higher education.

HISPANICS IN HIGHER EDUCATION

Just over one million Hispanics enrolled in higher education in 1998, a doubling from a decade earlier. However, 56 percent were enrolled in two-year colleges (compared to 42 percent of blacks, 37 percent of whites, and 30 percent of Asian/Pacific Islanders) (National Center for Education Statistics [NCES], 1998). Unfortunately, Hispanics are less than half as likely to graduate from college as whites. Only 13 percent of 25- to 28-year-old Hispanics had earned a bachelors degree or more, compared to 30 percent of whites. The gap did not close between 1971 and 1998 (NCES, 1998). Hispanics also take longer to complete college than whites. In 1990, 72 percent of whites graduated in five years or less, while 73 percent of Hispanics graduated in six years or less. Forty-four percent of whites graduated in four years or less, compared to 31 percent of Hispanics (NCES, 1995).

Hispanics enrolled in graduate school at about half the rate of whites and Asian/Pacific Islanders and somewhat less than blacks. In 1994, only 7 percent of Hispanic students in higher education were enrolled at the graduate level, compared to 14 percent of whites, 13 percent of Asian/ Pacific Islanders, and 9 percent of blacks (NCES, 1996).

Gender differences in college enrollment have grown more pronounced among all racial and ethnic groups. More women than men enrolled as undergraduates starting about 1980 and as graduates starting about 1984. Hispanic males in 1998 make up 42 percent of enrolled Hispanic undergraduate students. At the graduate level, the proportions are about the same. Hispanics are split 42 percent male, 58 percent female (NCES, 1998). Hispanics were awarded 32,400 associate degrees in 1997–98, about double the number from the mid-1970s. Bachelors degrees were up significantly, from 19,000 in 1976–77 to 50,000 in 1997–98. This number still represents only 4 percent of all bachelors degrees awarded in that year. Hispanic students garnered just 2 percent of both masters and doctoral degrees awarded in the same year (NCES, 1998).

More relevant data from the University of California (UC) Latino Eligibility Task Force (University of California, 1997) addresses a set of myths that are relevant here in assessing Hispanic student participation in higher education:

- Myth: Hispanic student growth in the nation is stabilizing as immigration wanes.
  Reality: Hispanic K–12 enrollments are now growing by more than 200,000 students per year and are projected to continue that explosive growth through the beginning of the 21st century. About 2,200,000 enrolled in 1985; 5,100,000 are expected in 2005.
- Myth: Hispanic high school dropout rates are high and limit access to higher education.
  Reality: The rate of Hispanics dropping out of high school continues to remain high. However, Hispanic high school graduation, in absolute numbers, has increased significantly in the last decade. In California, for example, nearly 80,000 Hispanics graduated from California's public high schools in June 1996—8,000 more than the year before and 32,000 more than graduated in 1990.
- Myth: Hispanic families and students do not aspire to higher education.
  Reality: Hispanic parents express great interest in higher education. More than 85 percent of Hispanics surveyed agreed or strongly agreed that special measures should be taken to ensure that the same percentage of Hispanics as others groups is admitted to college.
- Myth: Hispanic females in particular are discouraged and do not participate in higher education.
  Reality: Ninety-four percent of Hispanics surveyed agreed or strongly agreed that married women have the right to continue their education, and more than 81 percent agreed that it is acceptable for women to earn as much as their husbands. In the fall of 1997, total UC undergraduate Hispanic females outnumbered Hispanic males.
- Myth: Hispanics are applying and enrolling at institutions of higher education in proportion to their growing enrollments in public schools.
  Reality: The number of Hispanic participants has not kept pace with growing Hispanic K–12 enrollments and the rapidly increasing number of Hispanic high school graduates. In California, just 8.9 percent of Hispanic high school graduates applied to the University of Cali-

fornia in 1997–98 compared to 10.2 percent in 1989–90. Furthermore, the proportion of Hispanics of the regularly admitted applicants
to the University of California has steadily declined in each of the last
four years.

- Myth: There are no clearly demonstrable programs that positively influence college participation rates for Hispanic students.
Reality: The Early Academic Outreach Programs (EAOPs), established in K–12 schools throughout the United States, are ably preparing Hispanic public high school graduates. Nearly 50 percent of
EAOP-served Hispanic high school graduates were eligible to attend
a four-year college or university. Hispanic "graduates" of programs
like Advancement Via Individual Determination (AVID) attend college at a rate 75 percent higher than the overall rate of comparable
student cohorts, while two-thirds of the community college–enrolled
Hispanics participating in the Puente Project enrolled in four-year institutions.

- Myth: The community college is an effective alternative route for Hispanic student matriculation into the four-year college or university.
Reality: Actual Hispanic transfer enrollment to the University of California reached just 1,204 students in 1998, representing only 2 percent
of the total Hispanic high school graduating cohort two years earlier.
The same limited transfer rate is true nationwide (Nora, Rendon, and
Cuadraz, 1999).

- Myth: Hispanic dropout rates at the University of California continue
to be high and graduation numbers low for Hispanics.
Reality: Only about 20 percent of Hispanic students drop out after two
years at the university—nearly the same rate as for white students.
Two-thirds of Hispanic students graduate within six years. On average, they appear to take a year longer to graduate than Asian Americans and whites, but within this extended time period they graduate
at the same rate.

- Myth: The elimination of affirmative action will have no significant
effect on Hispanic student participation at the University of California.
Reality: Without affirmative action, Hispanic enrollment dropped by
an average of 40 percent at the university. At UC Berkeley and
UCLA, Hispanic enrollment dropped more than 50 percent. This level
of admission takes these two universities back to mid-1980s levels of
admissions for Hispanic students. In Texas, however, adaptation of a
10 percent eligibility plan after elimination of affirmative action has
not negatively affected Hispanic student enrollment at the University
of Texas, Austin.

This information helps in situating Hispanics in higher education. However, it does not go very far in identifying the specific barriers and opportunities that might help us address this situation. In attempting to make these issues more visible, I will address some data that identify individual/familial variables, including the financial tensions of the family and the absence of instrumental knowledge regarding college attendance, and, institutional variables including those which limit preparation and admissions to college. I will also take some time to examine an array of programs that have demonstrated their effectiveness in expanding Hispanic student participation in four-year institutions of higher education.

Keep in mind that most research on Hispanics and education has focused on understanding the overall low levels of achievement and high dropout rates for this group. For example, a research volume attending to this issue, *Chicano School Failure and Success* (Valencia, 1991), is a good example of the majority of research conducted on the topics related to Hispanics and educational inequality. Topics include bilingualism, segregation, and dropout rates. Two articles root Chicano underachievement in the "cultural conflict" between Chicano socialization and the culture of the schools. Another article describes how Chicano students are the victims of the tradition of standardized testing that discriminates. Studies of Hispanics dropouts have been based on large-scale national surveys, census data, and smaller fieldwork studies (Valverde, 1987; Romo and Falbo, 1996; Warren, 1996). Most quantitative research has been conducted in the traditional manner of status attainment, which includes examining the effect of individual background characteristics such as family socioeconomic status (SES) and behaviors in the school setting, such as confrontation, family size, family structure, and grade retention (Fligstein and Fernandez, 1982; Fernandez, Henn-Reinke, and Petrovich, 1989; Fernandez and Velez, 1989; Valdés, 1996).[1] Researchers modeling Hispanic educational attainment have expanded traditional models to include the effects of migration history, language usage, enrollment in a bilingual program in high school, and nativity of parents in addition to tradition measures of family background characteristics (Fligstein and Fernandez, 1982; Warren, 1996).

In short, a significant amount of the literature on education inequality and Hispanics has been confined to understanding this group's scholastic underachievement and high school dropout rates. Less research has been devoted to understanding college choice among college-bound Hispanic high school graduates. As stated previously, a significant number of college-going Hispanic students are choosing to enroll in community colleges compared to their similarly academically qualified black and white counterparts, who are enrolling in four-year institutions. This is clearly an issue that must be addressed.

Further Explaining College Choice among Hispanics

Several policymakers and scholars have argued there is a strong relationship between changes in financial aid policies and access to four-year institutions for underrepresented groups (Orfield, 1992; McPherson and Schapiro, 1997). The argument in these studies is the following: Tuition at public and private four-year universities and colleges increased dramatically during the late 1980s and early 1990s and has not been offset by increases in grant aid. Instead, student loans as opposed to scholarships and grants constitute the majority of federal funds, and the substantial increase in loan volume since 1992 has benefited primarily the middle-income students. While postsecondary enrollments have increased for all income and racial groups, the enrollment gap between low-income and middle-/high-income students has increased, as has the gap between whites and minority groups such as blacks and Hispanics. Likewise, the percentage of low-income students attending private institutions has decreased, while it has increased at community colleges. Therefore, these studies conclude that equal access to postsecondary education is declining for the very group that financial aid is meant to help, while the majority of aid in the form of loans is going to students who would probably attend anyway. It is argued that the relationship between financial aid and access is based on a variety of indirect mechanisms: Low-income students and minorities are less willing to take out loans, so they cannot afford the net costs at private colleges and enroll at public four-year institutions instead; others cannot afford the net costs at public four-year institutions and are forced to enroll in community colleges, where grants cover a greater percentage of the expenses; still others are discouraged from applying to four-year colleges, believing that they would be unable to meet the expenses (Olivas, 1997). In each scenario, access is effectively denied.

The argument that links declining grant aid and the underrepresentation of low-income and minority students at four-year colleges and universities implicitly assumes that students across the income distribution and from different racial/ethnic groups are similar in academic preparation and dissimilar only in attitudes toward borrowing and ability to afford the net costs at the colleges of their choice. In fact, low-SES, Latino, and black high school seniors are less likely to be in a college preparatory program. The argument also assumes that those low-income and minority students who do have the academic qualifications to be admitted to most four-year institutions have taken appropriate steps toward securing admission to a four-year institution: taking a college entrance examination and submitting an application for admission. In other words, this argument assumes that these underrepresented students have secured admission to four-year institutions yet choose to attend two-year community colleges only when they realize that their financial aid packages are insufficient. In fact, among all four-year-college-qualified 1992 high school graduates, the proportion both taking a college entrance examination (SAT or ACT) and submitting an application for admission to a four-year institution is directly related to family income. Furthermore, college-qualified Latinos were less likely than Asians, whites, and blacks to have taken these necessary steps for college admission.

One possible explanation, then, for the Alexander et al. (1987) finding—that Hispanics enrolled in college were less likely to be at four-year colleges compared with their similarly academically prepared white and black counterparts—is that academically prepared Hispanics did not apply to four-year institutions, nor did they take the proper entrance exams. Unfortunately, Alexander and his associates did not include these variables in their model. Other researchers, on the other hand, have modeled the effects of individual student ability, achievement, and socioeconomic background on application to four-year colleges (for an analysis of 1972 high school graduates, see Manski and Wise, 1983; for a replication of the Manski and Wise study with 1982 high school graduates, see Ozden, 1996). The general findings of these studies have been that individual ability (measured by SAT scores) followed by achievement (high school class rank) are the best predictors of application to four-year colleges and selectivity of four-year colleges. Ozden, summarizing his results in comparison to those of Manski and Wise, concludes that "academic preparation and high school achievement continue to determine the college application decisions and college choices of youth" (1996, 24). In other words, students make rational decisions about applying to four-year colleges: Using their SAT scores and class rank as guides, they apply only if they think they will be admitted. Low-income students are underrepresented at four-year colleges because they have lower achievement levels. In short, the higher education system is working meritocratically. This conclusion is similar to that made by researchers modeling status and educational attainment who concluded that while SES is strongly related to educational attainment, it operates primarily through ability, aspirations, and significant others.

Economic approaches to the study of college choice view the individual as making rational decisions about where to apply to college based on their ability to be accepted. This perspective assumes that students have perfect information about all the options available to them in the higher-education system. More concretely, it assumes that students know how to apply to college, what types of college entrance exams are needed for admission to most four-year institutions, and, even more important, when one needs to apply and take appropriate exams (which is usually a full year before expected enrollment).

Stanton-Salazar (1997) also goes beyond viewing "rational economic

factors" in the formation of Hispanics students' educational and occupational aspirations. He defines social capital as relationships and ties with
"individuals who have the capacity and commitment to directly transmit,
or negotiate the transmission of, institutional resources and opportunities"
(5). Like Useem (1992) and Lareau (1989), Stanton-Salazar argues that
Hispanic working-class students must rely on people within the educational institution to facilitate their success. In particular, unlike middle-
class students, whose parents are more likely to be aware of the processes
involved in, for example, attending college, working-class students are extremely dependent on what he calls "institutional agents": "The parents of
working-class students are less likely to be in positions to act as mobility
resources for their children as they move through the educational system,
and therefore their choices, knowledge, and outcomes are reliant largely
on having relationships with these crucial institutional agents whose
'power' also comes from their ability to situate youth within resource-rich
social networks by actively manipulating the social and institutional forces
that determine who shall 'make it' and who shall not" (Stanton-Salazar,
1997, 13–14).[2]

Social capital, as defined by Stanton-Salazar and by McDonough, is a
useful concept for understanding the question of why Hispanics who are
as qualified as whites and blacks are more likely to choose to attend two-
year institutions than four-year institutions because it situates the decisions
students make within both their family background and the information
they have available to them. For example, Hispanics who aspire to earn a
bachelors degree yet are unaware of the proper college board exams they
need to take as well as the application process are unlikely to attend four-
year colleges and instead will opt to attend a two-year college—unless
someone intervenes and explains the bureaucratic hoops to them. Similarly, Hispanics who perceive Harvard, Stanford, Berkeley, and so on as
being schools for "rich people" will also be more likely to attend a two-
year college so that they can live at home and work part time—unless
someone intervenes and, for example, explains that financial aid is available.

The research described here focused largely on the effect of economics,
instrumental knowledge, and cultural capital. Taking the traditional college choice model beyond the level of the individual, it seems clear that
Hispanic students' choices with regard to four-year colleges are influenced
largely by their families economic and social circumstances coupled with
their school staffs' understandings of the appropriate schools to apply to.
McDonough's (1992) qualitative study of college bound girls in northern
California shows that girls from working-class families apply to fewer
schools and rarely consider prestigious schools (private as well as public)
as feasible choices for college. Gandara's (1997) examination of Hispanic
college graduates reports the same findings. These women tend to apply

to less prestigious campuses and to more accommodating ones, expecting to enroll in these in case they are not accepted to their first choices, which tend to be flagship schools. Furthermore, they receive little guidance from the school counselors at the large schools they attend, as these counselors are overworked and hardly know them. Girls from upper-middle-class families with similar grades and SAT scores, on the other hand, apply to many different prestigious private schools, rarely consider less prestigious options, and treat public flagship schools as "backups" in case they are not accepted to their first choices. Their parents understand the significance of selectivity of college and potential earnings and encourage them to apply to a variety of different schools. Furthermore, their high school counselors communicate the idea that certain schools are appropriate while others are not. In short, McDonough's and Gandara's work shows the mechanisms by which social class affects one's choice of a four-year college. This relationship is mediated by students' social and economic circumstances, which are shaped by their social capital, that is, their relationships with significant others.

Barriers to College Admission: The SAT as a Case Study

In recent years, sociologists (Ozden, 1996) who study access to postsecondary education have argued that academic preparation is a key ingredient to college participation. However, when comparing college enrollment rates across income and racial/ethnic groups—holding academic preparation constant—one finds that merit and motivation become more important in explaining the variation. Put differently, this finding overpredicts the extent to which access is actually being denied to students who have the motivation as well as the merit to attend four-year institutions.

Less research has been devoted to understanding the motivation to attend college and especially to the effects of traditional college entrance requirements and related barriers for Hispanic students. More attention is being paid to this issue now because of the eroding support for affirmative action (Bowen and Bok, 1998). At least for public universities in California and Texas, admissions criteria have been contorted by recent regental, legislative, or court action. The bans there on utilizing race/ethnicity/gender as an admissions criterion has sent women and underrepresented students tumbling off the playing fields of select public universities. For instance, Hispanics are rapidly becoming the largest ethnic group in California public schools, now accounting for 33 percent of high school graduates. Meanwhile, at selective UC campuses like Berkeley, only 7.6 percent of the 1998 admitees are Hispanic (down from 15.4 percent from the 1997 admitted class). Similarly, UCLA rates have dropped to 9.6 percent of the entering class. For all campuses, UC Hispanic admitees make up only 11.9 percent of the projected entering class.

College-bound students from middle- and high-SES families are in the best positions to have concrete knowledge about the process of applying to college by virtue of their parents' higher levels of education. In contrast, low-SES students, such as many Hispanic students, whose parents did not attend college cannot rely on them for crucial information related to post-secondary enrollment (McDonough, 1992). They must receive this information from teachers and counselors in their high school (Stanton-Salazar and Dornbusch, 1995; Stanton-Salazar, 1997). Thus, Hispanics are disadvantaged by how this kind of test plays out in three ways: absence of instrumental knowledge regarding the use of the test (Hurtado and Garcia, 2001), low quality of schooling that they receive (Oakes, 1985), and inappropriate use of the SAT in college admissions (University of California, 1997).

Growing Reliance on the SAT to Determine Admission

The SAT was first used experimentally in 1958 at the University of California. In 1959, it was required for the first time—for students from nonaccredited high schools including all out-of-state schools. It was adopted for all students in 1968. In 1977, it was made part of a linear formula combining grade-point average (GPA) and test scores: the "academic index" (Douglass, 1997). More recently, at the most selective UC campuses, the SAT has usurped as much as half the weight in the overall admissions score. The SAT and other eligibility tests were originally just one part of a student's academic dossier. High school GPA, leadership, community activity, and social circumstances were to be included in substantial proportion as well. However, the SAT has become perceived as a more "objective" tool than some attributes of character and achievement and more reliable than grade-inflated GPAs. Thus, the SAT plays a great role in determining who gets into the university and especially into the most selective campuses.

Other Concerns about the SAT

Criticism about the SAT and other standardized tests of college admission is not new. In recent decades, critics have questioned the validity of these tests and their predictability for the college outcomes of ethnic and linguistic minority students. Admittedly, organizations administering these tests have offered articulate rebuttals to these arguments and have promoted their tests as a means of admission and predictability of first-year performance at colleges and universities (Ramist, Lewis, and McCamley-Jenkins,

1994). These rebuttals, however, have not diminished the criticism that these tests fail to accurately measure students' academic achievement (Beaver, 1996) or the complaint that they exclude otherwise qualified students who might do very well (Crouse and Trusheim, 1988). The following sections lay out the sustained concerns about the misuse of aptitude tests, namely the SAT, in order to encourage a dialogue about achieving equitable college access.

Underrepresented Students Do Poorly

Underrepresented students and students of low SES do not score as well on aptitude tests. By their own admission, the Educational Testing Service (ETS)—the SAT's creator—agrees that students of higher SES tend to do better on these standardized tests than those students who come from poorer backgrounds (Crouse and Trusheim, 1988; Miller, 1995). Miller (1995) reinforces this connection of "aptitude" and educational outcomes. His meta-analysis shows that students who fall into lower-SES categories and whose parents were educated at less than the college level do less well on the SAT (needless to say, many of these students fall into underrepresented racial and ethnic groups).

Effects of Low Expectations

The scores achieved are not predicted only by family income or parental educational level. Minority students who do come from higher-SES categories still do not do as well as those white students who come from a lower-SES category (Miller, 1995). This raises a troubling and persistent problem, but the answer is likely associated with motivation and expectations. Controlled studies of test-taking motivation in students who attended Stanford back up this conclusion. When African American and white students were told that the test they were to take was meaningless, they scored virtually on par with each other. However, when the test was promoted as one that reflected the Graduate Record Exam (GRE, a graduate-level equivalent to the SAT), then African American students scored significantly lower (Steele and Aronson, 1995). Steele and Aronson's results help explicate the chasm between the success of white and African American students. They pointed out that students could very well internalize a stereotyped image of themselves when put into judgment situations. This hypothesis points to a particularly troubling possibility: Our "objective" forms of measurement are indeed subjective. Similarly, Gandara and Lopez (1998) found that Latino students' high school records were not accurately reflected in their SAT scores. In interviews, these students often explained that they were told that "the SAT doesn't really matter";

rather, it was their high school academic record that would gain them entrance into the college of their choice. What they found, however, was that SAT did matter, and ultimately it counted against them. The researchers also found that these students' low performance on the SAT led to a lower feeling of academic self-worth and, as a consequence, lower performance in college.

Coaching's Effect on Test Outcomes

The effect of coaching has remained contentious. An entire industry has sprung up around test preparation. Organizations such as the Princeton Review and the Kaplan Educational Center have offered coaching for students who wish to gain an edge in their testing. These organizations can charge upward of $700 for preparation classes for the SAT I and more for each subject examination on the SAT II. Obviously, such fees are out of reach for many students from lower-SES categories.

Does coaching help? The College Board argues that students see very little improvement in their test scores after coaching. Others further removed from the SAT have estimated the range of improvement from as few as 24 points overall (both tests) to 110 points in certain coaching situations (Zuman, 1988; Smyth, 1990). Yet measuring the success of coaching remains murky. Becker (1990) reports on a number of coaching programs and concluded that there were not enough well-described and well-designed studies to reach a clear understanding of the contributions of coaching interventions.

Coaching may or may not help, but it is certainly perceived to do so and, as such, may in itself raise performance. If coaching helps, how accurately is aptitude being measured? And is the growth of the coaching industry itself not a tribute to the growing power of the SAT? In a world where as few as 10 points can make the difference between admission and rejection or in receiving grants for scholarship, any edge not available to everyone is simply unfair.

The SAT's Predictive Validity of College/University Success Is Questionable

Institutions of higher education are beginning to admit that the tests add very little predictive validity over and above that of high school GPAs. Baron and Norman (1992) found that tests used by their particular institution did not add significant predictability to the students' overall performance. More important, it failed to predict the academic persistence of the students who entered. On the basis of an analysis of the applicants' GPAs and their resulting freshman grades, Crouse and Trusheim (1988) discovered that when SATs were used as a tool to exclude certain applicants, those same students would have succeeded at the institution.

Bowdoin College and Bates College in Maine chose to eliminate tests requirements they felt "unnecessarily discourage[d] students from applying to certain schools; and [furthermore] minorities, women and students from low-income families consistently score below white males" (Vobejda, 1987). What happened without tests? Bates College discovered that its applicant pool broadened after it no longer required students to submit their SATs. Following up, Bates determined that those students who did not choose to submit scores still had an academic survival rate of from 92 to 99 percent. Yet their test scores averaged 160 points lower than those of submitters (Shabazz, 1995).

Why the Predominance of the SAT?

Despite detrimental evidence and lingering concerns, admission professionals and faculty committees continue to require aptitude tests like the SAT. Their reasons might include the convenience of utilizing the only "objective" tool at their disposal, a feeling that they are protecting the current definitions of academic standards or presumptive applicant success, or influence from the almost boundless self-promotion of the ETS and the College Board (Beaver, 1996). They might also see the test as a comfortable means to measure the relative quality of the institution's applicant class and the institution itself (Hiss, 1990; Pitsch, 1991).

The Educational Testing Service, the College Board, and their proponents defend the continued use of aptitude tests in admission decisions. They have rightly pointed out that test score variations indicate that some students have experienced insufficient educational opportunities. A favorite metaphor is that the test is like a thermometer that indicates symptoms of an illness; throwing out the thermometer will not make the virus vanish. True enough. Yet real-life thermometers do not prevent the patient from getting well. Standardized aptitude tests play a large part in determining eligibility. As such, they prevent otherwise qualified students from entering college, therefore perpetuating the currently inequitable status quo. This cost is much too high for the convenience offered by the numeric scores of "aptitude."

Are There Alternatives?

A number of alternatives are available to counter the growing overreliance on the SAT in admissions decisions. However, the suggestions that follow should not be seen as substitutes for the long-term solution to equitable access to higher education, namely, choosing and training first-class teachers; creating high expectations for all students, backed by rigorous curriculum standards and testing; and acquiring the resources to remediate shortcomings in achievement as they arise. These recommendations are ordered here from the immediate term to the midterm.

IMMEDIATE

- Eliminate standardized aptitude tests as gatekeepers to college admission. Increase opportunities for students, regardless of race or ethnicity, by eliminating a test that does not accurately reflect the circumstances in which the students learn and, more important, that does not accurately reflect their potential.

SHORT TERM

- Develop criteria to assemble a class of freshmen that collectively meet the mission of the campus. At most universities, each individual applicant is compared only to every other, ignoring the opportunity to create a coherent class that would be diverse in terms of academic interests, background, SES, geography, and so on.
- Level the playing field by weighting more heavily the records of students who attended high schools that did not sponsor sufficient college prep courses. Alternatively, give more weight to applicants from heavily impacted low-income (i.e., segregated) high schools.
- Consider rewarding students who have succeeded in spite of schools that are resource poor. Such students may have succeeded in their education despite their families low SES and parental educational attainment, overcome placements in nonacademic tracking, or improved markedly through their high school years.
- Pay particular attention to references from high school staff—teachers, counselors, and principals. Reward these staffs who have supported successful students by allowing them to nominate others to follow in their paths.
- Expand admissions of community college transfers. At most universities, the SAT is not a transfer requirement; rather, only a certain GPA in selected courses, combined with sufficient overall credits, is needed.

MIDTERM

- Reexamine the SAT as a predictor of university academic success. This would require commissioning a comprehensive examination regarding the ability of SATs and various admissions criteria to predict student outcomes, including college graduation and success in careers.

- Evaluate and consider proposals that would admit a certain proportion of the graduating class in each high school. The University of Texas has adopted the policy of guaranteeing admissions to the top 10 percent of performing students by GPA. The University of California will soon guarantee admission to the top 4 percent of each high school graduating class. Moreover, it has lessened the significance of the SAT I aptitude test for purposes of determining admissions to a campus. Instead, the SAT II achievement tests will be given more weight.
- Develop and utilize achievement tests for determining eligibility, particularly tests that are aligned directly with high school curriculum standards. Most state are moving toward the establishment of content and performance standards with accompanying "standardized" tests that are aligned with those standards. Such standards-based systems would also reflect the curriculum that students should receive at the state level. Meanwhile, achievement tests like the SAT II that are developed to assess content-based knowledge might serve as a surrogate.

In summary, the rapid demise of affirmative action may bring a silver lining. It has exposed the huge role that standardized aptitude tests have come to play in determining college eligibility since the 1960s. (Their widespread use, perhaps coincidentally, began at about the same time affirmative action was initiated.) Ample evidence exists that these tests stand in the way of college opportunities for many underrepresented or poor students who, because of their test results, are denied access to the colleges and universities of their choice. To the extent that aptitude tests are heavily shaping high-stake admission decisions, their creators and supporters must answer to their misuse. If the SAT were not required in determining the UC eligibility of Hispanic students, the number of eligible students would immediately double. While the absolute numbers would still be small, it would send a clear signal that colleges are open to those who have achieved and who want to reach their potential, regardless of the obstacles they have had to overcome.

K–12 PROGRAMS THAT WORK TO ENHANCE COLLEGE PARTICIPATION

Programs to better serve the aspirations of minority students to participate in higher education have evolved in recent decades, tending to grow more comprehensive and to address more subtle obstacles to academic, social, and economic advancement. De Acosta (1996) describes the history of such programs as beginning with meeting needs for financial aid, moving to the improvement of academic skills (e.g., a focus on language arts and strengthened college prep curriculum) to attending to psychological and social factors (e.g., adding academic and career counseling) to helping students negotiate the institutional culture of college. She and others (Gandara and Maxwell-Jolly, 1998) find common characteristics of successful programs: sensitivity to individual students, to student cultures, and to the institution where the program is located; proactive interventions; a focus on accelerated, enriched learning; small size; and partnering with family and community.

What we know much less about is how these programs evaluate themselves, how successful they are, how much they cost, how well they can be replicated, and how well they can scale as the population they are serving grows. At least in California, we have found very little evidence of increases in funding, even to meet general population growth, not to speak of the phenomenal growth of the Hispanic population.

This review of successful programs looks first at efforts to increase Hispanic student access to higher education. Key barriers to be overcome include lack of information, counseling, and advisement; tracking; test requirements; course-taking patterns; underprepared teachers; low aspirations, expectations, and motivations; and the cost of higher education (Policy Analysis for California Education [PACE], 1997). A helpful typology is the one utilized in a recent study of outreach programs performed by PACE (1997): Student-centered outreach embodies predominantly academic development programs (and sometimes include financial aid), and school-centered outreach includes teacher development, recruitment, and retention and scholarship programs. Some programs combine features from these different categories, but regardless of the orientation, their focus is on removing obstacles to participation in higher education. This section highlights both student- and school-centered programs.

Student-Centered Programs

Early Outreach

The first of the systemwide outreach programs in California, the Early Academic Outreach Program (EAOP), began in 1976. It serves grades 7 through 12 in 131 school districts in California and is operated by eight UC campuses. It "enrolls" more than 50,000 students per year at nearly 500 schools. The program has evolved to include academic skills development, motivational activities, and parent involvement activities (PACE, 1997). Nearly half its "graduating" seniors (constituting only about 2.5 percent of the statewide Hispanic public high school graduating class) were eligible to attend the University of California, but only about one-quarter of those seniors actually do matriculate to the university. The majority enroll instead on campuses of other California higher-educational systems. Like other academic support programs, its goal has become fostering students' resilience in demanding academic work rather than remediating deficiencies (Cooper et al., 1995).

MESA

The Math, Engineering, Science Achievement (MESA) program, sponsored by the University of California, provides an academic enrichment program for precollege students at elementary, junior high, and senior high schools. A new effort, the Mathematics, Engineering, Science and Agriculture Achievement (MESA2) program introduces rural precollege students to high-tech opportunities in agriculture.

Founded in 1970, MESA has organized 20 centers serving 13,857 students from 259 schools at all levels in California. In addition, seven other states have joined California's program to form MESA USA. The main elements of the MESA model include academic enrichment, group study, academic and financial aid advising, career exploration, parent involvement, and teacher training. For the latter element (which stretches beyond the original student-centered focus), MESA offers training opportunities for its advisers, those math and science teachers who work with MESA students. MESA provides a three-day MESA Annual Training Institute so that advisers can learn new teaching techniques and hands-on activities. Other regional training opportunities have been funded by companies and foundations. Many training sessions call for attendees to train other teachers, including non-MESA educators.

MESA high school seniors average a 3.13 GPA, compared to the statewide average of 2.78; they average 903 on the SAT, comparable to national averages for all groups and much higher than average scores for African Americans or Hispanics, and they complete physics, for example, at double the rate of students statewide. Most impressive are the college-going rates of MESA "graduates": 97 percent go on to college (75 percent of whom enroll in four-year colleges). Hispanic students make up approximately 55 percent of the precollege MESA enrollment.

School-Centered Programs

AVID: Untracking for Hispanics

The Advancement Via Individual Determination (AVID) program was developed as an alternative to compensatory education and remedial tracking for underachieving high school students, especially those from ethnic and linguistic minority backgrounds. Mary Catherine Swanson, a member of the English department, introduced the idea of untracking underachieving students to San Diego in 1980 at Clairemont High School, a predominantly white school. Untracking became a way to educate minority students bused to Clairemont from predominantly ethnic minority schools in southeast San Diego under a court-ordered desegregation decree. Unwilling to segregate African American and Latino students into a separate, compensatory curriculum, Swanson and the Clairemont faculty placed the bused students who had high test scores but low grades into regular college prep classes. In addition, these students were provided special mentoring through an elective class. AVID soon spread beyond Clairemont High School, and by 1997 more than 500 secondary schools in eight states and the Department of Defense's Dependents Schools overseas had introduced AVID programs.

Those eligible for AVID are high school students who are members of low-income, ethnic, or linguistic minorities who have average to high achievement test scores but whose grades average C. After these high-potential, underachieving students are identified and selected by AVID co-ordinates, parents are advised. Those parents who agree to support their children's participation in the academic program sign contracts to have their children participate in AVID in high school.

The previously underachieving students who are placed in college prep classes are not left to sink or swim. AVID has arranged a system of supports to assist students to make the transition from low-track to high-track high school classes. Among the most visible supports in the AVID untracking program is a special elective class that meets for one academic period a day, 180 days a year, for three or four years. In addition to a classroom teacher, students are assisted by college tutors on a 7:1 student-to-tutor ratio.

AVID promotes a basic plan for the weekly instructional activities within AVID classrooms. Two school days are designated tutorial days. On these days, students are to work in small groups with the assistance of a tutor. On two other days, writing as a tool for learning is emphasized. On these days, students are to engage in a variety of writing activities, including essays for their English, social studies, science, and history classes. Other important activities that occur within the classroom are instruction in note taking, test taking, and study strategies. One day a week, usually Friday, is a "motivational day." Guest speakers are invited to address the class, and field trips to colleges are scheduled on these days. By dispensing these academic techniques and exposures to opportunities, AVID gives its students explicit instruction in the implicit or hidden curriculum of the school.

Institutional support of the students augments this explicit socialization process. AVID coordinates help remove impediments to students' academic achievement by intervening on their behalf with high school teachers, administrators, and college admissions officers. AVID connects its students to social networks; that is, it provides its students with the social capital at school that is similar to the social capital that more economically advantaged parents are able to provide their children at home through their family connections. If schools and their agents act collectively in a deliberate, intensive, and explicit fashion to generate a socialization process that produces the same sorts of strategies and resources deployed in privileged homes and institutions, then working-class and minority youth can enjoy the same advantages as their more privileged peers.

Peer group relations also support untracking. AVID publicly marks the students' group identity. Their notebooks clearly display the AVID logo, as does the AVID classroom that is used for lunch, social gatherings, and academic instruction. Within the social space demarcated for them, AVID students form new academically oriented friendships and develop academic identities. The time that students spend together on field trips to colleges, in collaborative study groups, and in informal discussions with college tutors and guest speaks from local colleges and businesses facilitates this process.

From 1990 to 1992, the AVID program was studied in eight San Diego high schools to see whether previously underachieving students from low-income ethnic and linguistic minority backgrounds who are placed in college-bound courses with high-achieving students benefit academically and socially by the experience (Mehan et al., 1996). During the period of study, 1,053 students who had participated for three years in the AVID untracking experiment graduated from 14 high schools in the San Diego City Schools (SDCS) system. In those same years, 288 additional students started the program but left after completing one year or less. Two hundred forty-eight of the three-year AVID students and 146 of the one-year AVID students were interviewed.

Of the 248 students (mostly Hispanic) who "graduated" from AVID, 120 (48 percent) reported attending four-year colleges, 99 (40 percent) reported attending two-year colleges, and the remaining 29 (12 percent) said that they are working or doing other things. This is particularly impressive given that fewer than 20 percent of California's Hispanic high school graduates in the same years attended a college or university. Of specific importance, 43 percent of the three-year AVID experience went on to a four-year college. Nationally, this figure is 29 percent (Nora et al., 1999). Therefore, in AVID we find a program providing the academic and social supports that significantly influence Hispanic student college participation. It addresses the highly tracked conditions that these students experience and

alters the academic, curriculum, and social dimensions of that experience
with highly positive results.

High School Puente

Puente means "bridge" in Spanish; the Puente Project was conceived of
as a bridge from one segment of education to another. The Puente High
School Project is an outgrowth of Puente's successful community college
program, which was begun at Chabot College in Hayward, California, in
1981 to address the problem of the low transfer rate of Hispanic students
to four-year colleges and universities. The program combines innovative
teaching and counseling methods with community involvement to provide
a focused, supportive, and culturally sensitive learning environment to foster student success. The academic focus is on the development of critical
analysis and writing skills, areas in which Latino students consistently underachieve. Since 1981, the program has expanded to 38 community colleges throughout California.

High School Puente project began in 1993 with a four-year pilot to be
tested in 18 schools in California. The goal of the project is to increase the
number of Hispanics graduating from high school and enrolling in college.
At each pilot high school, Puente students, who represent a wide range of
skill and motivation levels, are enrolled in a Puente college prep English
class grades 9 and 10. The course is taught by a Puente-trained English
teacher and integrates community-based writing, portfolio assessment,
and Latino-authored literature into the regular core curriculum. The Puente
counselor works closely with the Puente students and their parents to ensure that students are enrolled in college prep courses and that parents have
the information they need to support their children's academic progress.
In addition, a community mentor liaison (CML) both recruits mentors
from the community to work directly with students and seeks resources
from the business and professional communities to help support the program.

The High School Puente model is "front ended" in its resource alloca-
tions. Students are placed in the Puente classroom for the first two years
of high school with the hope that this will provide the foundation to successfully mainstream them into the core college preparatory English
classes. Counselors work most intensively with the students during these
first two years, and the assigned mentor is asked to maintain the relationship with the students for the first two years. It would be ideal, though not
required, if the mentoring relationship lasted longer than two years, but to
date most have not done so. Hence, the first two critical years of high
school are carefully monitored by adults associated with the Puente program. In subsequent years, students are encouraged to maintain the rela-

tionship with their Puente counselor and, where possible, with the Puente teacher. The Puente Club is also an avenue for maintaining the Puente connection. This extramural club allows students get together for social events that support their college preparatory activities (e.g., plan for car washes and bake sales in order to support a field trip). The counselor—and in some cases the teacher—works to maintain the club and its activities in an attempt to preserve the integrity of the Puente group and encourage the students to support one another. Another strategy used by counselors to monitor the Puente students is to group them into one or more classes in the junior and senior years where the counselor can maintain contact with the students and organize activities through a single visit to the classroom. The design of the program emphasizes a strong start in the first two years, with continued counseling and monitoring of students in the final two years of high school.

The Puente intervention has three major components: instructional, counseling, and mentoring. Associated with each component is a cluster of activities and interventions.

Instructional component. The instructional component consists of a two-year-long class in which students are enrolled in grades 9 and 10. The class is composed entirely of the heterogeneous Puente cohort of 30 students. A specially trained Puente teacher focuses on intensive process writing instruction, the interweaving of acclaimed Latino literature into the regular grades 9 and 10 literature curriculum, and training and experience in the use of writing portfolios so that students may learn to critique writing, assess their own progress, and set their own (high) performance standards. Each year that they are in the program, Puente teachers receive several weeks of training in Hispanic literature and cultural awareness, process writing, heterogeneous classroom instruction, and portfolio assessment. A portion of this training is provided during summer vacation, but an important element of the staff development is also continual contact and training throughout the school year. These sessions are of shorter duration than the summer program but occur at frequent intervals during the year and may occur on site or regionally, generally for one or two days at a time. The importance of these sessions is seen not only in providing continuous instruction for teachers (as well as counselors and community mentor liaisons) but also in monitoring implementation of the program and allowing local staff to more broadly disseminate practices that are developed at the site level.

Students generally are required to write daily, in journals and in other forms; they cover the regular English curriculum in addition to the Latino literature component, and they must maintain their own writing portfolios and help fellow students polish their work, which is seen as an important element in becoming a good writer. The Puente class is also an important

forum for cultural discussions as well as frequent presentations and conversations about colleges, careers, and personal aspirations.

Counseling component. The counseling component provides oversight
of the student's high school program, assuring that the student will be
placed in college preparatory classes; that any deficiencies will be quickly
noted and addressed; and that the student is supplied with the information
necessary to prepare him- or herself for postsecondary education. Counselors also participate in some Puente classroom activities to integrate
themselves into the daily activities of the students. These activities may
include a planned writing experience, a session on university admission
requirements, or some other focused activity. Counselors also arrange for
college visits and other field trips and parent and mentor meetings and
events, and most oversee the Puente Club.

Mentoring component. The mentoring component is coordinated by a
CML who seeks out appropriate mentors from the community for the students, trains them, and then matches these mentors to students in the program. The CML also works with the counselor to arrange for appropriate
activities for the students and mentors and monitors these relationships.
Mentors are encouraged to maintain relationships with students for a minimum of two years, during which time the goal is to meet with students,
either individually or in groups, at least monthly. Mentors are also urged
to meet with the students' families, preferably in the family home, in order
to get to know more about the student. Ensuring that these meetings occur
regularly and that they are productive and satisfying for both mentor and
the student is a labor-intensive activity.

In addition to locating, training, and monitoring mentors, the CML is
also charged with a more vaguely defined community relations role: making presentations to local community groups and raising the profile of
Puente in order to encourage greater community participation in the program in the form of donations, resources, and mentors. For example, the
CML may find companies that are willing to sponsor field trips, site visits,
or even internships for Puente students. Some of these companies may be
willing to make cash or in-kind donations to Puente activities. However,
the primary role of the CML is the rather arduous task of locating and
training Hispanic professionals to mentor and provide role models for high
school students.

The results of High School Puente are impressive (Gandara et al., 1998).
At the end of the junior year, Puente students are significantly ahead of the
control group in college preparatory courses taken and their success (GPA)
in them. A constant growth in GPA overall characterizes Puente students
in later grades, while the reverse is true for non-Puente control group students. In addition, 95 percent of Puente students feel confident that they
know what it takes to apply to college; less than 33 percent of non-Puente

students report this same confidence. And by grade 12, 91 percent of Puente students have taken necessary college entrance exams compared to 35 percent for non-Puente students. Also, by grade 12, 53 percent of Puente students actually have completed application to a four-year college compared to 25 percent for non-Puente students. The college matriculation rate is also double for Puente students.

In short, Puente students are more likely than non-Puente students to stay in school and at the same school, they take and pass more college preparatory courses, their attitudes toward school are significantly more positive, their preparation for making college applications is stronger, their aspirations are higher, and they are more eager to identify with the label of a "good student." Because we know that willingness to put forth effort makes the greatest difference in long-term academic success (Gandara, 1995), the reported willingness of Puente students to give up other things in favor of school and to identify themselves as good students is especially compelling evidence that Puente can make a difference in the lives of these students over the long run. A more positive attitude toward schooling, combined with enhanced preparation for college, would appear to be providing the Puente students with a substantial advantage as they look toward their futures (Gandara, 1997).

CONCLUSION

The findings of the programs discussed here and those reviewed by others (Hope and Rendon, 1997; Gandara et al., 1998) have several implications for programs that seek to enhance Hispanic academic achievement and move them successfully up the educational ladder:

- The evidence points to the critical importance of interventions that are consistent, intensive, and well articulated from grade to grade and that provide consistent monitoring of students throughout the secondary years. There is no point at which it appears safe to let down one's guard (Datnow et al., 1998). Students growing up in risky environments remain at risk throughout adolescence, even when they may appear to be on track. Sustaining gains requires that the intervention be sustained.
- All programs attribute much of their success to the fact that at least one adult in the school setting takes personal responsibility for each student in the program. This adult may be a teacher, counselor, social worker, or mentor, but he or she must know and understand the student and his or her family situation and be ready and able to intervene on the student's behalf. Adolescence is not too late a period to make

a substantial difference in kids' lives; even high-risk, low-income youth can be educationally engaged and can dramatically improve their achievement if provided with a comprehensive program that involves caring adult advocates.

- These programs have designed intervention components that address the issue of locating students in supportive peer groups that reinforce achievement-oriented behavior. It is essential that students receive consistent messages about the importance of staying in school and doing well, and program effects are strengthened when students band together to support a shared achievement ideology.

- The findings point to the need for increased time to achieve high academic goals. These findings are consistent with Puente's focus on providing supportive resources for students outside of school hours. Even before considering modifying or improving the quality of classroom practices, it seems necessary to increase the amount of time that previously low-achieving students spend on math, science, literature, and history. In effect, this is the approach that the highly celebrated Garfield High School teacher Jaime Escalante took with his previously underachieving Hispanic calculus students. Although he was rightfully applauded for his charismatic motivational efforts, it cannot be overlooked that Escalante increased exponentially the number of hours, days, and weeks that his students spent in the classroom. Instead of spending 180 hours in business or consumer math in one academic year, his students spent three times that amount each year in advanced math courses (Escalante and Dirmann, 1990).

- Puente and PDP relied extensively on heterogeneous, collaborative grouping practices. Cooperative learning, the classroom practice of grouping heterogeneously for the purpose of accomplishing tasks collaboratively, seems to help underachieving students improve their classroom performance while helping high-achieving students maintain theirs.

- The success of these programs has been built on a sensitivity to the particular circumstances of the students' families they serve and the creation of "strategic" places for them to interact in the school. The personal connections, however, must be predicated on honoring the cultural and linguistic practices in the students' homes. These programs have shown that parents can be recruited, if given respect and care, as powerful allies for enhancing the educational outcomes of their children and, by virtue of increasing the aspirations and achievement of significant numbers of students, strengthening the schools that they attend.

If we know that programs attending to these attributes for Hispanic students work, why are there not more of them?

NOTES

1. One paper found that SES had a negative effect on dropping out for whites, while it had no effect for blacks and Latinos (Fernandez, Henn-Reinke, and Petrovich, 1989). Another paper looking specifically at Mexican-origin students found that SES had an independent effect on dropping out (Velez, 1989).

2. In a study based on a large-scale national survey, McDonough and Antonio (1996) found that visiting a teacher's home in high school was positively related to selectivity of four-year college attended for Chicano and black students but not for whites.

9

Theoretical Perspectives on the Present and Future Educational Circumstances of the Hispanic Student

WHY THEORY?

Like any student, I was introduced to a multitude of theories that expanded my conceptualizations of "why things are the way they are" while in the formal processes of schooling. These theories of physics, biology, chemistry, and mathematics were central in my early educational pursuits. Theories, however, became highly prominent in my undergraduate training and not just in the hard sciences. Theories of sociology and psychology fascinated me since they seemed more relevant to my own circumstances—they were more helpful in helping me make sense of my own personal situation. Theories became important, therefore, not only in understanding the physical world that surrounded me but also in the social world in which I immersed myself. Theories became consciously very important in making sense of old and new information and created a context in which to act on that information. They organized that knowledge base in ways that were intellectually helpful, but most significantly they organized my further intellectual pursuits as well as my everyday activity. It was theories of social stratification, for instance, that led me to protest against the Vietnam War and to volunteer my services as an English-as-a-second-language (ESL) tutor for Hispanic farmworkers. I "realized" that disadvantaged social structures, which led to the overrepresentation of Hispanics in the war and their underrepresentation in high-level educational opportunities, are, in theory, the result of the same set of social processes. It was evident, then, that such a theoretical understanding not only provided me with a knowledge base but also determined how I might act to change that which I perceived to be detrimental.

In graduate school, theories became even more important in the intellectual work that I chose to perform. I had trained to be a behavioral psychologist. My brand of theoretical "behaviorism" put great stock on the environmental influences of behavior (Skinner, 1957). Through this theoretical lease, I focused on a set of environmental "stimuli" that, if arranged in a specific manner, would significantly affect learning—changes in behavior. That theoretical perspective guided how I tried to make sense of the world: what questions to ask, how to ask them, where to ask them, and how to assess the effect of any interventions in learning I might implement. It called for scientific precision, objectivity, and a focus on empiricism.

I have to admit that my concern for and influence of theories began in the family. My parents, particularly my mother, had given me a theory, a worldview, about making sense of my surroundings. Her theory was much more "spiritual." It was not very precise, and it relied heavily on faith and trust—faith in God (and fear of the Devil) and trust in others. In trying how to understand the world and act on it, my mother instructed me to look for good and evil and to promote good while avoiding evil while working in concert with others who were working in the same way. I still try to do that. This theory, in an adapted form, continues to guide much of what I do—and my mother reminded me of these tasks until her dying day. My brothers and sisters also rely on this theory; almost all quite "Christian" in their world and intricately involved in institutions aligned with this "theory."

Professionally, I must admit that I am no longer a "behaviorist," and personally my own view of the world has been morally complexified. In particular, new theories of human development and learning seem better for understanding my work. Therefore, theories still guide me. I am not without a conceptual framework that guides my present professional task of understanding the world, particularly issues of development, learning, teaching, and schooling. In a recent study I completed (Garcia, 1999), I found that teachers also have theories of how children develop and learn and their own role in such processes. In short, whether we articulate them or not, we all have theories that guide us in making meaning of the world we live in. That is why theories are important to all of us, not just to physical, social, or behavioral "scientists," despite their being solely linked to the use of theories.

For this reason, it is important to look more explicitly at conceptual frameworks, or theories, that might help us understand the educational circumstances of Hispanics. Such explanations, although not in agreement, can help us understand the present situations in which Hispanics find themselves and may be useful in understanding how to rectify those circumstances that we find unacceptable. Such explanations come in many shapes and forms. I will likely not do justice to the varied positions, their intricacies, or their implications. However, I will attempt to address the major ways in which colleagues working to understand the education of Hispanics have organized the information about their circumstances and have attempted to explain those circumstances. Such explanations have very direct implications on what might need to be done to enhance the educational outcomes of this student population.

Of particular focus in this chapter are theories and explanations that emphasize the social processes and institutions in which these students reside, their individual and psychological attributes, and their cultural "roots." Social stratification theories, which focus on social class, and particularly social organizations have attempted to explain why poor students continue to underachieve. Other social theories add the ingredient of race and ethnicity to the variable of class as a way to "enrich" explanations for academic underachievement of selected populations, including Hispanics. Other theories concentrate on the individual student as learner in the schooling enterprise. This more "psychological" approach emphasizes both inherent learning capabilities with issues related to opportunities to learn. In such theories, Hispanic students are perceived more as individual learners who can be motivated to achieve under teaching and learning circumstances within the schooling experience itself. Beyond the social and psychological explanations are new theories that recognize the interactions of the social, psychological, and cultural attributes of the Hispanic student. This integrated theory recognizes the contribution of various factors in its explanation, but, significantly, it makes the case that it is important to consider the "Hispanic" character of the student—not in a general sense, but in a way that recognizes who the student is, what social structures he or she is immersed in, and how schooling can be adapted to address his or her success academically, socially, and economically. In this process of reviewing theories that attempt to account for the present educational circumstances of Hispanics in the United States, my intent is not just to list these as alternative forms of explanation. Instead, it is to make clear that each theory adds value to our understanding while at the same time collectively establishing the rationale and importance to act on such understandings. For in education, it is not enough just to know why things are the way they are; it is important to use such knowledge in a way that moves us closer to realizing our pursuit of equity and excellence. For Hispanics in particular, we need not continue to puzzle over this population's historic educational underachievement given the conceptual understandings we now possess.

SOCIAL PROCESS THEORIES

Theories of Social Stratification

The steering of young Hispanics in schools toward different educational and economic fates is rooted within the social processes that create unequal "fates" to be steered into. There is, according to Connell (1993), a social stratification cycle: the production, shaping, legitimization, and reproduction of structures of inequality. It is an "advantaging cycle" as well as a "disadvantaging cycle." For some select students, these processes and social organizations are highly advantageous; for others, they are just as disadvantageous.

In this view of social stratification, educational opportunities for Hispanics are not just a mirror image of economic inequalities. Education systems are busy institutions that are vibrantly involved in the production of social hierarchies. They are not just passive institutions. They select their students, organize them in very predictable ways, and produce and disseminate particular kinds of knowledge to particular users. They determine who succeeds and who fails. Centrally involved, education contributes to the creation of social identities for groups who are stakeholders in the system. These identities range from narrow old-school-tie networks to ethnic group identities. On a wider scale again, education is central to the modern mosaic of inequality. Most significant, education systems persistently promote the belief that people who are advantaged in the distribution of social assets deserve their advantages. They deserve a better deal because they are more intelligent, better trained, or more hard-working or because they and their parents have sacrificed to get those assets.

In this view, the education system is part of the social construction process. Relationships between education and other social institutions are constantly being reconstructed. Compensatory education programs for Hispanics, particularly bilingual education and immigrant education programs, emerged in the later stages of the civil rights movement. These educational programs were a product of socially constructed efforts to serve "disadvantaged" students. Schools were forced by the courts and enticed by new federal resources to reconstruct the schooling of Hispanic students. In addition, the widespread belief in continuous economic growth and the moral imperative for "equity" during this civil rights era made it possible to get political support for measures to expand "opportunity." But within a few years, other social forces, including the limited or curtailed support for education, the increasing pressure of immigration, and the resulting growth of child poverty, were undermining these measures.

The growing importance of organized knowledge in production and distribution systems has intensified the class struggle for advantage in education and training. In this particular theoretical framework for "explaining" Hispanic student underachievement, this is the key reason why compensatory programs for Hispanics have never been enlarged to the scale where they would have major redistributive effects (Garcia and Gonzalez, 1995). Though the school is a distinct institution, education is not a closed system. Schools are interwoven with their milieus. Their design and functioning presuppose relationships with families, workplaces, labor markets, and neighborhoods, and the way the schools are designed presupposes the organization of these other institutions. Looking at it from the other end, particularly from the perspective of Hispanic neighborhoods and families, conducting these relationships with schools requires various resources. Some of these are very familiar and are the "bread and butter" of conventional thinking on educational disadvantage: health, nutrition, physical security, emotional security, attention from helpful adults, peer support, time available for school work, books in the home, scholastic know-how in the home, and so on (Garcia, 1998). We might call these "contextual resources for schooling." They represent the material and personal supports of formal schooling, focused on the individual learner.

Less familiar, but just as critical for student success, are the kinds of resources involved when property owners withdraw support of public schools—as happened in California with the passage of Proposition 13 in 1978, producing a long decline in that state's school financing. Similarly, universities dominate curricula in such a way that advantages certain sectors of the population. This capacity to shape a school system is typically outside the realm of any individual student's or family's capability. The inequalities of such resources in a given time and place and the deployment of these resources by the groups involved define the situation that an education system finds itself in. The central feature of this situation for Hispanic students, families, and communities is that they have been and continue to be outside the realm of influence when it comes to these important resources.

Nine out of 10 educational researchers emphasize the importance of some cultural match between school and home (Garcia, 1999). However, in a more robust social stratification conceptual framework, such an emphasis is perceived as a "little off the beam." Most formulations of this point, including Pierre Bourdieu's well-known conceptions of "cultural capital" and "social reproduction," are too static for more recent theories of social stratification. Even dominant groups do not seek simple "reproduction" through education (Connell, 1993). They know that the world is changing, and they want the schools to help their children get ahead of the game. Hispanics, as a group, are no different. The absence of critical social resources can affect the social organization of schooling and may help to account for inequities in their schooling success more than any perceived mismatch between home and school.

In short, social stratification theories help us understand the powerful social forces that act to advantage some populations of students and to disadvantage others. The absence of social resources to counter such forces by those who become disadvantaged is key in understanding that disadvantage. Add to this view an additional set of variables that imply the importance of social processes on the development of individual and collective ethnic identity and its negative effects on the schooling of minorities (Ogbu, 1999). From these perspectives, action is needed to counter this unbalance, not by acting on the individual student but by acting on the social forces that restrict or enhance educational opportunities for the disadvantaged. The focus is not just on schooling or educational institutions since they are only a mix of government, private-sector, religious, and community institutions that act together in ways that shape one another and help explain the present and future circumstances of Hispanic students in the educational enterprise. Other theories of social construction have called on more explicit attention to race and ethnic relations in this country to understand the educational underachievement of Hispanics, African Americans, and other minority groups.

Theories on Minorities/Majorities, Race, and Ethnic Relations

Race and Ethnic Conflict

In 1968, sociologist Donald Noel published a seminal paper, "A Theory of the Origin of Ethnic Stratification," in which he proposed that if two or more groups come together in a contact situation defined by ethnocentrism, competition, and differentials in power, then some form of racial or ethnic stratification will result. Drawing on earlier social science contributions to race relations theory, Noel further proposed that if the contact situation has all three of these characteristics, some system of inequality between these groups will create, for example, a dominant versus minority group structure. Trueba (1999) suggests that such a construction helps us understand the educational circumstances of Hispanics in this country.

Robert Blauner, in his book *Racial Oppression in America* (1972), elaborated on Noel's theory by proposing that the key factor in shaping relationships between a minority group and the dominant group is their initial relationship, and he distinguished between two major types of initial relationship: colonization and immigration. He classified Native Americans and African Americans as "colonized" groups—a population forced into minority status by the military or political power of the dominant group and thus becoming involuntary participants in a system of subordination and discrimination that is reinforced by their visible racial and cultural characteristics. Acuña (1972) characterized Mexican Americans particularly as products of this American "internal colonization."

In contrast, white ethnic Europeans were classified as "voluntary" groups. They are voluntary participants in a host society, and they share more racial and cultural similarities with the dominant group, which allows them to assimilate by the second and third generation. More recent immigrants from Africa, Asia, and Latin America, however, do not fit the mold of white European immigrants, primarily because they are dissimilar in racial and cultural characteristics from the dominant majority group. For Blauner (1972), they represent a "mixed type of enclave or middleman minorities," voluntary immigrants who often bring economic resources, establish economic niches, and serve as "colonized" minorities (e.g., Korean grocers) or play a specialized role in the broader economy (e.g., Chinese restaurants and laundries or Mexican gardeners and farmworkers). Finally, there is consensus among race relations theorists that for all minority groups, the differentials of economic and political power and the barriers to upward mobility are pronounced and exacerbated for groups identifiable by racial and selected cultural or linguistic difference (Ogbu, 1987a). Race and ethnicity serve, then, as an additional significant variable in accounting for differential treatment and related educational, social, and economic status.

This social theory perspective has spawned various analyses of inequity that examine social structures of schools and their related social networks. Stanton-Salazar (1997) presents such an analysis of social support networks and help-seeking experiences of low-income Mexican-origin adolescents from immigrant families. Using network survey data and excerpts from transcribed interviews, he documents the many constraints and social forces inside and outside schools that prevent these youths from constructing the kinds of social networks that provide access to important forms of social support (e.g., academic assistance, career decision making, emotional support, and crisis intervention). Special attention is paid to those forms of support that privileged youth normally receive and that Hispanic working-class youth in particular do not (e.g., expert guidance pertaining to college opportunities). Among the many constraints studied, specifically high was the lack of trust and rapport with various significant others (e.g., teachers and counselors). Even though teachers and counselors indicate that they are available to serve all students, they organize their work in ways that exclude Hispanic students. The analysis also reveals how some working-class Hispanic youths become exceptional cases, "weaving social webs" that promote persistence in school as well as forms of resiliency. In such cases, the access to and utilization of external social resources—

outside of one's own intellectual, linguistic, and cultural "capital" in shaping young people's life chances—become illuminated.

Because the main focus of the study was Hispanics, it begins to deliver an explicit examination of how class, race, and ethnic forces influence the development of resources in the form of social networks and how such resources can either mediate or obstruct the "social reproduction" of inequality in society. Unlike the approach taken in most of the research on social and interpersonal networks, this analysis provides a view of social inequality in school- and community-based resources. In short, being Hispanic in this school and community was disadvantageous in the ways that the individual student was incapable of achieving success.

Other social researchers have also attempted to understand the link between social and educational inequality by focusing directly on issues of race and ethnicity in the United States. In a speech in 1998, President Bill Clinton initiated the most recent national "dialogue" regarding this issue:

> What do I really hope we will achieve as a country? If we do nothing more than talk, it will be interesting but it won't be enough. If we do nothing more than propose disconnected acts of policy, it would be helpful, but it won't be enough. But if ten years from now people can look back and see that this year of honest dialogue and concerted action helped to lift the heavy burden of race from our children's future, we will have given a precious gift to America.

Essentially, the president seemed to be seeking a change in consciousness, a "new thinking," concerning one's relations with others to create new conceptualizations of race in the United States and to generate ways to come to terms with the changing demographics of the nation. This national effort seems to make clear that addressing the role of race is a precondition to the types of change needed in this country.

In considering explicit theories of the importance of race, Delgado (1995) described features of a Critical Race Theory (CRT). Critical Race Theory begins with one basic insight: Racism is normal, not aberrant, in American society. Formal equality can do little about the business-as-usual forms of racism that people of color confront every day and that account for much misery, alienation, and despair. Critical Race Theory's challenge to racial oppression and the status quo sometimes takes the form of storytelling, in which writers analyze the myths, presuppositions, and received wisdom that makes up the common culture about race and that invariably render Hispanics, African American, American Indians, and other minorities one-down (Delpit, 1988; Renato, 1993; Ladson-Billings and Tate, 1995; Vizenor, 1998).

Moreover, CRT proposes an analysis of "interest-convergence." Developed by Derrick Bell (1980c), this idea holds that white elites will tolerate or encourage racial and ethnic advances only when they also promote white self-interest. President Clinton had hopes that as the nation entered the 21st century, the attention on blacks and other minorities in America would be different than they were at the beginning of the 20th. Unfortunately, as Cornel West (1999) argues, for nearly a century, since the writings of W. E. B. DuBois, the nation confines discussion about race in American to the "problems" that people of color pose for society, meaning the white majority, rather than consider what this way of viewing people of color reveals about us as a nation. National discussions, with different spins and various twists, have recently begun to place a particularly negative tone on black, Hispanic, Asian, and white relations. Race and ethnicity seem to continue to drive us apart, but they do so, conclude the race theorists, to the disadvantage of nonwhites and to the advantage of whites. Conclusions are recognizing not to ignore race.

Implications for Education

This set of theories relies on socially constructed disadvantages and takes on special significance for schooling in the United States. At one level, it means that the society as a whole must come to understand the social constructions that may lead academic underachievement for Hispanic students. The curriculum must therefore take on a special mission for all students to engage in learning about this social construction. In essence, we are all responsible for the social construction of these inequities and therefore similarly responsible for their deconstruction (Banks, 1994). But of special significance is the direct engagement of the "disadvantaged" in understanding their own circumstances, the reasons for those circumstances, and the critical analysis of how they might overcome such circumstances (Aronowitz and Giroux, 1991). It becomes incumbent on educational institutions to embrace a "critical pedagogy" (Giroux, 1992) that seeks to equip those disadvantaged by existing social structures and organizations with the intellectual means to remove those encumbrances.

THE HISPANIC STUDENT AS A LEARNER

Placing an emphasis on the student as learner and on schools as the major instrument of imparting learning led the American Psychological Association (APA) to construct a portrait of psychological variables that enhance the teaching and learning enterprise within educational settings (Lambert and McCombs, 1998). Identified as a blueprint for "learner-centered schools," the APA made clear that psychological research in the field of human development, cognition, social development, and specifically teaching and learning could be organized in a set of constructs that could be highly useful in reforming the learning environments of schools. At the center of this set of psychological underpinnings were five universal "theoretical" propositions about the learning process:

1. Learning progresses through various common stages of development influenced by inherited and experiential factors—young children and not just "young" adults learn differently, and all learners come equipped to learn even though unique individual experiences determine the course of that learning.
2. One's existing knowledge serves as a foundation of all future learning by guiding organization and representations and by serving as a basis of association with new information—what we already know and how we know it determines how we learn from new experiences.
3. The ability to reflect on and control one's thoughts and activities is essential—the ability to self-regulate new experiences and to "think about" the significance of those activities given what one already knows are critical for learning.
4. Motivational factors, including reasons for learning and achieving personal goals along with the intrinsic motivational characteristics of learning tasks themselves, play a substantial role in the learning process—individual interests for learning coupled with the nature of the teaching activity are critical.
5. Learning is both a social and an individually constructed enterprise—the learner is engaged in learning within socially constructed and individual contexts that are critical in the learning process. (adapted from Alexander and Murphy, 1998, 5–20)

These conceptual universals further delineate into a set of principles that might guide instruction that is learner centered (table 9.1). These principles, considered theoretical universals based on our best understanding of the psychological literature regarding learning, have much to offer those educators who serve Hispanic students. Evident in this psychological landscape is the importance of previous experience, the motivational attributes of learning activities, and the social context of learning. Stretching beyond the individual potential and aptitude to learn, this recent psychological learning theory places great weight on the "roots" of the learner and how those "rooting" experiences in social contexts organize and embed social and cultural learning opportunities. This theory suggests strongly that new learning will best benefit from a recognition of the previous set of learning contexts and the personal beliefs, motivational structures, and "filters" acquired.

In other words, psychological theory has discovered that the cultural at-

Table 9.1   American Psychological Association's Learning-Centered Psychological Principles.

Principle 1: The nature of the learning process. Learning is a natural process of pursuing personally meaningful goals, and it is active, volitional, and internally mediated; it is a process of discovering and constructing meaning from information and experience, filtered through the learner's unique perceptions, thought and feelings.

Principle 2: Goals of the learning process. The learner seeks to create meaningful, coherent representations of knowledge regardless of the quantity and quality of data available.

Principle 3: The construction of knowledge. The learner links new information with existing and future-oriented knowledge in uniquely meaningful ways.

Principle 4: Higher-order thinking: Higher order strategies for "thinking about thinking"—for overseeing and monitoring mental operations—facilitate creative and critical thinking and the development of expertise.

Principle 5: Motivational influences on learning. The depth and breadth of information processed, and what and how much is learned and remembered, are influenced by (a) self-awareness and beliefs about personal control, and ability; (b) clarity and saliency of personal values, interests, and goals; (c) personal expectations for success or failure; (d) affect, emotion, and general states of mind; and (e) the resulting motivation to learn.

Principle 6: Intrinsic motivation to learn. Individuals are naturally curious and enjoy learning, but intense negative cognitions and emotions (e.g., feeling insecure, worrying about failure, being self-conscious or shy, and fearing corporal punishment, ridicule, or stigmatizing labels) thwart this enthusiasm.

Principle 7: Characteristics of motivation-enhancing learning tasks. Curiosity, creativity, and higher-order thinking stimulated by relevant, authentic learning tasks of optimal difficulty and novelty for each student.

Principle 8: Development constraints and opportunities. Individuals progress through states of physical, intellectual, emotional, and social development that are a function of unique genetic and environmental factors.

Principle 9: Social and cultural diversity. Learning is facilitated by social interactions and communication with others in flexible, diverse (in age, culture, family background, etc.), and adaptive instructional settings.

Principle 10: Social acceptance, self-esteem, and learning. Learning and self-esteem are heightened when individuals are in respectful and caring relationships with others that see their potential, genuinely appreciate their unique talents, and accept them as individuals.

Principle 11: Individual differences in learning. Although basic principles of learning, motivation, and effective instruction apply to all learners (regardless of ethnicity, race, gender, physical ability, religion, or socioeconomic status), learners have different capabilities and preferences for learning mode and strategies. These differences are a function of environment (what is learned and communicated in different cultures or other social groups) and heredity (what occurs naturally as a function of genes).

Principle 12: Cognitive filters. Personal beliefs, thoughts, and understandings resulting from prior learning and interpretations become the individual basis for constructing reality and interpreting life experience.

Source: Alexander & Murphy (1998)

tributes of the learner are critical ingredients of the teaching and learning formula. As Saxe (1996) concluded, a student's intellectual adaptations relate to the cultural practices in which they were and are participants. In more recent formulations of cognitive development, such development and learning are imbued directly by the social experiences in which the student is embedded, previous to as well as inside and outside schools. From this theoretical perspective, there is an assumption that all knowledge is constructed by either innate cognitive structures or those cognitive structures that are themselves products of continued construction (Noddings, 1973; Davis, Maher, and Noddings, 1990; Cole, 1995). Noddings (1996) states the following:

1. All knowledge is constructed.
2. There exist cognitive structures that are activated in the process of construction.
3. Cognitive structures are under continual development.
4. Purposive activity induces transformation of existing cognitive structures.
5. The environment presses the organism to adapt.

Learning is best described in the traditions of this approach as requiring constructions, not passive reception of new information. More directly, Vygotsky (1956) has provided a conceptual framework related to teaching and learning. In his constructivist theory, Vygotsky identified the developmental level of a child by what the child can do unassisted. Moreover, what the child can do with assistance is called the "zone of proximal development" (ZPD). It is in this zone that teaching is important. Vygotsky (1956) has indicated that effective teaching "awakens and rouses to life those functions that are in the stage of maturing, which lie in the zone of proximal development" (278). Teaching, in this theoretical view, is perceived as assisted performance, thus making it a highly social endeavor embedding the learner's cultural surroundings that serve as the "roots" of future development and learning. Learning is performance achieved through assistance.

Viewing the learner as an active participant engaged in a set of socially organized learning opportunities, constructing and not just imbibing new knowledge, places a premium on understanding what the learner is. Important in that understanding is the information regarding the previous learning opportunities of that individual, the social nature of those opportunities, and the products of that previous learning. In planning for future learning, all this information must be taken into consideration. As the title of this book suggests, enhanced learning opportunities for Hispanics must consider these culturally determined "roots" if we are to organize instructional settings that will result in high performance—the educational "wings" of the student.

HISPANICS AND INSTRUCTION

Coupled with this new psychological perspective of the Hispanic learner, it is important to turn now to more direct theories of instruction that recognize this perspective regarding the Hispanic learner. Tharp and Gallimore (1988), in their research related to the schooling of Hawaiian native children, proposed in a formal way the interconnections between the culture of home and the culture of schooling. Put simply, they asked about the significance of cultural membership for the education of children: Are there forms of education that are specifically suited for the education of different cultures? Garcia (1999) has proposed a theoretical answer to this question: The more compatible the organization of instruction mirrors the organization of instruction in the home, the more likely school can enhance learning for students. (Keep in mind that schools have been operating quite readily in the opposite mode as well by sending with the student the types of "homework" that are typified by the instructional activities of the classroom—these might be perceived as conscious efforts to make the home like the school.)

Such compatibility theories argue against the notion that there are learning universals that can be prescriptively applied to members of any cultural group with the same learning outcomes. The extreme of the compatibility theory would suggest that each individual is a "culture" unto him- or herself and that instruction must be tailored to that unique culture. Placed somewhere in between these two extreme theoretical alternatives is a theoretical middle ground. That perspective recognizes the existence of universal principles—much like those of the APA discussed earlier in this chapter—that themselves make clear the interrelationship of the individual learner as a product of culture(s) and the significant relevance of that culture(s) to the instructional enterprise.

A RESPONSIVE PEDAGOGY

In broader theoretical terms, allow me to introduce the foundations for this new thinking. Embedded in this new perspective for Hispanic students are the understandings that language, culture, and their accompanying values are constructed in the home and community environments, that children come to school with some constructed knowledge about many things, and that children's development and learning is best understood as the interaction of previous and present linguistic, sociocultural, and cognitive constructions. An appropriate perspective of learning for Hispanic students, then, is one that recognizes that learning becomes enhanced when it occurs in contexts that are socioculturally, linguistically, and cognitively meaningful for the learner—they bridge previous "constructions" to present "constructions."

Such meaningful events, however, are not generally accessible to Hispanic children without critical adaptations to the generally observed instructional activity within today's schools. Those schooling practices that contribute to the academic vulnerability of this student population and that tend to dramatize the lack of fit between the student and the school experiences are reflected in the monolithic culture transmitted by the schools in the forms of pedagogy, curricula, instruction, classroom configuration, and language. Such practices include the systematic exclusion of the students' histories, language, experience, and values from classroom curricula and activities; the use of "tracking," which limits access to academic courses; learning environments that do not foster academic development and socialization and perception of self as a competent learner; and limited opportunities to engage in developmentally and culturally appropriate learning that are outside teacher-led instruction.

The implication of this rethinking has profound effects for the teaching/ learning enterprise related to Hispanic students. This new responsive pedagogy is one that redefines the classroom as a community of learners in which speakers, readers, and writers come together to define and redefine the meaning of the academic experience. It might be described as a pedagogy of empowerment, as cultural learning, or as a cultural adaptation of instruction that provides optimal instructional assistance/guidance. A responsive pedagogy presupposes the respect and integration of the students' values, beliefs, histories, and experiences and recognizes the active role that students must play in the learning process. However, this responsive pedagogy expands students' knowledge beyond their own immediate experiences while using those experiences as a sound foundation for appropriating new knowledge. For many Hispanic students, this includes the utilization of the native language and/or bilingual abilities that are a substantive part of a well-functioning social network in which knowledge is embedded.

Furthermore, a responsive pedagogy for academic learning requires a redefinition of the instructor's role. Instructors must become familiar with the cognitive, social, and cultural dimensions of learning. They need to recognize the ways in which diversity of instruction, assessment, and evaluation affect learning. They should become more aware of the classroom curriculum, its purpose, and the degree of its implementation. The configuration of the classroom environment and the nature of interaction of students with teachers and students are of significance. Further, instructors must recognize that the acquisition of academic content also requires helping students display their knowledge in ways that suggest that they are competent as learners and language users. Analysis of these dimensions will underscore the potential for equipping the classroom for the particularly sensitive task of ensuring student success with Hispanic students.

In addition, teachers must destroy preconceived myths about learning processes and the potentially underprepared student and, in particular, myths about those who come from lower socioeconomic households and/ or homes in which English is not the primary language. For those embracing this new idea of responsive pedagogy, new educational horizons for themselves and their students are not only possible but also inevitable. Table 9.2 summarizes these important dimensions of a responsive pedagogy within a responsive learning community. This recasting, theoretically, of education for Hispanics lays a distinct and important shift in understanding the future education for this population of students.

Table 9.2   Conceptual Dimensions of a Responsive Pedagogy: Addressing Cultural and Linguistic Diversity in Responsive Learning Communities

Schoolwide Practices

- A vision defined by the acceptance and valuing of diversity—Americanization is NOT the goal
- Professional development characterized by collaboration, flexibility, and continuity with a focus on teaching, learning, and student achievement
- Elimination (gradual or immediate) of policies that seek to categorize diverse students thereby rendering their educational experiences as inferior or limiting for further academic learning
- Reflection of and connection to community—particularly with the families of the students attending the school

Teacher Practices

- Bilingual/bicultural skills and awareness
- High expectations of diverse students
- Treatment of diversity as an asset to the classroom
- Ongoing professional development on issues of cultural and linguistic diversity and practices that are most effective
- Basis of curriculum development to address cultural and linguistic diversity:
  1. Attention to and integration of home culture/practices
  2. Focus on maximizing student interactions across categories of Spanish and English proficiency and academic performance
  3. Focus on language development through meaningful interactions and communications

Just as there are certain elements of schoolwide and classroom practices that increase the likelihood that Hispanic students can be academically successful, the theoretical perspective articulated here provides considerable guidance in the particular questions that can serve as a starting point for developing useful strategies for schools that serve Hispanics:

- What is the school vision and mission? How are issues of language, culture, and diversity addressed in these? How are these articulated with teachers, students, district and school administrators, policy bodies, and parents?
- How is language, culture, and student diversity incorporated into the curriculum, instruction, and assessment practices?
- What are the resources, experiences, and structures that contribute to the professional development of the school community? How are these related to student achievement?
- How do power relationships in society and the educational and local communities get embedded in the school?
- What are the prevailing norms and underlying beliefs that shape the roles, expectations, and standards? How do these change as schools create and implement new policies and practices aimed at developing responsive learning communities?

A RESPONSIVE RESEARCH AGENDA

Olsen (1997), Romo and Falbo (1996), and Valdés (1996, 1998) have recently paved the way for a new research agenda that can be very useful for understanding and acting on the educational circumstances of Hispanic students. Each of these colleagues has started with a set of acknowledged presuppositions regarding their research:

1. Their "subjects" live in complex worlds that they inhabit; one of those is the school, and others are made up of families, neighborhoods, and other social institutions (e.g., private, government, religious, and peer oriented).
2. These same subjects are directly and indirectly influenced by their past experience in these and other organizations and the present action of various social entities.
3. Understanding the student and the social institutions and processes that influence the student requires the "tracking" of the perceptions, interactions, and changes of the student and the institutions over a reasonable period.

Olsen spent three years investigating the educational circumstances of recently arrived immigrant students in California. She did so by visiting the schools, homes, and communities of these students. She observed the students in those environments, asked the students about those environments, and included an analysis of information from the institutions and the individuals who inhabited those social entities—parents, teachers, other students, community members' school administrators, and so on (Olsen, 1997). Romo and Falbo (1996) followed the same research agenda in providing an in-depth analysis of some 100 Hispanic students in a Texas high school over the life of the student in that high school. Valdés (1996) followed a set of Hispanic immigrant families and their students/children as they engaged with schools and other social institution in the United States for many years.

We need to follow the guidance of these researchers. This is not to say those snapshot analyses of Hispanic students individually or collectively are not worthwhile. Rather, it is to suggest that the complexity of student circumstances, coupled with their individual navigation through a diverse and complex set of social circumstance, each changing over time, provides us with a much more in-depth, theoretical, and practice-rich understanding of the student.

Considering what we now know about the lives of Hispanic students, two issues seem paramount in a new research agenda: "what works best for who and why" and "maintenance of effects." Recommended as the basis of organizing future research, these two issues are addressed more specifically in the following critical questions:

1. Which education practices maximize benefits for Hispanic children and families with different characteristics under what types of circumstances? Why?
2. Are gains sustained for children and families after the education experience?

Both questions take into account the present conditions emerging in educational research strategies. The focus is on producing a knowledge base that can provide a foundation for ongoing program improvement and for upgrading quality within educational partners, both inside and outside of schools. It is the lack of answers to these two questions that places educational services to Hispanic students in jeopardy of haphazard and highly politicized policy initiatives, such as California's Proposition 227.

The first question acknowledges the diversity and related understanding of the required flexibility of educational interventions for Hispanics. Average outcomes of average programs, which were the aim of an earlier generation of studies, pose the risk of misleading findings and fail to provide the information needed to tailor services to identifiable subgroups of children and families. Developing strategies must respond to the different information needs that support quality improvements and that will achieve the hoped-for societal benefits in moving toward highly specific educational reforms. Put simply, what works in El Paso may not work in Los Angeles, New York City, or Miami. We need not only "effective" or generic "best practices" but also rich contextual information about the interventions and the students served by those interventions. The question Why? implicates the need for an intellectual/theoretical foundation for the research as that research intersects with practices in the field. We need a set of theories or constructs that help us better understand why some interventions work and others do not for the diverse populations being served. Such theories/constructs allow us more readily to adapt new interventions that are different than those we have studied.

The second question reflects issues that have come to the fore in the policy and research communities as a result of findings of socially meaningful, lasting gains for children who have participated in educational programs. For example, Wong-Fillmore (1991) found that English emphasis programs for Hispanic students generated significant intergeneration communication gaps that negatively affected children, parents, and grandparents. Attention to this type of social consequence has been sorely absent. Moreover, attention directed to issues related to lasting effects should not be interpreted to imply that the bilingual education experience, by itself, would necessarily be responsible for producing long-term benefits. On the contrary, the most plausible scenario is that the long-term outcomes are a product of the combined influences of the schooling experience, influences in the family, and follow-up actions of other community agencies that serve to extend or attenuate the effects of schooling efforts.

Even keeping in mind these critical questions and the importance of addressing them in new research with Hispanic students, it is important to realize that policy- and practice-related research does require clarity in causal inference. In such research, it is the impact of policies and practices that are examined: Did this or that intervention work? Reforms, revisions, and add-ons to policies and practices are implemented to make a difference. While much of social science can avoid the troubled issues of the direction of causal effects, "reforms" or "ameliorative programs" cannot. Policy and practice research and, in particular, program evaluation for Hispanic students have a commitment to causal inference and a need to optimize the clarity of the inference. Description is not enough.

Unfortunately, there is a general perception that most of the evaluations of government programs are low-quality products of dubious value (August and Hakuta, 1997). This perception is shared both by those applied scientists in the universities who attempt to use this research in cumulative scholarship and by those federal administrators whose policy choices are supposed to be guided by it.

Lastly, honesty and integrity in reporting results must be directly reinforced. The ancient tyrant executed the messenger who brought bad news. At every level in the research process, the present system biases the data in the same way. At the level of the local program, participants and staff evaluations and refunding should be totally separated. In particular, it should clear that reporting on failures and imperfections will not jeopardize future funding. Policy- and practice-relevant research instruments should not be mixed with report forms used for managerial control, where "bias" is impossible to avoid. Researchers and program alternative implementers should not be punished (nor should their receipt of future contract and grants be jeopardized) by honest reporting of failed implementations, lack of effects, and other factors. In other words, our future research agenda should be guided by research with varied populations in varied places with a direct link in learning from both successes and failures. This is not what is done in the present research world, particularly with research related to Hispanic students.

CONCLUSION

An optimal learning community for Hispanic student populations recognizes that academic learning has its roots in both out-of-school and in-school processes. When diversity is perceived and acted on as a resource for teaching and learning instead of a problem, there is a focus on what students bring to the process that generates an asset-oriented approach rather than a deficit-assessment approach. Within this knowledge-driven, responsive, and engaging learning environment, previous knowledge is seen as a tool for acquiring and using new knowledge.

In addition, the search for general principles of learning that will work for all students must be redirected. This redirection considers a search for and documentation of particular implementations of general and nongeneral principles of teaching and learning that serve a diverse set of environments in and out of school. This mission requires an understanding of how individuals with diverse sets of experiences, packaged individually into cultures, make meaning, communicate that meaning, and extend that meaning, particularly in social contexts we call schools. Such a mission requires in-depth treatment of the processes associated with producing diversity, issues of socialization in and out of schools, coupled with a clear examination of how such understanding is actually transformed into schools and broader communities to promote high achievement as well as a clear understanding that some aspects of the social fabric in which students reside may serve to directly or indirectly impede academic success. It is also important to indicate that promoting achievement for Hispanic students can beneficially affect the performance of all students. Although the tenets of a theory of responsive pedagogy may have focused here on the Hispanic student, they can be seen as valuable contributions to any educational treatment devised and implemented for any individual or group of students.

10

Of "Raíces y Alas"

THE PROBLEM WITH METAPHORS

This book has at its core the metaphorical notion that the education of Hispanics in this country is all about understanding and acting on their linguistic and cultural attributes—their *raíces*—in ways that can lead to educational success—develop their academic *alas*. I need to admit that no metaphor is perfect in conveying meaning. Absent in these metaphorical efforts related to this topic is the ambiguity of the metaphorical ingredients: What raíces? All raíces? Is there something particularly significant in Hispanic raíces? What alas—academic, social, economic?

I admit that I have not conquered the lack of precision and overall ambiguities inherent in this "raíces y alas" metaphor. Perhaps one should not expect that I would have. What I hope I have done is make important in a very few words—in an image, metaphorically—the ingredients that help one understand the circumstances of the U.S. Hispanic students, why they are where they are, and what we might do to enhance their future educational outcomes. Let me also admit that the metaphor can be critiqued even in its best moments of clarity.

On one end of the criticism is a host of voices that insist that attending to Hispanic raíces stereotypes a very heterogeneous population while at the same time promoting multiculturalism and thwarting social assimilation—creating ethnic enclaves. These manifestations of ethnic pride, the

241

argument goes, hide dangerous undercurrents of discrimination, privilege, social and economic fragmentation, and resegregation that can easily erode the American way of life (Chavez, 1991; Schlesinger, 1992; Unz, 1998). Such "tribalization," a term considered quite negative since the era of European colonization in which "tribes" were consider uncivilized, keeps the United States from achieving a harmonious society in which racial, linguistic, and ethnic differences are of no personal or social consequence. In such a world, equity in education and social and economic well-being are independent of these physical/cultural attributes.

On the other side of this issue, promoters of a strong multiculturalism philosophy contend that insistence on the development of English-language competency for Hispanics, combined with "adding" other mainstream cultural attributes, undermines the goals of cultural maintenance and leads to rapid assimilation and debilitating cultural loss (Trueba, 1999). Under an "additive" model, there is the assumption that the nation "wants" to be united, particularly in the face of long-standing inequity in schools, voting, political representation, and economic well-being. Inequities that could have been rectified in the country's history still exist and may even be growing in some sectors. Moreover, for Hispanics in particular, it is only a matter of time before the results of the demographic "reconquest" will provide political and economic power. California specifically and the Southwest and, to some extent, the Southeast are undergoing rapid levels of "Hispanicization." The United States is undeniably linked economically to the future "American common market," much like European countries are now linked economically, socially, and culturally in the European Common Market. This argument concludes that the route to equality in U.S. society is not surrendering one's Hispanic cultural and linguistic heritage but, rather, strengthening it in ways that help counter the relentless inequalities thrust on Hispanic ethnic, racial, and linguistic minorities, themselves soon to become majorities. In other words, the Hispanic cultural "meek" will not inherit the earth. The U.S. motto—*e pluribus Unum* (out of many, one)—needs to be changed to *Unum e multis* (one with many).

These philosophical positions and the related disagreements associated with these positions are long-standing and will likely continue. I am certain that we will not soon resolve this assimilationist-versus-multiculturalist debate. What we may need to do is develop a framework that allows us to engage in discussions about individual and group differences that minimize an emphasis on negative consequences for any individual and for any group.

With some attention to this debate, what I have attempted to make evident in this book are the realities of what we know and how what we know can elucidate our actions with regard to the growing and significant population of Hispanic students in this country. We do know so much more now about the education of these students then we ever did. You need only run a computer search of education literature and materials related to key words like "Hispanic," "Mexican American," "Chicano," "Cuban American," "Puerto Rican," "Latino," and so on. I recall when I did such a search in 1976 in preparation for the writing of my first book, I found some 100 or so references. In preparation for this book, I stopped looking after finding over 3,000 references. National, statewide, and local attention to the educational circumstances of Hispanic students demonstrates unequivocally that education programs can and do successfully fulfill their mission for Hispanic student educational success. They do so in rural and urban locals, in early childhood and K–12 sectors, and in institutions of higher education and with students who represent the heterogeneity and homogeneity of the "Hispanic" label. Is there any "one way" that works? No, local variety in methodology is the rule in these programs. Are there "good" programs" and "not-so-good" programs? Yes, but the evidence is clear: Programs can and do work. What I have attempted to communicate are the attributes that make them work in all their many ways. And overwhelmingly, these programs consistently attend to and are responsive to the raíces of these students while at the same time providing the direct opportunities to develop their educational alas. The metaphor seems to be appropriate.

PUBLIC POLICY IMPLICATIONS

Because I have served for four years as a member of a local board of education and served for two years as a political appointee and senior officer in the U.S. Department of Education, I can assure you that policymaking and its implementation cannot be ignored. Whether as a policymaker in these two positions, an "expert witness" in national, state, and local litigation, or as a critic of policy as an applied researcher, public policy has and will continue to have a meaningful influence on the future educational success of Hispanic students. The demographic trends that so vividly proclaim the phenomenal growth of Hispanic families and students, coupled with the continued "conflict" in our society between majorities and minorities, between "haves" and "have-nots," ensure that public policy will take on a particularly important forum for debate and action. Three specific issues seem of primary relevance in this public policy arena for Hispanics in the new millennium: affirmative action, bilingual education, and immigration reform.

Affirmative Action

This federal government program, initiated during the Nixon administration, was intended to increase access of underrepresented minorities and women in a variety of sectors but had a direct target of providing equal educational opportunity in higher education. After two decades of uneven and at times hotly contested implementation, a backlash of major proportions developed in the late 1980s fueled by the notion that such policies were themselves highly discriminatory and produced "reverse discrimination" against whites. In 1995, the University of California Board of Regents adopted SP-1, eliminating the use of race, gender, and ethnic status as variables that could be taken into consideration in student admission to the University of California's nine campuses. Subsequently, in 1996 California voters passed Proposition 209, which directly outlawed affirmative action in public education, employment, and contracting. After a year of legal challenges, the U.S. Supreme Court, on November 3, 1997, refused to hear an implementation appeal, leaving Proposition 209 well entrenched as new law in California. In similar Supreme Court action in a related affirmative action case in Texas, *Hopwood v. University of Texas at Austin,* the court directed the University of Texas system to dismantle scholarship and admissions procedures that included the use of race, ethnicity, and gender. In 1998, the voters of the state of Washington approved an anti–affirmative action initiative, while other states, including Arizona and Oregon, are considering such initiatives. Even further adjudication of high school affirmative action programs, like those at historically highly regarded Latin High School in Boston that reserved places for underrepresented minorities, has eroded efforts to ensure K–12 preparation opportunities for Hispanics.

Implementation of Proposition 209 has already had adverse effects on Hispanics in California. At a time when Hispanic high school graduation is actually on the rise in the state, fewer Hispanics are applying to, being admitted to, and attending the University of California. This is particularly the case at the three "flagship" campuses at Berkeley, Los Angeles, and San Diego. The net effect of this policy is that of severely limiting access to highly competitive undergraduate as well as critically important professional programs in law, medicine, and the sciences—higher-education domains in which Hispanics are sorely underrepresented. These programs are acknowledged as producing the majority of future professionals and leaders in the state. Hispanics are now systematically excluded from such opportunities, which were available under affirmative action policies.

Beyond Affirmative Action

Public policy that attempts to achieve and surpass the goals of affirmative action is critical for Hispanics. In Texas and California, legal challenges continue and will be need to be exhaustive in efforts to overturn Proposition 209 and *Hopwood*. The State of Texas, with the strong leadership and bipartisan legislative action, has taken steps to address this public policy concern at the level of university admission. In 1997, the Democratically controlled state legislature and a Republican governor enacted new locally driven policies regarding the admission of high school graduates into the state's two university systems. In this new articulation of admissions policy, any student graduating from any Texas high school in the upper 10 percent of his or her class—determined by cumulative grade-point average—is automatically admitted into the system. These students are "guaranteed" a place in the Texas university of choice. The immediate effects of this policy have been to make more Hispanic and other underrepresented high school graduates immediately university eligible. In addition, the policy has staved off predictions that the elimination of affirmative action in Texas as a result of the *Hopwood* decision would result in lower application, admission, and attendance of Hispanic students at the University of Texas at Austin. These have remained at pre-*Hopwood* levels. Moreover, it is important to point out that this policy has not had a negative influence on the application, admission, or attendance of white students.

The University of California is considering implementing a similar policy. That initiative, known commonly as the "4 percent solution" after Texas's "10 percent solution," identifies all high school juniors in the top 4 percent of their graduating class as automatically eligible for the University of California. Coupled with this statewide initiative, each campus has revised and is continuing to revise specific admissions criteria to take into consideration factors that would consider an individual student's effort, opportunity, and achievement in the local high school context. This policy, coupled with the limited use of standardized test scores on the SAT or ACT in the admissions process, is seen as an effort to recognize and respond to the goal of ensuring that access to higher education is not denied to underrepresented students.

To the credit of the California legislature and the higher-education systems in the state, new efforts are engaging university faculty's students and programs with educational reform efforts in the K–12 sector. These outreach efforts have spawned a new consciousness that the educational system in this country should be perceived as "all one system" instead of individual and independent sectors, one system sending students to another in some hierarchical manner. In 1998, the University of California system received a $38 million augmentation to its budget for these K–12 and intersegmental outreach efforts with the contingency of matching these funds with other nonuniversity resources.

Although these policy initiatives are steps in the right direction, they are efforts that treat the severe underachievement and underrepresentation of Hispanics only in ways that either hold the line in the present absence of affirmative action or potentially lay the foundation for longer-term solutions to these educational dilemmas for Hispanics. They in no way offer immediate relief, nor are they removed from the political backlash of affirmative action and related arguments that they are no more than a means to subvert present anti–affirmative action laws and court judgments and promote white "reverse discrimination." Bowen and Bok's (1998) longitudinal study in their recent book *The Shape of the River* makes a very forceful case regarding the benefits of affirmative action for African Americans. These students, admitted into prestigious four-year universities, excelled within those universities and in the professions that they pursued on graduation, many times filling significant leadership roles within their profession, the African American community, and the community at large. Although such an analysis is absent for Hispanics, it seems reasonable to suggest that similar positive outcomes exist. We can expect more public policy attention to these matters of race, ethnicity, and access.

Bilingual Education

Bilingual education, another recent controversial issue in public education, often divides Hispanics and non-Hispanics and also exposes major ideological differences within the Hispanic/Latino population (Chavez, 1995a; Garcia, 1999). Both proponents and opponents of bilingual education have found research to support their positions, although recent studies generally conclude that, over the long term, Spanish-speaking children placed in bilingual programs in the early elementary grades perform equally or better than children not placed in these programs (Valencia, 1994; Garcia and Gonzalez, 1995; August and Hakutu, 1997; Garcia, 1999).

Since one of eight children entering public schools in California in 1990 had limited English proficiency, conflicts over bilingual programs have come to symbolize more than differences in educational philosophy. Rather, they represent fundamental differences in perspectives on cultural diversity and access to equal educational opportunities through our tax-supported public educational system. Thus, as other linguistic minorities increase in the state's population, this debate over bilingual education has the potential to exacerbate ethnic and racial tensions, particularly between whites and Asians (11 percent of California students are Asian) and between Hispanics and non-Hispanics.

In addition, the issue of bilingual programs versus English immersion programs has become a lightning rod for groups that advocate declaring English the official language of the United States and eliminating all other languages—in the workplace, on election ballots, on consumer products, on street signs, and more. By 1995, 23 states had passed laws making English the official state language, but in April 1998, the Arizona Supreme Court struck down the state's law mandating that state and local government business be conducted in English.

In the November 1996 local elections, the voters of Orange County, California, approved an advisory measure supporting a school district decision to eliminate bilingual education in their schools. This measure was forerunner of Proposition 227, an initiative outlawing most forms of bilingual education and mandating one year of English-language classes for the state's 1.4 million non-English-speaking students. California voters passed this proposition in the June 1998 statewide election primaries by a margin of 61 to 39 percent. Although some polls had predicted that a majority of Latinos would support this measure, the final vote indicated that more than 60 percent of Latinos had voted against dismantling bilingual education programs, as they considered it detrimental to their children's educational success.

In a set of interesting developments, Arizona is gearing up for a Proposition 227 campaign, while Texas and Florida are making policy efforts to maximize Spanish/English bilingualism for all students. In California, legal assaults on the implementation of 227 continue and have produced court judgments in several large school districts, such as San Jose and San Francisco, that permit the continuation of bilingual education programs while blocking the implementation of Proposition 227. The bilingual education debate is likely to continue into the 21st century without any clear resolution. Such a debate will be carried out in national, state, and local forums, and, however addressed at the policy level, it will continue to significantly impact Hispanic students.

Immigration Reform

National efforts to reform immigration policies, which traditionally have been under the exclusive jurisdiction of the federal government, are continuing at all policy levels and will continue to have a direct effect on Hispanics. With the passage of Proposition 187 in 1994, the voters of California overwhelmingly supported (59 percent) the denial of basic social services, health care, and public education to undocumented ("illegal") immigrants as a way to discourage further influxes from Mexico and Central America.

Despite claims that these undocumented immigrants take jobs from native-born workers, do not pay their fair share in taxes, and cost the state's economy more than they contribute, researchers at both the Rand Corporation and the Urban Institute (Passell, 1994) point out that these immigrants take unskilled and service jobs that native-born workers reject, pay their proportionate share of taxes, create new jobs, and contribute more to the state economy than they cost the state in services (Fierman, 1994). As Suarez-Orozco (1996) suggests, Proposition 187 symbolizes ambivalence about immigrants, who have become the scapegoats of the economic, demographic, and cultural anxieties created by the uncertainties of rapid technological and social changes in a global economy.

As the battle over benefits for undocumented immigrants heats up again in California, it also will inflame tensions between Hispanics and non-Hispanics because, say a number of scholars, it targets nonwhite immigrants (Armbruster, Geron, and Bonacich, 1995; Smith and Tarallo, 1995). The impact of Propositions 187 and 209 on educational and occupational opportunities for all immigrants of color has energized Hispanics and Asian civil rights organizations, which have launched legal assaults against both propositions. On March 17, 1998, the U.S. District Court for the Central District of California overturned all but one provision of Proposition 187 because it unconstitutionally infringed on the federal government's right to set immigration policy. This initial decision was upheld by the U.S. Supreme Court.

Welfare reform also has been linked to immigration reform, resulting in punitive policies aimed at terminating benefits even to legal immigrants. For example, a group of Hmong refugees recently appealed to the federal government to restore their benefits because many of them had fought against the Communists in Vietnam and had been promised sanctuary and support in the United States. Since many have been unable to find employment and have had difficulties in adjusting to this society, their leaders strongly urged the U.S. government to honor its commitment to them. By denying benefits to legal immigrants, the government may have unintentionally dramatized the inequalities in our current system of multitiered levels of citizenship. These discriminatory policies also have had the unintended effect of arousing the "sleeping giant" of immigrant civil rights organizations that were unable to organize effective coalitions to defeat Proposition 187 or 209 (Armbruster et al., 1995; Smith and Tarallo, 1995). It is important to note, however, that the level of support for both propositions varied within each ethnic minority group, partly reflecting the range of political opinions within the groups and partly reflecting the language used to craft the propositions.

It also is significant that all three recent controversial propositions were crafted and promoted by a few committed individuals or small groups with conservative ideological agendas. They were worded in simplistic yet misleading language that confused many voters. Moreover, none of these propositions was based on reliable research findings, reasoned public debate, or responsible public policy. The unintended consequences of these policies may not be visible or calculable for years to come, as was the case with Proposition 13, California's 1978 antitax initiative that resulted in severe cutbacks in education, social services, public safety, and recreational facilities throughout the state.

Extrapolating from developments these three policy areas, one can predict several major implications for the formulation of future American public policy initiatives addressing racial and ethnic issues that have a direct bearing on Hispanics:

- Racial controversies in the 21st century will transcend the traditional black–white polarity, with conflict continuing between whites and people of color and potential conflicts emerging among ethnic minority groups.
- To make the policy issues politically palatable, they will increasingly be framed as matters of cultural and class differences rather than as racial differences.
- Controversial public policy issues will heighten tensions between whites and Hispanics and result in greater discord, but the tensions also may mobilize Hispanic groups to form more effective coalitions to minimize interethnic competition for social and economic resources.

EDUCATIONAL PRACTICE IMPLICATIONS

Concluding that the educational failure of Hispanic students in the United States was reaching crisis proportions, the U.S. Department of Education assembled a group of "experts" to assess the educational circumstances of Hispanic students, the reasons for these circumstances, and educational practices that were effective and/or promising. I was fortunate to serve on the Hispanic Dropout Project, which guided the work of this endeavor, and to participate in developing its final report: *No More Excuses: The Final Report of the U.S. Hispanic Dropout Project* (U.S. Department of Education, 1998). I can take no credit for the report's eloquent conclusion:

> We submit this report with a sense of urgency and impatience because of the slow pace of improvement. . . . There are dozens of proven programs, replicable programs capable of increasing Hispanic students' achievement, increasing high school completion, and increasing their college going rate . . . why, then the persistent gap in Hispanic student achievement? Many explanations have been offered: student characteristics such as social class, language, and entering achievement levels, especially among recent immigrants; school-based forces such as student retention, ability grouping, and tracking; and, non-school forces such as family and/or neighborhood violence and criminal activity, lack of community-based opportunity, and the historical and social

and political oppression of different ethnic and racial groups. Many of these "reasons" have assumed mythic proportions. They are used to explain a phenomenon that is portrayed as too large and too complex for schools to address. In short, these reasons have become little more than excuses for our schools' and society's failure to act. We as a people, need to say: *No more excuses, the time to act is now.* (U.S. Department of Education, 1998, 61–62)

Coupled with the sense of urgency, this report recommended specific practices that were in need of attention. In an effort to be comprehensive in its practice reform agenda, the report separately addressed recommendations for Hispanic students themselves, their parents and families, their teachers, and the schools in which they are served.

For students, the report highlighted a set of individual responsibilities that could not be ignored if educational success was to be accomplished. Specifically, each student should seek out the assistance and support of someone who understands how schools work and who is willing to take on personal responsibility for ensuring academic progress in school, that is, who can serve as both advocate and mentor. This may require active searches inside and outside the core or extended family into domains that are often out of bounds for these students. Parents and families of Hispanic students also were identified as important in any equation of educational success. Parents need to understand and serve to negotiate their children's education system—they cannot assume that others will do this work. They should participate in the schooling process as partners, not as passive recipients of school policies or practices. That requires monitoring their students educational progress, assisting students to achieve schooling goals, working to minimize antischool and antisocial behavior, and standing ready to take responsibility for their students' actions or inaction. Moreover, Hispanic parents were called on in the report to help their children envision a future and a reasonable means by which to plan for and achieve that future (U.S. Department of Education, 1998).

As other research and synthesis have indicated, teachers were identified in this report as crucial in the intellectual and academic development of Hispanic students. They were urged to do the following:

1. Teach content so that it interests and challenges Hispanic students.
2. Communicate high expectations, respect, and interest in each of their students.
3. Understand the roles of language, race, culture, and gender in schooling.
4. Engage parents and community in the education of their children.
5. Become knowledgeable about and develop strategies to educate Hispanic students and to communicate with their parents.

6. Seek and obtain the professional development needed to engender these attitudes, knowledge bases, and specific instructional skills.

Schools serving Hispanic students were similarly urged to adopt programmatic features and related attributes of effective programs that had been replicated in various school settings:

1. Schools should emphasize the prevention of academic problems. They need to become more aggressive in responding to early warning signs that a student may be doing poorly, losing interest, or in some other way becoming disengaged from school.
2. Schools, especially high schools, need to personalize programs and services that work with Hispanic students.
3. Schools should be restructured to ensure that all students have access to high-quality curricula. They should recognize time, space, and staffing patterns that provide students with the support necessary to achieve.
4. Schools should replicate programs that have proven effective. In addition to using new funding, schools should redeploy existing resources to run these programs.
5. Schools should carefully monitor the effectiveness of what they do for Hispanic students by requiring the desegregation of student progress data and acting on that data to improve or replace failing strategies. (Adapted from U.S. Department of Education, 1998, 35–38)

Such a listing of specific actions has been reinforced by more direct research in one way or another and has been addressed earlier in this book—in particular, the research by Larson and Rumberger (1995a), Rose (1995a), Rossi (1995), Romo and Falbo (1996), Olsen (1997), Soto (1997), Zentella (1997), and Trueba (1999). They are also echoed in other syntheses of research that have considered the linguistic and cultural character of the Hispanic student and particular education practices: the report of the National Research Council regarding the education of language-minority students in 1997 (August and Hakuta, 1997); the report of the National Academy of Sciences regarding the teaching of reading, particularly to non-English-speaking students (National Research Council, 1997); the report of the University of California Task Force on Latino student eligibility (University of California, 1997); and the Report of the National Task Force on Minority High Achievement (College Board, 1999). Over and over again, a similar call to action resonates in these reports and directs educational institutions to take on specific practices that can enhance Hispanic student achievement.

Eugene, Gene, and Geno Recommendations

These summonses to change educational practices in the face of continued Hispanic student underachievement are not to be ignored. However, my own personas have not been silent regarding these calls. I have often been called on to translate such calls in ways that might be helpful to policy-makers, educators, and the public at large. In so doing, I have often called on a set of recommendations that use a particular mnemonic, as in "remember the five R's." Educational programs, initiatives, strategies, and policies that assist Hispanic students are *respectful, responsive, responsible, resourceful,* and *reasonable.* Attending to these five "R's" should serve as a shorthand guide for those concerned with the practical translation of today's theory and research and the implications of that theory and research for the education of Hispanic students.

Respectful

Everyone wants respect. Parents want to be respected and want their children respected. Over and over again, it is common to hear from Hispanic parents and their children that they do not receive that respect in school. They are too often seen as the foreigner, the immigrant, the non–English speaker, the disadvantaged, or someone who does not belong or is "less than," and the school's mission is to change them so that they can belong. The most detrimental lack of respect for Hispanic might be identified as the *"el pobrecito"* or *"el bendito"* syndrome—"Oh, you poor thing— unwashed, of and in poverty, immigrant, non–English speaking; we sympathize with your circumstances and lower our expectations for what you might be able to learn." Sympathy is not what Hispanic students need. Such "sympathy" is shown when an educator or an educational system begins the slippery slope of lowering expectations and academic standards and begins to devise selection devices that separate the deserving from the nondeserving, the smart from the dumb, those with and those without a future. Hispanic students find themselves at the bottom end of this continuum through no fault of their own. Educational programs, teachers, and administrators who serve Hispanics well will respect the students for what they bring—their language, culture, and worldview—and do not see disadvantages that place students only "at risk" but as we see in these students' resources that can be marshaled to meet learning goals, particularly high learning goals. There is an acceptance and a respect that is to be honored and displayed for all students and their families and the communities from which they come. "Pobrecitos" they are not.

It was at Pajaro Middle School that I first encountered this "pobrecito" phenomenon (Garcia, 1989). The school was serving primarily Mexican

American students, many first-generation immigrants. Some teachers actually felt that these students should not be in the country and, by this logic, in this school. Several years later, the voters of California formally articulated this view in passing Proposition 187, which called for the elimination educational services for noncitizens. Since they did not speak English, they were poor, they were members of gangs, and they came from farmworker families, the majority of educators at the school felt that the most they could do for these students was provide them a basic, no-frills education—enough of an education to take them out of the fields. After we performed an analysis of the math and literacy curriculum for seventh-graders, we found that teachers, over an extended period of time, had arrived at teaching fifth-grade skills to these seventh-graders. This was not an instructional staff that purposely set out to downgrade instruction. They were not sinister in their goals or in their instructional behavior. When asked why they were teaching at these lower levels, the response was, "We sympathize with their disadvantages and don't want them to fail." In other words, they were "pobrecitos." That same staff, realizing and acting on the need to begin respecting the language and culture of the students and raising standards and academic expectations, developed and implemented organizational and instructional changes that resulted in significant gains in academic achievement in literacy, mathematics, and science (Garcia, 1999). For Hispanic students in particular, too much sympathy for their circumstances can be highly detrimental; too much respect is never handicapping.

Responsive

It is not enough just to have respect. Educational programs and those individuals who serve in them must be directly responsive to the students and families they serve. This requires an active assessment of the learning tools that the student brings to the schooling process, coupled with the utilization of those tools that optimize student learning. It means shifting the emphasis from "needs assessments" to "asset inventories." However, it is not enough to just to know students well; one must take that knowledge and make it come alive in organizing and implementing teaching and learning environments for those students. Borrowing from an unknown educational colleague whose name I cannot recall, "The general can be understood only in its specifics." That is, we can come to know our Hispanic students in various intellectual ways, but until we can translate that knowledge into the very specific ways in which we teach them, the maximum benefits of the intellectual knowledge will go unrealized.

My first encounter with the Puente Project resulted from a search of educational programs that supported Hispanic students in their efforts to attend four-year colleges (University of California, 1993). This program is an English literature–based program for community college students preparing to transfer to a four-year college (for details, see chapter 8). The project adapted the community college English literature course for Hispanic students, most first-generation college attendees, in several important ways. First, it made sure to bring the instructors in the program together to learn about the students they served; many of these instructors were the "standard" English professors, themselves personally unacquainted with the culture and the language of their students but highly competent instructors. Second, the curriculum of the course incorporated literature that uses Spanish, Spanish and English code switching, and standard English texts that reflected the students' personal or family experience. Lastly, each student was paired with a mentor, usually a Hispanic college graduate working in the same community of the student and, if possible, having grown up in the same community as the student. The role of this mentor was not only to monitor/promote student progress but also to provide direct knowledge about how the "system" works while directly and indirectly providing a vision of what the future held for a college graduate. Students were expected to read, write, and otherwise meet the high and challenging standards of this course. I was amazed to find that Hispanic students who participated in the Puente Project had five times the four-year college-going rate than did similar students who had not participated in the project. This phenomenon continues today, and the Puente Project has been extended to the high school and middle school. It is a real and productive example of educational responsiveness to Hispanic students.

Responsible

In constructing new federal legislation in the Improving American Schools Act, U.S. Department of Education colleagues and I were continually confronted with the unequal achievement outcomes for selected students in U.S. schools (Garcia and Gonzales, 1995) (for details of these academic achievement incongruencies across race, class, ethnicity, and gender, see chapter 2). It became evident that, nationally, we did not have policy mechanism in place for holding educational institutions accountable for these disparate educational results. Moreover, general aggregation of achievement data did not reveal how subgroups of students were actually doing. For this reason, the Improving American Schools Act in Title I of that law now requires schools receiving federal Title I funds to report student achievement by race, ethnicity, gender, and socioeconomic status.

Unfortunately, local schools and states do not always adopt disaggregation practices for achievement data on the basis of historically and new relevant demographic categories. For Hispanics, failures to make distinctions in this data for immigrants versus nonimmigrants, Spanish speakers versus English speakers, and previous educational background make interpreting these data confusing and unproductive. Most significant, Hispanic limited-English-speaking students are often out of the bounds of accountability simply because they were not assessed at all. In this case, educational entities have no knowledge regarding the academic effects of schooling for this population. Absence of such achievement data has often been defended on the basis that it is best not to take such measures rather than to do so with inappropriate (unreliable and invalid) assessments. Confused at this policy level is the failure to develop appropriate assessments as opposed to using inappropriate ones. These are clearly two different issues, each placing Hispanic students outside any system of accountability.

The state of Texas has taken an important lead in resolving this set of issues. A statewide accountability system administers achievement tests to each student in its schools on a yearly basis, publishes the results of those tests by school, and provides school-based rewards in the form of new resources to those schools that make substantial progress. And, much like the legislation that the U.S. Department of Education promoted and the U.S. Congress passed in the Improving American Schools Act of 1994, desegregation of achievement data by ethnic, racial, gender, and economic status is required. In addition, Hispanic students who are limited English proficient and have been receiving instruction in Spanish are administered academic achievement assessments in Spanish. Some have observed that the tests may still not meet high standards of content and may even be suspect because of their questionable reliability and validity. Yet we now have in one state a system that attempts to seriously address the issues of educational accountability for Hispanic students. This type of responsibility is still the exception, not the rule. It must become commonplace as Hispanic students grow in number throughout the United States so as inform practices that can hold education agencies accountable for the educational progress of these and all students.

Resourceful

We often are encouraged, particularly in education, that less is more and that throwing money at a problem is not the solution. Jaime Escalante, as portrayed in the popular movie *Stand and Deliver,* takes low-achieving Hispanic students and, with little more than engendering *"ganas"* (effort) in these students, produces a cadre of mathematics success stories. For many Hispanics, these adages sound hollow in the face of the challenges that they confront in everyday educational settings. Ganas is good, but a systematic effort to improve education on a variety of fronts is needed.

We learned in our own work that Hispanic students and parents resisted any notions of going to college because of the perceived and real high cost of such education (University of California, 1993). Families, averaging in size of four to eight members and earning less than $30,000 per year, cannot afford tuition and colleges costs averaging $12,000 per student per year in a public university. Scholarships for these students have actually been declining nationwide, while a system of student loans has proven very difficult to negotiate by a population of Hispanic students who are the first in their families to go to college. In the K–12, sector, we learned that serving immigrant, non-English-proficient students does cost more—anywhere for $200 to $1,000 per year (Garcia, 1994a). The types of curriculum and assessment and the expertise of the instructor are critical resources in need of attention if Hispanic students are to do well. Teachers with bilingual and English development instructional skills, reduction of class size, and resources (time and money) for professional development can enhance the educational responsiveness in preschools and the early grades. At high schools, access to college-bound, honors, and advanced placement courses requires redeployment and new resources in schools that have been historically organized to respond to probrecitos.

After-school programs, specifically targeted in-school reading programs, and community-based support programs are not free. They require public and private resourcefulness that are usually nonexistent. And, it does not always take a lot of resources. I was struck by the development and implementation of a high school completion program in Houston, Texas, that addressed very directly this issue of resourcefulness in response to a high dropout rate of Hispanic students. Simply, the high school redeployed a cadre of its physical space and instructional/support staff so as to hold the school open from 7:00 a.m. to 12:00 midnight every day of the week. This allowed many low-income Hispanic students who needed to help their families by working during the normal operational hours of the school to attend classes, complete assignments, and obtain related counseling services within times most accessible to them. High school completion rates and academic achievement of Hispanic students tripled within one year. Its added costs were estimated at approximately $220 per year, but its benefits, as articulated by parents, students, teachers, and administrations, undeniably justified this added expenditure. We pay for what we receive—Hispanics and the general society will need to pay.

Bambi Cardenas, a professor of education at the University of Texas at San Antonio and a recognized leader in the U.S. Hispanic community, tells a story about her personal concern for the general education of Hispanic students. That concern comes even though her son, like my daughters, has been highly successful academically. Her son is now completing his tenure at a prestigious Ivy League university, while both my daughters have graduated from institutions of higher education. She, like Eugene, Gene, and Geno, worries that even though her son and my daughters may be, as individuals (professionally and even economically), successful, the overall quality of life they will lead in a future U.S. society is greatly dependent on the success of Hispanic students collectively. Without their educational well-being, the well-being of all our children is unnecessarily placed at risk. Too often we, collectively, are unwilling to allocate and redistribute resources to critically alter this situation.

Reasonable

We are right to pursue and insist on immediate solutions to the education circumstances of Hispanic students. The U.S. Department of Education concluded that U.S. education needed "No More Excuses" (U.S. Department of Education, 1998). The University of California forcefully concluded, "*Ya Basta*" (enough) concerning university underrepresentation of Hispanics. Yet the urgency of such conclusions must be tempered and coupled with reasonable actions.

In California and Texas, the elimination of affirmative action—once perceived as a "reasonable" solution to the problem of underrepresentation that empirical evidence indicates helps those it targets while not imposing harm on those it does not—was unilaterally disposed of on the basis of "reason and principle." Similarly, the anti–bilingual education movement, led by California's Proposition 227 but with extensions into other states and into proposed federal initiatives aimed at immigrant students, seeks to unreasonably restrict the flexibility of states and local school districts to respond to these students. These new policies mandate prescriptive instructional treatments, limit temporal access of programs to these students (from one to three years), and focus their efforts only on English-language development instead of high academic achievement without any concern for the accountability of the mandates they impose. New proposed assessment practices in the U.S. Department of Education's "Reading-by-Third-Grade" initiative would require all students to be assessed in English reading, although the department presently funds programs whose direct goal is to teach children to read in their native language, with English reading competencies expected after the third grade. Does this incongruency seem reasonable? Similarly, in California, English tests in reading and mathematics for non-English-speaking students have been mandated by executive order of the governor with the support of the California State Board of Education. Luckily, in the case of the U.S. Department of Education, Congress refused to fund the proposed testing program. In California, a "reasonable" judge found it of no use to test non-English-speaking students in an English achievement test that was not aligned with the students' language of instruction while placing the student in very awkward and potentially harmful testing situation. In our urgency and goodwill, we need not act unreasonably.

Reasonable people who attend to Eugene, Gene, and Geno's five "R's" are often seen nodding their heads. In almost all cases, these general guidelines are relevant to all students. I have tried, however, to make the strongest case possible that for Hispanic students and their present and future educational success, these guides are absolutely critical. Educational practices that respect who the students are, that respond directly to that knowledge base, that hold themselves responsible for academic outcomes, and that provide for and maximize new and existing resources organized in ways that are reasonable can make a huge difference. We need no more excuses, and enough is enough.

PREPARING HISPANICS AND THE
UNITED STATES FOR THE FUTURE

As the United States enters the 21st century, it is even more important to understand the seismic changes in technology, globalization, and democratization that are reflected in similar seismic changes in demography. Unfortunately, the general U.S. population is far more attuned to and comfortable with engaging in aspects of the technological, globalization, and political challenges than those challenges confronting us by our demographic changes. They are almost characterized a blind spot when it comes to the new demographic reality—they are "demographically challenged."

However, all changes are inextricably intertwined. Some 60 percent of new jobs in the near future will be in the fields of information technology and communications. The spoils go to those students who master and control this new technology—locally, regionally, nationally, and internationally. They will be like those who controlled the capital and labor in the 20th century. This link creates an obvious imperative to educate those who will enter this country prosper or serve as its growing weak link. To educate our underachieving but growing Hispanic students is a "no-brainer." This youth will serve as our foundation for national preeminence in the fields of high technology in a global workplace that promotes democratic principles and practices.

These circumstances pose a particular challenge to educators and those among us who look to educational agencies for help in realizing the moral imperatives of equity and social justice. These agencies are being called on to develop and implement models of culturally competent practices in treating and delivering services to growing numbers of Hispanic students and families. As Wilson (1978) has noted, class has become increasingly more important than race in determining access to opportunities, power, and privilege in American society. West (1993) reminds us that race is still important. This book, with its emphasis on the education of Hispanics in the United States, has attempted to further complexify our understanding of the education in this country through the discussion of culture. If class and race count, so does culture.

If these findings are valid, then one could predict that as more Hispanics and other linguistically and culturally diverse students enter the "right" kind of schools, barriers to their academic, social, and economic success and mobility will fall. Likewise, as ethnic majorities become more attuned to the cultural diversity around them and the resources inherent in that diversity, cultural distinctions will blend with other features of our society to create a more equalitarian, multicultural society. This is a highly optimistic scenario of our future for Hispanic students and American society in general. Yet it is most certainly a preferable prediction to one that argues that America could become another Bosnian nightmare where racial and ethnic conflicts could escalate into major avenues of social unrest.

If the treatment of Hispanics in our educational institutions is like the seismic indicators of an impending earthquake, a set of indicators that are now sending signals of coming dangers, then how we react to those signals is important. We can ignore these, but the dangers will not go away. We can respond to them minimally, study them some more, and prepare for the worst. Or we can marshal the intellectual resources in ways that will make the inevitable an opportunity from which we can benefit.

Simply put, our challenge for Hispanic students is to help America arrive at a truly multiracial, multiethnic democracy. We must both learn about and create new ways (1) to honor diversity and the social complexity in which we live—to give the individual integrity and a place where he or she develops as a human being a similar integrity—and (2) to unify, but not to insist on it without recognizing that the underpinnings of unifying are individual and collective dignity.

References

Abi-Nader, J. 1990a. A house for my mother: Motivating Hispanic high school students. *Anthropology and Education Quarterly* 21 (1): 41–58.

———. 1990b. Helping minority high school students redefine their self-image through culturally sensitive instruction. Paper presented at the annual meeting of the American Educational Research Association, Boston, April.

Acuña, R. 1972. *Occupied America: The Chicano's struggle toward liberation.* San Francisco: Canfield Press.

Adler, M. 1982. *The paideia proposal: An educational manifesto.* New York: Macmillan.

Alexander, A. A., and K. P. Murphy. 1998. The research base for APA's learner-centered psychological principles. In N. L. Lambert and B. L. McCombs, eds., *Issues in school reform: A sampler of psychological perspectives on learner-centered schools* (1–56). Washington, D.C.: American Psychological Association.

Alexander, Karl L., et al. 1987. Social background and academic determinants of two-year versus four-year college attendance: Evidence from two cohorts a decade apart. *American Journal of Education* 96 (1): 56–80.

Allport, G. 1954. *The nature of prejudice.* Reading, Mass.: Addison-Wesley.

American Educational Research Association, American Psychological Association, and National Council on Measurements in Education. 1985. *Standards for educational and psychological testing.* Washington, D.C.: American Psychological Association.

Appleton, C. 1983. *Cultural pluralism in education: Theoretical foundations.* New York: Longman.

Armbruster, R., K. Geron, and E. Bonacich. 1995. The assault on California's Latino immigrants: The politics of Proposition 187. *International Migration Review* 20: 655–663.

Aronowitz, S., and H. A. Giroux. 1991. *Postmodern education: Politics, culture and social criticism.* Minneapolis: University of Minnesota Press.

August, D., and E. Garcia. 1988. *Language minority education in the United States: Research, policy and practice.* Chicago: Charles C. Thomas.

August, D., and K. Hakuta. 1997. *Improving schooling for language-minority children: A research, policy, and practice.* Chicago: Charles C. Thomas.

Baden, B., and M. Maehr. 1986. Conforming culture with culture: A perspective for designing schools for children of diverse sociocultural backgrounds. In R. Feldman, ed., *The social psychology of education* (289–309). Cambridge, Mass.: Harvard University Press.

Baker, K. A. 1990a. Bilingual education's 20 year failure to provide rights protection for language-minority students. In A. Barona and E. Garcia, eds., *Children at risk: Poverty, minority status and other issues in educational equity* (29–52). Washington, D.C.: National Association of School Psychologists.

———. 1990b. Language minority education: Two decades of research. In A. Barona and E. Garcia, eds., *Students-at-risk* (3–41). Washington, D.C.: National Association of School Psychologists.

Baker, K. A., and A. A. de Kanter. 1983. An answer from research on bilingual education. *American Education* 56: 157–169.

Banks, J. 1981. *Multiethnic education: Theory and practice.* Boston: Allyn and Bacon.

———. 1984. *Teaching strategies for ethnic studies.* Boston: Allyn and Bacon.

———. 1994. *Multiethnic education: Theory and practice.* Boston: Allyn and Bacon.

Banks, J., and C. A. Banks. 1995. *Handbook of research on mulitcultural education.* New York: Macmillan.

Baron, J., and M. F. Norman. 1992. SATs, achievement tests, and high-school class rank as predictors of college performance. *Educational and Psychological Measurement* 52 (4): 1047–1055.

Basch, L., N. G. Schiller, and C. Szanton Blanc. 1994. *Nations unbound: Transnational projects, postcolonial predicaments, and deterritorialized nation-states.* Gordon and Breach.

Bean, F. D., R. O. de la Garza, B. R. Roberts, and S. Weintraub. 1997. *At the crossroads: Mexico and U. S. Immigration Policy.* Lanham, Md.: Rowman & Littlefield.

Bean, F. D., T. Espenshade, M. White, and R. Dymoski. 1990. Post-IRCA changes in the volume and flow of undocumented migration to the United States. In F. Bean, B. Edmonston, and J. Passels, eds., *Undocumented migration to the United States: IRCA and the experience of the 1980s* (111–158). Washington, D.C.: The Urban Institute Press.

Bean, F. D., and M. Fix. 1992. The significance of recent immigration policy reforms in the United States. In G. Freeman and J. Jupp, eds., *Nations of immigrants: Australia and the United States in a changing world* (41–55). New York: Oxford University Press.

Beauf, J. 1977. Development of ethnic awareness in Native American children. *Developmental Psychology* 13: 244–256.

Beaver, W. 1996. Is it time to replace the SAT? *Academe,* May–June, 37–39.

Becker, B. J. 1990. Coaching for the Scholastic Aptitude Test: Further synthesis and appraisal. *Review of Educational Research* 60 (3): 373–417.

Bell, D. A. 1980a. Brown v. Board of Education and the interest-convergence dilemma. *Harvard Law Review* 93 (3): 518–534.

———. 1980b. Humanity in legal education. *Oregon Law Review* 59 (2–3): 243–247.

———. 1980c. A reassessment of racial balance remedies—I. *Phi Delta Kappan* 62 (3): 177–179.

Bell, D., P. Kasschau, and G. Zellman. 1976. *Delivering services to elderly members of minority groups: A critical review of the literature.* Santa Monica, Calif.: Rand Corporation.

Ben-Zeev, S. 1977. The influence of bilingualism on cognitive strategy and cognitive development. *Child Development* 48: 1009–1018.

Berman, P. 1992a. Meeting the challenge of language diversity: An evaluation of California programs for pupils with limited proficiency in English. Paper presented at the meeting of the American Educational Research Association, San Francisco.

———. 1992b. *The status of bilingual education in California.* Berkeley, Calif.: Paul Berman and Associates.

Berman, P., R. Wyman, and K. Kunz. 1992. *The feasibility of statewide distance education.* Commission on Innovation Policy Discussion Paper No. 5. Berkeley, Calif.: BW Associates.

Bernstein, B. 1971. A sociolinguistic approach to socialization with some reference to educability. In B. Bernstein, ed., *Class, codes and control: Theoretical studies towards a sociology of language* (146–171). London: Routledge and Kegan Paul.

Bigler, E. 1999. *American conversations: Puerto Ricans, White ethnics, and multicultural education.* Philadelphia: Temple University Press.

Bilingual Education Act, P.L. 93–380, 88 Stats. 503 (1974).

Bilingual Education Act, P.L. 95–561, 92 Stats. 2268 (1978).

Bilingual Education Act, P.L. 98–511, 98 Stats. 2370 (1984).

Bjork, R. A. 1994. Institutional impediments to effective training. In D. Druckman and R.A. Bjork, eds., *Learning, remembering, believing: Enhancing individual and team performances* (295–306). Washington, D.C.: National Academy Press.

Blauner, R. 1972. *Racial oppression in America.* New York: Harper & Row.

Bloom, B. 1984. The search for methods of group instruction as effective as one-to-one tutoring. *Educational Leadership* 41 (8): 4–17.

Bowen, W. G., and D. Bok. 1998. *The shape of the river: Long-term consequences of considering race in college and university admissions.* Princeton, N.J.: Princeton University Press.

Boykin, A. W. 1983. The academic performance of Afro-Americans. In J. T. Spence, ed., *Achievement and achievement motives: Psychological and sociological approaches.* San Francisco: W. H. Freeman.

———. 1986. The triple quandry and the schooling of Afro-American children. In U. Neisser, ed., *The school achievement of minority children* (57–92). New York: New Perspectives.

Brophy, J. 1983. Research on the self-fulfilling prophecy and teacher expectations. *Journal of Educational Psychology* 75 (5): 631–61.

Brophy, J., and T. Good. 1986. Teacher behavior and student achievement. In M. Wittrock, ed., *Handbook of research on teaching.* 3rd ed. New York: Macmillan.

Brown v. Board of Education. 1954. 327 U.S. 483, 1954; 686.

Cafferty, P., B. R. Chiswick, A. M. Greeley, and T. A. Sullivan. 1984. *The dilemma of American immigration: Beyond the golden door.* New Brunswick, N.J.: Transaction Books.

California Commission on Teacher Credentialing. 1991. *Teacher credentialing in California: A special report.* Sacramento, Calif.: California Commission on Teacher Credentialing.

California Department of Education. 1990. *High school curriculum frameworks.* Sacramento, Calif.: California Department of Education.

———. 1997. *Mandate of excellence: A call for standards, assessment and accountability in the education of California's Hispanic students.* Sacramento, Calif.: California Department of Education.

California Tomorrow. 1995. *The unfinished journey: Restructuring schools in a diverse society.* San Francisco: California Tomorrow.

Campbell, D. T., and P. W. Frey. 1970. The implication of learning theory for the fade-out of gains from compensatory education. In J. Hellmuth, ed., *Compensatory education: A national debate. Vol. 3: Disadvantaged child* (455–463). New York: Brunner/Mazel.

Campbell, J. R., C. M. Reese, C. O'Sullivan, and J. A. Dossey. (1996). *NAEP 1994 Trends in Academic Progress.* Washington, D.C.: National Center for Education Statistics & Office of Educational Research and Improvement, U.S. Department of Education.

Cardenas, J. 1986. The role of native-language instruction in bilingual education. *Phi Delta Kappan* 67: 359–363.

Carroll, J. B. 1982. The measurement of intelligence. In R. J. Sternberg, ed., *Handbook on human intelligence* (29–120). Cambridge: Cambridge University Press.

———. 1993. *Human cognitive abilities: A survey of factor-analytic studies.* Cambridge: Cambridge University Press.

Carter, L. E. 1997. Intermediate scrutiny under fire: Will Plyler service state legislation to exclude undocumented children from school? *University of San Francisco Law Review* 31: 354–398.

Carter, T. P. 1968. The negative self-concept of Mexican-American students. *School and Society* 96: 217–219.

Carter, T., and M. Chatfield. 1986. Effective bilingual schools: Implications for policy and practice. *American Journal of Education* 95: 200–232.

Castaneda v. Pickard. 1981. 648 F.2d 989, 1007 5th Cir. 1981; 103 S. Ct. 3321.

Cavasos, E. 1990. An executive initiative for Hispanic education. Testimony before the U.S. House of Representatives, Committee on Education and Labor, Washington, D.C., November.

Chapa, J. 1990. The myth of Hispanic progress. *Journal of Hispanic Policy* 4: 3–18.

Chavez, L. 1991. *Out of the barrio: Toward a new politics of Hispanic assimilation.* New York: Basic Books.

———. 1995a. Bilingual education and its problems. *Reader's Digest,* February.

————. 1995b. One nation, one common language. *Reader's Digest,* August, 87–91.

Civil Rights Act of 1964, P.L. 88–352, 70 Stats. 241 (1964).

Clark, K. B., and M. P. Clark. 1939. Segregation as a factor in the racial identification of Negro preschool children. *Journal of Experimental Education* 8: 161–163.

Clark, R. M. 1983. *Family life and school achievement: Why poor black children succeed or fail.* Chicago: University of Chicago Press.

Clasen, D. R., and B. B. Brown. 1985. The multidimensionality of peer pressure in adolescence. *Journal of Youth and Adolescence* 14 (6): 451–468.

Clement, D., and J. Harding. 1978. Social distinctions and emergent student groups in a desegregated school. *Anthropology and Education Quarterly* 9 (4): 272–283.

Colangelo, N., C. H. Foxley, and D. Dustin, eds. 1982. *The human relations experience.* Monterey, Calif.: Brooks/Cole.

Cole, R. W. 1995. *Educating everybody's children: What research and practice say about improving achievement.* Alexandra, Va.: Association for Supervision and Curriculum Development.

Coleman, J. S. 1963. *The adolescent society: The social life of the teenager and its impact on education.* New York: The Free Press.

College Board. 1999. Report of the National Task Force on minority high achievement. New York: College Board.

College Board and the Western Interstate Commission for Higher Education. 1991. *The road to college: Educational progress by race and ethnicity.* New York: College Board.

Conley, C. H., P. Kelly, P. Mahanna, and L. Warner. 1997. *Street gangs: Current knowledge and practice.* Washington, D.C.: U.S. Department of Justice.

Connell, R. W. 1993. *Schools and social justice.* New York: Academic Press.

Cooper, C. R., H. Baker, D. Polichar, and M. Welsh. 1991. Ethnic perspectives on individuality and correctedness in adolescents' relationships with family and peers. Paper presented at the annual meeting of the Society for Research in Adolescence, Alexandria, Virginia.

Cooper, C. R., J. F. Jackson, M. Azmitia, E. M. López, and N. Dunbar. 1995. Bridging students' multiple worlds: African American and Latino youth in academic outreach programs. In R. F. Macías and R. G. García Ramos, eds., *Changing schools for changing students: An anthology of research on language minorities, schools and society* (245–267). Santa Barbara: University of California Linguistic Minority Research Institute, University of California, Santa Barbara.

Council of Economic Advisers. 1998. *Changing America: Indicators of social and economic well-being by race and Hispanic origin.* Washington D.C.: U.S. Government Printing Office.

Crawford, J. 1992. *Hold your tongue: Bilingualism and the politics of "English only."* Reading, Mass.: Addison-Wesley.

Crawford, J. 1999. *Bilingual Education: History, Politics, Theory, and Practice* (4th ed.). Los Angeles: Bilingual Educational Services.

Crouse, J., and D. Trusheim. 1988. *The case against the SAT.* Chicago: University of Chicago Press.

Cummins, J. 1979. Linguistic interdependence and the educational development of bilingual children. *Review of Educational Research* 19: 222–251.

———. 1981. The role of primary language development in promoting educational success for language minority students. In California State Department of Education, ed., *Schooling and language minority students: A theoretical framework* (3–50). Los Angeles: Evaluation, Dissemination, and Assessment Center, California State University.

———. 1984a. *Bilingualism and special education.* San Diego: College Hill Press.

———. 1984b. Wanted, a theoretical framework for relating language proficiency to academic achievement among bilingual students. In C. Riveral, ed., *Language proficiency and academic achievement.* Clevedon, England: Multilingual Matters.

———. 1986. Empowering minority students: A framework for intervention. *Harvard Educational Review* 56 (1): 18–35.

———. 1997. Minority status and schooling in Canada. *Anthropology and Education Quarterly* 28 (3): 411–436.

Darcy, N. T. 1953. A review of the literature of the effects of bilingualism upon the measurement of intelligence. *Journal of Genetic Psychology* 82: 21–57.

———. 1963. Bilingualism and the measurement of intelligence: Review of a decade of research. *Journal of Genetic Psychology* 103: 259–282.

Datnow, A., L. Hubbard, and H. Mehan. 1998. Educational Reform Implementation: A Co-Constructed Process. Research Report 5. Center for Research on Education, Diversity and Excellence, Santa Cruz, Calif. 1998.

Davis, R. B., C. A. Maher, and N. Noddings, eds. 1990. *Constructivist views on the teaching and learning of mathematics.* Reston, Va.: Council of Teachers of Mathematics.

De Acosta, M. 1996. *Characteristics of successful recruitment and retention programs for Latino students.* Research Report No. 15. Cleveland: Urban Child Research Center, Cleveland State University.

Delgado, R. 1995. *Critical race theory: The cutting edge.* Philadelphia: Temple University Press.

Delpit, L. D. 1988. The silenced dialogue: Power and pedagogy in educating other people's children. *Harvard Educational Review* 58 (3): 280–298.

Development Associates. 1984. *Final report descriptive study phase of the national longitudinal evaluation of the effectiveness of services for language minority limited English proficient students.* Arlington, Va.: Development Associates.

———. 1993. *Final report descriptive study phase of the national longitudinal evaluation of the effectiveness of services for language minority limited English proficient students.* Arlington, Va.: Development Associates.

DevTech Systems, Inc. 1996. *A descriptive study of the ESEA Title VII services provided for secondary school limited English proficient students.* Contract No. T294009001.Washington, D.C.: DevTech System, Inc.

Dewey, J. 1916. *Democracy and education: An introduction to the philosophy of education.* New York: Macmillan.

————. 1921. *Reconstruction and philosophy.* London: University of London Press.

Diaz, R. M. 1983. The impact of bilingualism on cognitive development. In E. W. Gordon, ed., *Review of research in education.* Vol. 10 (23–54). Washington, D.C.: American Educational Research Association.

————. 1985. Bilingual cognitive development: Addressing these gaps in current research. *Child Development* 56: 1376–1388.

Diaz, S., L. C. Moll, and H. Mehan. 1986. Sociocultural resources in instruction: A context-specific approach. In Bilingual Education Office, ed., *Beyond language: Social and cultural factors in schooling language minority students* (197–230). Los Angeles: Evaluation, Dissemination, and Assessment Center, California State University.

Douglass, J. A. 1997. *Setting the conditions of undergraduate admissions: The role of University of California faculty in policy and process.* Berkeley, Calif.: Universitywide Academic Senate Office and the Center for Studies in Higher Education.

Dryfoos, J. G. 1998. *Safe passage: Making it through adolescence in a risky society.* New York: Oxford University Press.

Dugger, W. E. 1999. Putting technology education standards into practice. *NASSP Bulletin* 83 (608): 57–63.

Duran, R. 1986. Improving Hispanics' educational outcomes: Learning and instruction. Unpublished manuscript. Graduate School of Education, University of California, Santa Barbara.

Dusek, J., and G. Joseph. 1986. The bases of teacher expectations: A meta-analysis. *Journal of Educational Psychology* 75: 327–346.

Dwyer, C. 1991. *Language, culture and writing.* Working Paper No. 13. Berkeley: Center for the Study of Writing, University of California.

Eckert, P. 1989. *Jocks and burnouts: Social categories and identity in high school.* New York: Teachers College Press.

Eder, D. 1982. Difference in communication styles across ability groups. In L. C. Wilkinson, ed., *Communicating in the classroom* (245–263). New York: Academic Press.

Edmonds, R. 1979a. Effective schools for the urban poor. *Educational Leadership* 37: 20–24.

————. 1979b. Some schools work and more can. *Social Policy* 9 (5): 28–32.

Ekstrom, R. B., M. E. Goertz, J. M. Pollack, and D. A. Rock. 1986. Who drops out of high school? Findings from a national study. *Teachers College Record* 87 (3): 356–373.

Elam, S. 1972. Acculturation and learning problems of Puerto Rican children. In F. Corradasco and E. Bucchini, eds., *The Puerto Rican community and its children on the mainland* (37–45). Metuchen, N.J.: Scarecrow Press.

Elementary and Secondary Education Act of 1965, Title II, P.L. 89–10, Stat. 27 (1965).

Emanuel, S. 1983. *Constitutional law.* New York: Emanuel Law Outlines, Inc.

Equal Educational Opportunities and Transportation of Students Act of 1974, 294(f).20 U.S.L.

Erickson, F. 1987. Transformation and school success: The politics and culture of educational achievement. *Anthropology and Education Quarterly* 18 (4): 335–355.

Escalante, J., and J. Dirmann. 1990. *The Jaime Escalante math program.* Washington, D.C.: National Education Association.

Federal Interagency Forum on Child and Family Statistics. 1997. America's children: Key national indicators of well-being. Washington, D.C.: Federal Interagency Forum on Child and Family Statistics.

Feldman, C., and M. Shen. 1971. Some language-related cognitive advantages of bilingual five-year-olds. *Journal of Genetic Psychology* 118: 235–244.

Fernandez, R., K. Henn-Reinke, and J. Petrovich. 1989. *Five cities high school dropout study: Characteristics of Hispanic high school students.* Washington, D.C.: ASPIRA Association, Inc.

Fernandez, R. R., and W. Velez. 1989. *Who stays? Who leaves? Findings from the ASPIRA five cities high school dropout study.* Working Paper No. 89–1. Washington, D.C.: ASPIRA Association, Inc.

Fierman, J. 1994. Is immigration hurting the U.S.? In T. Mills, ed., *Arguing immigration* (146–168). New York: Simon & Schuster.

Fin, J. D., and D. A. Rock. 1997. Academic success among students at risk for school failure. *Journal of Applied Psychology* 82: 221–234.

Finley, M. K. 1984. Teachers and tracking in a comprehensive high school. *Sociology of Education* 57 (4): 233–243.

Fishman, J. 1990. What is reversing language shift (RLS) and how can it succeed? *Journal of Multilingual and Multicultural Development* 11 (1–2): 5–36.

Fix, M., and J. S. Passel. 1994. Immigrants and social services. *Migration World Magazine* 22 (4): 22–25.

Fligstein, N., and R. M. Fernandez. 1982. *Educational transitions of whites and Mexican Americans.* Washington, D.C.: National Commission for Employment Policy.

Flores, W. V., and R. Benmayor. 1997. *Latino cultural citizenship.* Boston: Beacon Press.

Ford, D. Y., and J. J. Harris. 1996. Perceptions and attitudes of minority students toward school, achievement, and other educational variables. *Child Development* 67: 1141–1152.

Fordham, S. 1988. Racelessness as a factor in black students' school success: Pragmatic strategy or pyrrhic victory? *Harvard Educational Review* 58 (1): 54–83.

Fradd, S. 1997a. *Language differences or learning disabilities? Identifying and meeting the needs of students from non-English-language backgrounds.* Language in Education: Theory and Practice 86. Washington, D.C.: ERIC Clearinghouse on Languages and Linguistics.

———. 1997b. School–university partnerships to promote science with students learning English. *TESOL Journal* 7 (1): 35–40.

Freeman, Y. S., and D. E. Freeman. 1997. *Teaching reading and writing in Spanish in the bilingual classroom.* Portsmouth, N.H.: Heinemann.

Freire, P. 1970. *Pedagogy of the oppressed.* New York: Seabury Press.

Galambos, S. J., and K. Hakuta. 1988. Subject-specific and task-specific characteristics of metalinguistic awareness in bilingual children. *Applied Psycholinguistics* 9: 141–162.

Gamoran, A., and M. Berends. 1987a. The effects of stratification in secondary schools: Synthesis of survey and ethnographic research. *Review of Educational Research* 57 (4): 415–435.

———. 1987b. *The effects of stratification in secondary schools: Synthesis of survey and ethnographic research.* Madison, Wis.: National Center on Effective Secondary Schools.

Gandara, P. C. 1995. *Over the ivy walls: The educational mobility of low-income Chicanos.* Albany: State University of New York Press.

———. 1997. High school Puente evaluation. Report No. 3. University of California, Davis, October.

Gandara, P., L. Larson, R. Rumberger, and H. Mehan. 1998. *Capturing Latino students in the academic pipeline.* Berkeley: Chicano Latino Policy Project, University of California, Berkeley.

Gandara, P., and E. Lopez. 1998. Latino students and college entrance exams: How much do they really matter? *Hispanic Journal of Behavioral Sciences* 20 (1): 17–38.

Gandara, P., and J. Maxwell-Jolly. 1998. *Priming the pump: A review of programs that aim to increase the achievement of underrepresented minority undergraduates.* Report to the Task Force on Minority High Achievement of the College Board, New York.

Garcia, E. 1983a. *Bilingualism in early childhood.* Albuquerque: University of New Mexico Press.

———. 1983b. *The Mexican-American child: Language, cognition, and socialization.* Tempe: Arizona State University.

———. 1988. Effective schooling for language minority students. In National Clearinghouse for Bilingual Education, ed., *New focus.* Arlington, Va.: National Clearinghouse for Bilingual Education.

———. 1989. Instructional discourse in "effective" Hispanic classrooms. In R. Jacobson and C. Faltis, eds., *Language distribution issues in bilingual schooling* (104–120). Clevedon, England: Multilingual Matters, Ltd.

———. 1991a. Attributes of effective language minority teachers: An empirical study. *Journal of Education* 173: 130–141.

———. 1991b. Bilingualism, second language acquisition in academic contexts. In A. Ambert, ed., *Bilingual education and English-as-a-second language: A research annual* (181–217). New York: Garland.

———. 1991c. *Characteristics of effective teachers for language minority students: A review.* Education Report No. 1. Santa Cruz, Calif.: National Center for Research on Cultural Diversity and Second Language Learning.

———. 1991d. *The education of linguistically and culturally diverse students: Effective instructional practices.* Santa Cruz, Calif.: National Center for Research on Cultural Diversity and Second Language Learning.

———. 1994a. Addressing the challenges of diversity. In S. L. Kagan and B. Weissbourd, eds., *Putting families first* (243–275). San Francisco: Jossey-Bass.

———. 1994b. The impact of linguistic and cultural diversity in American schools: A need for new policy. In M. C. Wang and M. C. Reynolds, eds., *Making a difference for students at risk* (156–182). Thousand Oaks, Calif.: Corwin Press.

———. 1994c. *Understanding the needs of LEP students.* New York: Houghton Mifflin.

———. 1997. The education of Hispanics in early childhood: Of roots and wings. *Young Children* 52 (3): 5–14.

———. 1998. Promoting the contributions of multicultural students in the work force of the 21st century. In S. H. Fradd and O. Lee, eds., *Educational policies and practices for students learning English as a new language* (VII 1–VII 13). Tallahassee: University of Florida and the Florida Department of Education.

———. 1999. *Understanding and meeting the challenge of student cultural diversity.* 2nd ed. New York: Houghton Mifflin.

Garcia, E. 2001. Bilingualism and schooling in the United States. *International Journal of the Sociology of Language* (at press).

Garcia, E., and R. Gonzalez. 1995. Issues in systemic reform for culturally and linguistically diverse students. *College Record* 96 (3): 418–431.

Garcia, E., and G. B. Stein. 1996. Multilingualism in the U.S. schools: Treating language as a resource for instruction and parental involvement. *Early Childhood Development and Care* 127–128: 141–155.

Garcia, R. 1979. *Teaching in a pluralistic society.* New York: Harper & Row.

Gay, G. 1975. Organizing and designing culturally pluralistic curriculum. *Educational Leadership* 33: 176–183.

George Washington University Center for Equity and Excellence in Education. 1996. *Promoting excellence: Ensuring academic success of limited English proficient students.* Arlington, Va.: Evaluation Assistance Center East.

Gibson, M. A. 1987. The school performance of immigrant minorities: A comparative view. *Anthropology and Education Quarterly* 18 (4): 262–275.

———. (1995). Promoting additive acculturation in the schools. *Multicultural Education* 3(1): 10–12.

———. 1997. Complicating the immigrant/involuntary minority typology. *Anthropology and Education Quarterly* 28 (3): 431–454.

Gibson, M. A., and J. Ogbu, eds. 1991. *Minority status and schooling: A comparative study of immigrant and involuntary minorities.* New York: Garland.

Giroux, H. A. 1992. *Border crossings: Cultural workers and the politics of education.* New York: Routledge.

Giroux, H. A., and P. McLaren. 1986. Teacher education and the politics of engagement: The case for democratic schooling. *Harvard Review* 56: 213–238.

Goals 2000: Educate America Act. 1994. P.L. 103–227, 108 Stats. 125 (1994).

Goldenberg, C. 1996. The education of language-minority students: Where are we, and where do we need to go? *Elementary School Journal* 96 (3): 353–361.

Goldman, S., and H. Trueba, eds. 1987. *Becoming literate in English as a second language: Advances in research and theory.* Norwood, N.J.: Ablex Corporation.

Gollnick, D. M., and P. C. Chinn. 1986. *Multicultural education in a pluralistic society.* New York: Maxwell Macmillan International Press.

———. 1990. *Multicultural education in a pluralistic society.* 3rd ed. Columbus, Ohio: Merrill.

Gonzalez, G. 1990. *Chicano education in the segregation era: 1915–1945.* Philadelphia: The Balch Institute.

———. 1999. Segregation and the education of Mexican Americans, 1900–1940. In J. M. Moreno, ed., *The elusive quest of educational equality: 150 years of Chicano/Chicana education* (53–76). Boston: Harvard Educational Review.

Goodenough, W. H. 1981. *Culture, language, and society.* 2nd ed. Menlo Park, Calif.: Benjamin/Cummings.

Goodlad, J. 1984. *A place called school.* New York: McGraw-Hill.

Goodman, Y. 1980. The roots of literacy. In M. P. Douglass, ed., *Reading: A humanizing experience* (286–301). Claremont, Calif.: Claremont Graduate School.

Government Accounting Office. 1987. *Bilingual education policy and practice.* Washington, D.C.: Government Accounting Office.

Grant, C. A. 1977a. The mediator of culture: A teacher role revisited. *Journal Research and Development in Education* 11 (1): 102–117.

———, ed. 1977b. *Multicultural education: Commitments, issues, and applications.* Washington, D.C.: Association for Supervision and Curriculum Development.

———. 1999. *Multicultural research.* Philadelphia: Falmer Press.

Grant, C. A., and C. Sleeter. 1988. Race, class, and gender and abandoned dreams. *Teachers College Record* 90 (1): 19–40.

Hakuta, K. 1986. *Mirror of language: The debate on bilingualism.* New York: Basic Books.

Hakuta, K., and L. J. Gould. 1987. Synthesis of research on bilingual education. *Educational Leadership* 44 (6): 39–45.

Hall, N. 1987. *The emergence of literacy.* Portsmouth, N.H.: Heinemann Educational Books.

Harklau, L. 1994. Tracking and linguistic minority students: Consequences of ability grouping for second language learners. *Linguistics and Education* 6 (3): 217–244.

Haycock, K., and S. M. Navarro. 1988. *Unfinished business: Fulfilling our children's promise. A report from the achievement council.* Oakland, Calif.: Achievement Council.

Haynes, N. M., and C. L. Emmons. 1997. *Comer school development program effects: A ten year review, 1986–1996.* New Haven, Conn.: Yale University Study Child Center.

Heath, S. B. 1981. Towards an ethnohistory of writing in American education. In M. Farr-Whitman, ed., *Variation in writing: Functional and linguistic cultural differences.* Vol. 1 (225–246). Hillsdale, N.J.: Lawrence Erlbaum Associates.

———. 1982. Questioning at school and at home: A comparative study. In G. D. Spindler, ed., *Doing the ethnography of schooling: Educational anthropology in action* (102–131). New York: Holt, Rinehart and Winston.

———. 1983. *Ways with words: Language, life, and work in communities and classrooms.* Cambridge: Cambridge University Press.

———. 1986. Sociocultural contexts of language development. In California Department of Education, ed., *Beyond language: Social and cultural factors in schooling language minority students* (143–186). Los Angeles: Evaluation, Dissemination, and Assessment Center, California State University.

————. 1989. Oral and literate traditions among black Americans living in poverty. *American Psychologist* 44 (2): 367–373.

Henze, R., K. Regan, L. Vanett, and M. Power. 1990. An exploratory study of the effectiveness of the lower Kuskokwin school district's bilingual program. Paper prepared for the Lower Kuskokwin School District, Oakland, California.

Herrnstein, R. J., and C. Murray. 1994. *The bell curve: Intelligence and class structure in American life.* New York: The Free Press.

Hetherington, E. M., and R. D. Parke, eds. 1988. *Contemporary reading in child psychology* 3rd ed. New York: McGraw-Hill.

Hispanic Dropout Project. 1998. *Improving opportunities: Strategies from the secretary of education for Hispanic and limited English proficient students.* Washington, D.C.: U. S. Department of Education.

Hiss, W. 1990. Optional SATs: Six years later. *The Alumni Magazine,* September, 15–17.

Hoffman, D. M. 1988. Cross-cultural adaptation and learning: Iranians and Americans at school. In H. Trueba and C. Delgado-Gaitan, eds., *School and society: Learning content through culture* (131–149). New York: Praeger.

Hope, R. O., and L. I. Rendon. 1997. Educating a new majority: Mandate for the new century. In L. I. Rendon and R. O. Hope, eds., *Educating a new majority: Mandate for a new Century* (456–71). San Francisco: Jossey-Bass Publishers.

Hornberger, N. H. 1997. Indigenous literacies in the Americas. In N. H. Hornerberger ed., *Indigeneous literacies in the Americas: Language planning from the bottom up* (3–16). Berlin: Mouton de Gruyter.

Hudelson, S. 1987. The role of native language in literacy in the education of language minority children. *Language Arts* 64 (8): 827–841.

Hunt, J. McV. 1961. *Intelligence and experience.* New York: Ronald.

Hurtado, A., and E. Garcia. 1994. *The educational achievement of Latinos: Barriers and successes.* Santa Cruz: University of California Latino Eligibility Study.

————. 2001. The reconstruction of merit and the changing demographics in California. In E. Garcia, ed., *Latinos in higher education.* Berkeley, Calif.: Center for Latino Policy Research.

Hurtado, A., and P. Gurin. 1987. Ethnic identity and bilingualism attitudes. *Hispanic Journal of Behavioral Sciences* 9 (1): 1–18.

Hutton, E. R. 1942. Mexican children find themselves. In National Education Association, eds., *Americans all: Studies in intercultural education* (45–51). Washington, D.C.: National Education Association.

Irvine, J. 1990. *Black children and school failure: Politics, practices and prescriptions.* New York: Greenwood Press.

Jackman, M. R. 1973. Education and prejudice or education and response-set. *American Sociological Review* 38: 327–339.

Jaynes, G. D., and R. M. Williams Jr., eds. 1989. *A common destiny: Blacks and American society.* Washington, D.C.: National Academy Press.

Jencks, C. 1972. *Inequality: a reassessment of the effect of family and schooling in America.* New York: Basic Books.

Jessor, R. 1993. Successful adolescent development in high risk settings. *American Psychology* 48 (2): 117–126.

Johnson, D., and R. Johnson. 1981. Effects of cooperative and individualistic learning experiences on interethnic interaction. *Journal of Educational Psychology* 73(3): 444–449.

Johnson, D. L., K. Teigen, and R. Davila. 1983. Anxiety and social restriction: A study of children in Mexico, Norway, and the United States. *Journal of Cross-Cultural Psychology* 14: 439–454.

Joyce, B., C. Murphy, B. Showers, and J. Murphy. 1989. School renewal as cultural change. *Educational Leadership* 47 (3): 70–77.

Kagan, S. 1983a. Interpreting Chicano cooperativeness: Methodological and theoretical considerations. In J. L. Martinez and R. H. Mendoza, eds., *Chicano psychology.* 2nd ed. (289–333). Orlando: Academic Press.

———. 1983b. Social orientation among Mexican-American children: A challenge to traditional classroom structures. In E. Garcia, ed., *The Mexican-American child.* Tempe: Arizona State University.

Kagan, S., G. P. Knight, S. Martinez, and P. Espinosa-Santana. 1981. Conflict resolution style among Mexican children: Examining urbanization and ecology effects. *Journal of Cross-Cultural Psychology* 12: 222–232.

Kaufman, A. S. 1994. *Intelligence testing with the WISC-III.* New York: John Wiley & Sons.

Kaufman, P., and M. J. Frase. 1990. *Dropout rates in the United States: 1989.* Washington, D.C.: National Center for Education Statistics.

Keefe, S. E. 1979. Urbanization, acculturation, and extended family ties: Mexican-Americans in cities. *American Ethnologist* (summer): 349–362.

Keefe, S. E., and A. M. Padilla. 1987. *Chicano ethnicity.* Albuquerque: University of New Mexico Press.

Keefe, S. E., A. M. Padilla, and M. L. Carlos. 1979a. *Mental health issues of significance in Mexican American families.* Hispanic Mental Health Working Papers. Los Angeles: University of California.

———. 1979b. The Mexican-American extended family as an emotional support system. *Human Organization* 38: 144–152.

Kessler, C., and M. E. Quinn. 1986. Positive effects of bilingualism on science problem-solving abilities. In J. E. Alatis and J. J. Staczek, eds., *Perspectives on bilingual education* (289–296). Washington, D.C.: Georgetown University Press.

———. 1987. Language minority children's linguistic and cognitive creativity. *Journal of Multilingual and Multicultural Development* 8 (1): 173–185.

Knapp, M. S. 1995. *Teaching for meaning in high-poverty classrooms.* New York: Teachers College Press.

Knight, G. P., M. E. Bernal, and G. Carlos. 1988. Socialization and the development of cooperative, competitive, and individualistic behaviors among Mexican American children. In E. Garcia, L. Moll, and A. Barona, eds., *The Mexican American child: Language, cognition, and socialization.* Vol. 2. Tempe: Arizona State University.

Knight, G. P., and S. Kagan. 1977. Acculturation of prosocial and competitive behaviors among second- and third-generation Mexican American children. *Journal of Cross-Cultural Psychology* 8: 273–284.

Kozol, J. 1991. *Savage inequalities: Children in America's schools.* New York: Crown.

Kroeber, A. L., and D. Kluckhohn. 1963. *Culture: A critical review of concepts and definitions.* New York: Vintage Books.

Labov, W. 1972. The logic of nonstandard English. In W. Labov, ed., *Language in the inner city: Studies in black English vernacular* (201–240). Philadelphia: University of Pennsylvania Press.

Ladson-Billings, G., and W. F. Tate. 1995. Toward a critical race theory of education. *Teachers College Record* 97 (1): 47–68.

Lambert, N. L., and B. L. McCombs, eds. 1998. *Issues in school reform: A sampler of psychological perspectives on learner-centered schools.* Washington, D.C.: American Psychological Association.

Laosa, L. M. 1977. Nonbiased assessment of children's abilities: Historical antecedents and current issues. In T. Oakland, ed., *Psychological and educational assessment of minority children* (1–20). New York: Brunner/Mazel.

———. 1982. School, occupation, culture and family: The impact of parental schooling on the parent-child relationship. *Journal of Educational Psychology* 74 (6): 791–827.

———. 1984. Social policies toward children of diverse ethnic, racial, and language groups in the United States. In H. W. Stevenson and A. E. Siegel, eds., *Child development research and social policy* (1–109). Chicago: University of Chicago Press.

———. 1995. *Intelligence testing and social policy.* Research Report No. 95–32. Princeton, N.J.: Educational Testing Service.

———. 1996a. Intelligence testing and social policy. *Journal of Applied and Developmental Psychology* 17: 155–173.

———. 1996b. *Research perspectives on constructs of change: Intercultural migration and developmental transitions.* Princeton, N.J.: Educational Testing Service.

Lareau, A. 1989. *Home advantage: Social class and parental intervention in elementary education.* London: Falmer Press.

Larkin, R. W. 1979. *Suburban youth in cultural crisis.* New York: Oxford University Press.

Larson, K. A. 1989. Task-related and interpersonal problem-solving training for increasing school success in high-risk young adolescents. *Remedial and Special Education* 10 (5): 32–42.

Larson, K., and R. Rumberger. 1995a. Doubling school success in highest risk Latino youth: Results from a middle school intervention study. In R. Marcas and R. Garcia Ramos, eds., *Changing schools for changing students* (154–179). Santa Barbara: University of California Linguistic Minority Research Institute.

———. 1995b. *PACT manual: Parent and community teams for school success.* ABC Dropout Prevention and Intervention series. Santa Barbara: Graduate School of Education, University of California, Santa Barbara.

Latino Eligibility Task Force. 1997. *Latino student eligibility and participation in the University of California: YA BASTA!* Report No. 5. Berkeley: University of California.

Lau v. Nichols. 1974. U.S. Supreme Court, 414 U.S. 563.

Lave, J. 1988. *Cognition in practice: Mind mathematics and culture in everyday life.* Cambridge: Cambridge University Press.

Lee, L. C. 1991. The opening of the American mind: Educating leaders for a multi-cultural society. *Human Ecology Forum* (winter): 2–5.

Leopold, W. F. 1939. *Speech development of a bilingual child: A linguist's record. Vol. I: Vocabulary growth in the first two years.* Evanston, Ill.: Northwestern University Press.

Levin, H. M. 1986. *Educational reform for disadvantaged students: An emerging crisis.* Washington, D.C.: National Education Association.

Levin, I. 1988. *Accelerated schools for at-risk students.* CPRE Research Report Series RR-010. New Brunswick, N.J.: Rutgers University Center for Policy Research in Education.

Lindholm, K., and A. Christiansen. 1990. *Directory of two-way bilingual programs.* Washington, D.C.: Center for Applied Linguistics.

Linn, R. L. 1989. Current perspectives and future directions. In R. L. Linn, ed., *Educational measurement.* 3rd ed. (1–10). New York: Macmillan.

Lockwood, A. T. 1996. *Tracking: Conflicts and resolutions. Controversial issues in education.* Report No. EA027994 (ERIC Document Reproduction Services No. ED 400 604). Thousand Oaks, Calif.: Corwin Press.

Lockwood, A. T., and W. G. Secada. 1999. *Transforming education for Hispanic youth: Exemplary practices, programs, and schools.* Madison: University of Wisconsin Press; New York: Teachers College Press.

Lubin, B., R. M. Larsen, and J. D. Matarazzo. 1984. Patterns of psychological test usage in the United States: 1935–1982. *American Psychologist* 39: 451–454.

Lucas, T. 1997. *Into, through and beyond secondary school: Critical transitions for immigrant youth.* Washington, D.C.: Center for Applied Linguistics.

Lucas, T., R. Henze, and R. Donato. 1990. Promoting the success of Latino language-minority students: An exploratory study of six high schools. *Harvard Educational Review* 60 (3): 315–339.

Mace-Matlock, B. J., R. Alexander-Kasparik, and R. Queen. 1998. *Through the golden door: Educational approaches for immigrant adolescents with limited schooling.* Washington, D.C.: Center for Applied Linguistics.

Madden, N. A., R. E. Slavin, N. L. Karweit, L. Dolan, and B. A. Wasik. 1991. Success for all. *Phi Delta Kappan* 72: 593–599.

Mahiri, M. 1998. *Shooting for excellence.* New York: Teachers College Press and the National Council of Teachers of English.

Manaster, G. 1992. Mexican American migrant students' academic success: Sociological and psychological acculturation. *Adolescence* 27 (105): 123–136.

Manski, C., and D. A. Wise. 1983. *College choice in America.* Cambridge, Mass.: Harvard University Press.

Massey, D. S., K. M. Donato, and Z. Liang. 1990. Effects of the immigration reform and control act of 1986: Preliminary data from Mexico. In F. D. Bean, B. Edmonston, and J. S. Passel, eds., *Undocumented migration to the United States: IRCA and the experience of the 1980s* (183–210). Washington, D.C.: Urban Institute Press.

Matute-Bianchi, E. 1990. *A report to the Santa Clara county school district: Hispanics in the schools.* Santa Clara, Calif.: Santa Clara County School District.

McAdoo, H. P., and J. L. McAdoo, eds. 1985. *Black children: Social, educational, and parental environments.* Beverly Hills, Calif.: Sage Publications.

McCarthy, K. F., and G. Vernez. 1998. *Immigration in a changing economy: California's experience—Questions and answers.* Santa Monica, Calif.: Rand Corporation.

McClintock, C. G. 1972. Social motivation: A set of propositions. *Behavioral Science* 17: 438–454.

———. 1974. Development of social motives in Anglo-American and Mexican-American children. *Journal of Personality and Social Psychology* 29: 348–354.

McClintock, E., M. P. Bayard, and C. G. McClintock. 1983. The socialization of prosocial orientations in Mexican American families. In E. Garcia, ed., *The Mexican American child: Language, cognition and social development* (143–162). Tempe: Arizona State University.

McDermott, R. P. 1987. The exploration of minority school failure, again. *Anthropology and Education Quarterly* 18 (4): 361–364.

McDonough, P., and A. L. Antonio. 1996, April. Ethnic and Racial Differences in Selectivity of College Choice. Paper presented at the Annual Meeting of the American Educational Research Association. New York.

McDonough, P. M. 1992. *Buying and selling higher education: The social construction of the college applicant.* San Francisco: Research Association Conference.

McLaughlin, B. 1995. *Fostering second language development in young children: Principles and practices.* Educational Practice Report No. 14. Santa Cruz, Calif.: National Center for Research on Cultural Diversity and Second Language Learning.

McLeod, B. 1996. *School reform and student diversity: Exemplary schooling for language minority students.* Washington, D.C.: Institute for the Study of Language and Education, George Washington University.

McNab, G. 1979. Cognition and bilingualism: A re-analysis of studies. *Linguistics* 17: 231–255.

McPherson, M. S., and M. O. Schapiro. 1997. Financing undergraduate education: Designing national policies. *National Tax Journal* 70 (3): 557–571.

Mead, M. 1937. *Cooperation and competition among primitive people.* New York: McGraw-Hill.

———. 1939a. *Culture of the islander.* New York: Academic Press.

———. 1939b. Native languages as field-work tools. *American Anthropologist* 41: 189–205.

Mehan, H. 1987. Language and schooling. In G. Spindler and D. Spindler, eds., *Interpretive ethnography of education at home an abroad* (109–136). Hillsdale, N.J.: Lawrence Erlbaum Associates.

———. 1992. Understanding inequality in schools: The contribution of interpretive studies. *Sociology of Education* 65 (1): 1–20.

Mehan, H., I. Villanueva, L. Hubbard, and A. Lintz. 1996. *Constructing school success: The consequences of untracking low achieving students.* Cambridge: Cambridge University Press.

Meier, K. J., J. Stewart Jr., and R. E. England. 1989. *Race, class, and education.* Madison: University of Wisconsin Press.

Messick, S. 1989. Validity. In R. L. Linn, ed., *Educational measurement.* 3rd ed. (13–103). New York: Macmillan.

———. 1995. Validity of psychological assessment: Validation of inferences from persons' responses and performances as scientific inquiry into score meaning. *American Psychologist* 50: 741–749.

Miller, L. S. 1995. *An American imperative: Accelerating minority educational advancement.* New Haven, Conn.: Yale University Press.

Minicucci, C., P. Berman, B. McLaughlin, B. McLeod, B. Nelson, and B. Woodsworth. 1995. School reform and student diversity. *Phi Delta Kappan* 77 (1): 77–80.

Minicucci, C., and L. Olsen, L. 1993. *Programs for secondary limited English proficient students: A California study.* Washington, D.C.: National Clearinghouse for Bilingual Education.

Miramontes, O., A. Nadeau, and N. Commins. 1997. *Linguistic diversity and effective school reform: A process for decision making.* New York: Teachers College Press.

Moll, L. 1988. Educating Latino students. *Language Arts* 64: 315–324.

———. 1992. Bilingual classroom studies and community analysis: Some recent trends. *Educational Researcher* 21 (2): 20–24.

———. 1996. Educating Latino students. *Language Arts* 64: 315–324.

Moll, L., and S. Diaz. In press. Bilingual communication and reading. *Elementary School Journal.*

Montgomery, A., and R. Rossi. 1994. *Educational reforms and students placed at risk: A review of the current state of the art.* Washington, D.C.: U.S. Department of Education, Office of Educational Research and Improvement.

Moran, C. E, and K. Hakuta. 1995. Bilingual education: Broadening research perspectives. In J. A. Banks and C. A. McGee Banks, eds., *Handbook of research on multicultural education* (445–462). New York: Macmillan.

Moreno, J. F., ed. 1999. *The elusive quest for equality: 150 years of Chicano/Chicana education.* Cambridge, Mass.: Harvard Educational Review.

Moreno, R. P. 1997. Everyday instruction: A comparison of Mexican American and Anglo mothers and their preschool children. *Hispanic Journal of Behavioral Sciences* 19 (4): 527–539.

Moss, M., and M. Puma. 1995. *Prospects: The congressionally mandated study of educational growth and opportunity.* First Year Report on Language Minority and Limited English Proficient Students. Cambridge, Mass.: Abt Associates.

Murray, C. 1984. *Losing ground: American social policy 1950–1980.* New York: Basic Books.

National Association for the Education of Young Children (NAEYC). 1996. NAEYC position statement: Responding to linguistic and cultural diversity—Recommendations for effective early childhood education. *Young Children,* September.

National Center for Children in Poverty. 1990. *Five million children: A statistical profile of our poorest young citizens.* New York: Columbia University.

————. 1998. *Young child poverty in the states: Wide variation and significant change.* New York: Columbia School of Public Health.

National Center for Education Statistics (NCES). 1991. *The condition of education.* Vols. 1 and 2. Washington, D.C.: U.S. Department of Education.

————. 1995. *The educational progress of Hispanic students: The condition of education 1995.* Washington, D.C.: U.S. Department of Education.

————. 1996. *Annual report, 1996.* Washington, D.C.: U.S. Department of Education.

————. 1998. *Annual report, 1998.* Washington, D.C.: U.S. Department of Education.

National Center of Effective Secondary Schools. 1991. *Annual report: Effective secondary schools.* Madison, Wis.: National Center of Effective Schooling.

National Commission on Children. 1991. *Beyond rhetoric: A new American agenda for children and families—Final Report of the National Commission on Children.* Washington, D.C.: National Commission on Children.

National Commission on Excellence in Education. 1983. *A nation at risk: The imperative for education reform.* Washington, D.C.: U.S. Department of Education.

National Council of Teachers of English and the International Reading Association. 1996. *Standards for the English language arts.* Urbana, Ill.: National Council of Teachers of English; Newark, Del.: International Reading Association.

National Research Council. 1997. *The new Americans: Economic, demographic, and fiscal effects of immigration.* Washington, D.C.: National Academy Press.

Nieto, S. 1996. *Affirming diversity: The sociopolitical context of multicultural education.* 2nd ed. White Plains, N.Y.: Longman.

Noddings, N. 1973. Comments on the wisdom of scientific inquiry on education. *Journal of Research in Science Teaching* 10 (3): 279.

————. 1996. Rethinking the benefits of the college-bound curriculum. *Phi Delta Kappan* 78 (4): 285–289.

Nora, A., L. I. Rendon, and G. Cuadraz. 1999. Access choice and outcomes: A profile of Hispanic students in higher education. In A. Tashakkori and S. H. Ochoa, eds., *Education of Hispanics in the United States* (261–283). New York: AMS Press.

Oakes, J. 1985. *Keeping track: How schools structure inequality.* New Haven, Conn.: Yale University Press.

————. 1990. *Multiplying inequalities: The effects of race, social class, and tracking on opportunities to learn mathematics and science.* Santa Monica, Calif.: Rand Corporation.

————. 1991. *Lost talent: The underparticipation of women, minorities, and disabled persons in science.* Santa Monica, Calif.: Rand Corporation.

————. 1992a. *Blurring academic and vocational boundaries in cultures of large high schools.* Berkeley: National Center for Research in Vocational Education, University of California, Berkeley.

————. 1992b. *Educational matchmaker: Academic and vocational tracking in comprehensive high schools.* Santa Monica, Calif.: Rand Corporation.

Ogbu, J. 1982a. Cultural discontinuities and schooling. *Anthropology and Education Quarterly* 13 (4): 168–190.

———. 1982b. Socialization: A cultural ecological approach. In K. M. Borman, ed., *The social life of children in a changing society* (253–267). Hillsdale, N.J.: Lawrence Erlbaum Associates.

———. 1983. Minority status and schooling in plural societies. *Comparative Education Review* 27 (22): 168–190.

———. 1986. The consequences of the American caste system. In Ulric Neisser, ed., *The school achievement of minority children: New perspectives* (126–132). Hillsdale, N.J.: Lawrence Erlbaum Associates.

———. 1987a. *Minority education and caste: The American system in cross-cultural perspective*. New York: Academic Press.

———. 1987b. Variability in minority school performance: A problem in search of an explanation. *Anthropology and Education Quarterly* 18 (4): 312–334.

———. 1999. *Collective identity and schooling*. Tokyo: Japan Society of Educational Sociology.

Ogbu, J., and M. E. Matute-Bianchi. 1986. Understanding sociocultural factors: Knowledge, identity and school adjustment. In Bilingual Education Office, ed., *Beyond language: Social and cultural factors in schooling language minority students* (73–142). Los Angeles: Evaluation, Dissemination, and Assessment Center, California State University.

Olivas, M. 1997. Research on Latino college students: A theoretical framework and inquiry. In A. Darder, R. Torres, and H. Gutierrezl, eds., *Latinos and education: A critical reader* (468–486). New York: Routledge.

Olsen, L. 1997. *Made in America: Immigrant students in our public schools*. New York: The New Press.

Olsen, L., and C. Dowell. 1989. *Bridges: Promising programs for the education of immigrant children*. ERIC Document Reproduction Service No. ED 314 544. San Francisco: California Tomorrow.

O'Malley, M. J. 1981. *Children's and services study: Language minority children with limited English proficiency in the United States*. Rosslyn, Va.: National Clearinghouse for Bilingual Education.

Orfield, G. 1992. Money, equity, and college access. *Harvard Educational Review* 62 (3): 337–372.

Osborne, J. W. 1997. Race and academic disidentification. *Journal of Educational Psychology* 89: 728–735.

Ovando, C. J., and V. P. Collier. 1985. *Bilingual and ESL classrooms: Teaching in multicultural contexts*. New York: McGraw-Hill.

Ozden, Y. 1996. Have efforts to improve higher education opportunities for low-income youth succeeded? *Journal of Student Financial Aid* 26 (3): 19–39.

Passell, J. 1994. *Immigrants and taxes: A reappraisal of Huddle's "The cost of immigration."* Washington, D.C.: Urban Institute.

Paul, B. 1965. Anthropological perspectives on medicine and public health. In J. K. Skipper Jr. and R. C. Leonard, eds., *Social interaction and patient care* (142–178). Philadelphia: Lippincott.

Peal, E., and W. E. Lambert. 1962. The relation of bilingualism to intelligence. *Psychological Monographs: General and Applied* 76 (546): 1–23.

Pearl, A. 1991. Democratic education: Myth or reality. In R. Valencia, ed., *Chicano school failure and success* (101–118). New York: Falmer Press.

Pease-Alvarez, L., E. Garcia, and P. Espinoza. 1991. Effective instruction for language minority students: An early childhood case study. *Early Childhood Research Quarterly* 6 (3): 347–363.

Pelto, P., and G. H. Pelto. 1975. Intra-cultural variation: Some theoretical issues. *American Ethnologist* 2 (1): 1–45.

Perry, J. 1975. Notes toward a multicultural curriculum. *English Journal* 64: 283–291.

Phelan, P., L. A. Davidson, and T. H. Cao. 1991. *Students' multipleworlds: Navigating the borders of family, peer, and school cultures.* New York: Teachers College Press.

Phillips, S. 1983. *The invisible culture: Communication in classroom and community on the Warm Springs Indian reservation.* New York: Longman.

Pitsch, M. 1991. Partners: Schools and colleges forge new bonds to advance reform. *Teacher Magazine* 3 (3): 12–13.

Plyler v. Doe, 457 U.S. 202 (1982).

Policy Analysis for California Education (PACE). 1997. *Higher education outreach programs: A synthesis of evaluations.* Appendix to the University of California Outreach Task Force Report. Berkeley, Calif.: PACE.

Portes, A. 1996. *The new second generation.* New York: Russell Sage Foundation.

Portes, A., and R. Rumbaut. 1990. *Immigrant America: A portrait.* Berkeley and Los Angeles: University of California Press.

Professional Development Program. 1993. *Lessons learned from FIPSE projects II.* Berkeley and Los Angeles: University of California Press.

Purkey, S. C., and M. S. Smith. 1983. Effective schools: A review. *Elementary School Journal* 83: 52–78.

Ramirez, M., and A. Castaneda. 1974. *Cultural democracy, bi-cognitive development and education.* New York: Academic Press.

Ramist, L., C. Lewis, and L. McCamley-Jenkins. 1994. *Student group differences in predicting college grades: Sex, language, and ethnic groups.* New York: College Entrance Examination Board.

Rand Corporation. 1994. *Educational achievement of generations: Executive summary.* Los Angeles: Rand Corporation.

Reddy, M. A. 1993. *Statistical record of Hispanic Americans.* Detroit: Gale Research.

Renato, R. 1993. *Cultures and truth: The remaking of social analysis.* Boston: Beacon Press.

Rendon, L. I., and R. O. Hope. 1996. *Educating a new majority: Transforming America's educational system for diversity.* San Francisco: Jossey-Bass.

Rodriguez, C. E. 1989. *Puerto Ricans born in the U.S.A.* Winchester, Mass.: Unwin Hyman.

Rodriguez, R. 1982. *Hunger of memory: The Education of Richard Rodriguez—An autobiography.* Boston: D. R. Godine.

Romo, H. 1999. *Reaching out: Best practices for educating Mexican-origin children and youth.* Charleston, W. Va.: Clearinghouse on Rural Education and Small Schools.

Romo, H., and T. Falbo. 1996. *Latino high school graduation: Defying the odds.* Austin: University of Texas Press.

Rose, M. 1989. *Lives on the boundary.* New York: The Free Press.

———. 1995a. Calexico: Portrait of an educational community. *Teachers & Writers* 26 (5): 1–15.

———. 1995b. *Possible lives: The promise of public education in America.* New York: Houghton Mifflin.

Rosenshine, B. 1986. Synthesis of research on explicit teaching. *Educational Leadership* 43 (3): 60–69.

Ross, J. L., and C. Pinchback. 1990. *The decline of blacks in mathematics: Implications for elementary secondary and higher education.* ERIC Document No. ED 327 392.

Rossell, C. H. 1992. Nothing matters? A critique of the Ramirez, et al. longitudinal study of instructional programs for language-minority children. *Bilingual Research Journal* 16 (1–2): 159–186.

Rossell, C., and J. M. Ross. 1986. *The social science evidence on bilingual education.* Boston: Boston University.

Rossi, R. J. 1995. *Education reform and students at risk. Volume III: Synthesis and evaluation of previous efforts to improve educational practice and development of strategies for achieving positive outcomes.* Studies of Education Reform. Washington, D.C.: American Institutes for Research.

Ruiz, R. 1984. *Language Teaching in American Education: Implications for Second Language Teaching.* Washington, D.C.: National Institutes of Education.

———. 1985. La crise des langues aux Etats-Unis. In J. Maurais, ed., La crise des Langues. Paris: Le Robert, 147–88.

———. 1988. Language policy: Additive or subtractive. In A. Gordon, ed., *U.S. policy and immigration.* New York: Falmer Press.

———. 1990. Official Languages and Language Planning. In K. L. Adams and D. T. Brink, eds., *Perspectives on Official English: The Campaign English as the Official Language of the USA.* Berlin: Mouton de Gruyter.

———. 1993. Bilingual education and the reauthorization of ESEA. *NABE Journal* 13 (3): 46–64.

Rumbaut, R. 1996. Ties that bind: Immigration and immigrant families in the United States. In A. Booth, A. C. Crouter, and N. Landale, eds., *Immigration and the family: Research and policy on U. S. immigrants* (3–45). Hillsdale, N.J.: Lawrence Erlbaum Associates.

———. 1997. *Children of immigrants: The adaptation process of the second generation.* Report to the Russell Sage Foundation. New York: Russell Sage Foundation.

Rumbaut, R. G., and W. A. Cornelius. 1995. *California's immigrant children.* San Diego: Center for U.S.-Mexican Studies.

Rumberger, R. W. 1993. Dropping out of high school: The influence of race, sex, and family background. *American Educational Research Journal* 20 (2): 199–220.

———. 1995. Dropping out of middle school: A multilevel analysis of students and schools. *American Educational Research Journal* 32 (3): 583–625.

———. 1998. Achievement for Latinos through academic success. In P. Gandara, L. Larson, R. Rumberger, and H. Mehan, eds., *Capturing Latino students in the academic pipeline* (3–12). Chicano Latino Policy Project, University of California, Berkeley.

Rumberger, R., and K. A. Larson. 1996. The impact of student mobility on high school completion. Unpublished manuscript.

Rutter, M., B. Maughan, P. Mortimore, and J. Ouston. 1979. *Fifteen thousand hours: Secondary schools and their effects on children.* Cambridge, Mass.: Harvard University Press.

San Miguel, G., and R. R. Valencia. 1998. From the Treaty of Guadalupe Hidalgo to "Hopwood": The educational plight of Mexican Americans in the Southwest. *Harvard Educational Review* 68 (3): 353–412.

Saxe, G. B. 1996. Studying cognitive development in sociocultural context: The development of a practice-based approach. In R. Jessor, A. Colby, and R. A. Schweder, eds., *Ethnography and human development* (275–303). Chicago: University of Chicago Press.

Scarr, S. 1994–95. What is equality? *Issues in Science and Technology* (winter): 82–85.

Schlesinger, A. 1991. The disuniting of America: What we all stand to lose if multicultural education takes the wrong approach. *American Educator* 15 (3): 14, 21–23.

———. 1992. *The disuniting of America.* New York: W. W. Norton.

Schneider, S. G. 1976. *Revolution, reaction, or reform: The 1974 bilingual education act.* New York: Las Americas.

Schuman, H., and J. Harding. 1964. Prejudice and the norm of rationality. *Sociometry* 27: 353–371.

Schuman, H., C. Steeh, and L. Bobo. 1985. *Racial attitudes in America: Trends and interpretations.* Cambridge: Cambridge University Press.

Schwartz, T. 1978. Where is the culture? Personality as the distributive locus of culture. In G. Spindler, ed., *The making of psychological anthropology* (37–50). Berkeley and Los Angeles: University of California Press.

Scribner, S., and M. Cole. 1981. Unpackaging literacy. In M. Farr-Whiteman, ed., *Variation in writing: Functional and linguistic-cultural differences. Vol. 1. Writing: The nature, development, and teaching of written communications* (71–88). Hillsdale, N.J.: Lawrence Erlbaum Associates.

Seginer, R. 1989. Adolescent sisters: The relationship between younger and older sisters among Israeli Arabs. Paper presented at the annual meeting of the International Society for the Study of Behavioral Development, Jyvaskyla, Finland.

Shabazz, M. 1995. The bandwagon: Some schools lessen weight of standardized tests scores. *Black Issues in Higher Education* 11 (25): 24–26.

Sharan, S. 1980. Cooperative learning in small groups: Recent methods and effects on achievement, attitudes, and ethnic relations. *Review of Education Research* 50 (2): 241–271.

Skinner, B. F. 1957. *Verbal behavior.* Englewood Cliffs, N.J.: Prentice Hall.

Slavin, R. E. 1988. Cooperative learning and student achievement. In R. E. Slavin, ed., *School and classroom organization.* Hillsdale, N.J.: Lawrence Erlbaum Associates.

———. 1989. The pet and the pendulum. Fadism in education and how to stop it. *Phi Delta Kappan* 70 (10): 752–758.

————. 1996. Success for all: A summary of research. *Journal of Education for Students Placed at Risk* 1: 41–76.

Slavin, R., N. Karweit, and N. Madden. 1989. *Effective programs for students at risk.* Needham Heights, Mass.: Allyn and Bacon.

Sleeter, C. E., and C. A. Grant. 1987. An analysis on multicultural education in the U.S. *Harvard Educational Review* 57 (4): 421–424.

Smith, M., and B. Tarallo. 1995. Proposition 187: Global trend or local narrative? Explaining anti-immigrant politics in California, Arizona and Texas. *International Migration Review* 20: 664, 676.

Smith, T. W. 1971. *Understanding reading.* New York: Holt, Rinehart and Winston.

————. 1990. *Ethnic images.* GSS Topical Report No. 19. Chicago: National Opinion Research Center, University of Chicago.

Smith, T. W., and P. B. Sheatsley. 1984. American attitudes towards race relations. *Public Opinion* 7 (14–15): 50–53.

Smyth, F. L. 1990. SAT coaching: What really happens to scores and how we are led to expect more. *Journal of College Admissions* 129: 7–17.

Snow, C. E. 1990. The development of definitional skill. *Journal of Child Language* 17 (3): 697–710.

Snow, C. E., M. S. Burns, and P. Griffin. 1998. *Preventing reading difficulties in young children. National Academy of Sciences.* Washington, D.C.: National Research Council, Commission on Behavioral and Social Sciences and Education.

Snow, D. 1997. Children's acquisition of speech timing in English: A comparative study of voice onset time and final syllable vowel lengthening. *Journal of Child Language* 24 (1): 35–56.

Soto, L. D. 1997. *Language, culture, and power: Bilingual families and the struggle for quality education.* New York: State University of New York Press.

Spencer, M. B. 1988a. Self-concept development. In D. T. Slaughter, ed., *Black children and poverty: A developmental perspective* (103–116). San Francisco: Jossey-Bass.

————. 1988b. Transitional bilingual education and the socialization of immigrants. *Harvard Educational Review* 58 (2): 133–153.

Spencer, M. B., and F. D. Horowitz. 1973. Effects of systematic social and token reinforcement on the modification of racial and color concept attitudes in black and in white preschool children. *Developmental Psychology* 9: 246–254.

Spindler, G. 1987. *Education and cultural process: Anthropological approaches.* Prospect Heights, Ill.: Waveland Press.

Spiro, M. E. 1951. Culture and personality: The natural history of a false dichotomy. *Psychiatry* 14: 19–46.

Stanford Working Group. 1993. *Language minority education and ESEA.* New York: Carnegie Corporation of America.

Stanton-Salazar, R. D. 1997. A social capital framework for understanding the socialization of racial minority children and youths. *Harvard Educational Review* 67 (1): 1–40.

Stanton-Salazar, R. D., and S. M. Dornbusch. 1995. Social capital and the reproduction of inequality: Information networks among Mexican-Origin high school students. *Sociology of Education* 68 (2): 116–135.

Steele, C. 1994. Ethnic identity and test performance. *Journal of Social Psychology* 47 (3): 114–128.

Steele, C., and J. Aronson. 1995. Stereotype threat and the intellectual test performance of African Americans. *Journal of Personality and Social Psychology* 69 (5): 797–811.

Steinhauer, N. 1996. Non-native teachers of native children: *Native Viewpoints. Canadian Social Studies* 31 (1): 9–10.

Suarez-Orozco, M. M. 1985. Opportunity, family dynamics and school achievement: The sociocultural context of motivation among recent immigrants from Central America. Paper read at the University of California Symposium on Linguistics, Minorities, and Education, Tahoe City, California, May.

———. 1987. Becoming somebody: Central American immigrants in U.S. inner-city schools. *Anthropology and Education Quarterly* 18: 287–299.

———. 1996. California dreaming: Proposition 187 and the cultural psychology of racial and ethnic exclusion. *Anthropology and Education Quarterly* 27 (2): 151–167.

———. 1997. *Some thoughts on the "new" immigration.* Keynote Speech: Immigration and Education. Chicago: Spencer Foundation.

Suarez-Orozco, M., and C. Suarez-Orozco. 1995. *Transformations: Immigration, family life, and achievement motivation among Latino adolescents.* Stanford, Calif.: Stanford University Press.

Sue, S., and S. Okazaki. 1990. Asian-American educational achievements: A phenomenon in search of an explanation. *American Psychologist* 45 (8): 913–920.

Sue, S., and A. Padilla. 1986. Ethnic minority issues in the United States: Challenges for the educational system. In Bilingual Education Office, ed., *Beyond language: Social and cultural factors in schooling language minority students* (35–72). Los Angeles: Evaluation, Dissemination, and Assessment Center, California State University.

Suzuki, B. H. 1984. Curriculum transformation for multicultural education. *Education and Urban Society* 16 (2): 294–322.

Tajfel, H. 1978. *The social psychology of minorities.* London: Minority Rights Group.

Tashakkori, A., and S. H. Ochoa, eds. 1999. *Education of Hispanics in the United States: Politics, policies, and outcomes.* New York: AMS Press.

Teachers College Record. 1995. New policy in the U.S. Department of Education. *Teachers College Record* 27 (1): 1–114.

Terman, L. M., and M. A. Merrill. 1973. *Stanford-Binet intelligence scale: Manual for the third revisions—Form L-M.* Boston: Houghton Mifflin.

Tharp, R. G. 1989. Psychocultural variables and k constants: Effects on teaching and learning in schools. *American Psychologist* 44: 349–359.

Tharp, R. G., and R. Gallimore. 1988. *Rousing minds to life: Teaching, learning and schooling in social context.* Cambridge: Cambridge University Press.

Thomas, W. P., and V. P. Collier. 1995a. *Language minority student achievement and program effectiveness. Research summary of ongoing study.* Washington, D.C.: National Clearinghouse for Bilingual Education.

———. 1995b. *A longitudinal analysis of programs serving language minority students.* Washington, D.C.: National Clearinghouse on Bilingual Education.

Thomas, S. V., and B. Park. 1921a. *Culture of immigrants.* Cambridge, Mass.: Newcome Press.

———. 1921b. *Culture and personality.* 2nd ed. New York: Random House.

Tollefson, N. 1986. Functional competencies in the U.S. refugee program: Theoretical and practical problems. *TESOL Quarterly* 20 (40): 649–664.

Torres, R. D., L. F. Miron, and J. X. Inda. 1999. *Race identity and citizenship: A reader.* Malden, Mass.: Blackwell.

Trioke, R. C. 1981. Synthesis of research in bilingual education. *Educational Leadership* 38: 498–504.

Trueba, H. T. 1987. *Success or failure? Learning and the language minority student.* Scranton, Pa.: Harper & Row.

———. 1988a. Peer socialization among minority students: A high school dropout prevention program. In H. Trueba and C. Delgado-Gaitan, eds., *Schools and society: Learning content through culture* (173–193). New York: Praeger.

———. 1988b. Rethinking learning disabilities: Cultural knowledge in literacy acquisition. Unpublished manuscript. Office for Research on Educational Equity, Graduate School of Education, University of California, Santa Barbara.

———. 1999. *Latinos unidos.* Lanham, Md.: Rowman & Littlefield.

Turnbaugh, A. L., and W. G. Secada. 1999. *Transforming education for Hispanic youth.* Madison: University of Wisconsin Press.

Ueda, R. 1987. *Avenues to adulthood: The origins of the high school and social mobility in an American suburb.* Cambridge: Cambridge University Press.

University of California. 1993. *Latino student eligibility and participation in the University of California.* Report No. 1 (March). Santa Cruz: University of California and the Latino Eligibility Task Force.

———. 1997. *Latino student eligibility and participation in the University of California. YA BASTA!* Latino Eligibility Task Force Report No. 5 (July). Berkeley: University of California and the Chicano/Latino Policy Project.

Unz, R. 1998. Personal communication with Eugene Garcia.

U.S. Bureau of the Census. 1990. *Social and economic characteristics in the U.S.: 1990 census of the population.* Washington, D.C.: U.S. Government Printing Office.

———. 1991. *Statistical abstract of the United States, 1991.* Washington, D.C.: U.S. Government Printing Office.

———. 1993a. *Hispanic Americans today.* Washington, D.C.: Economics and Statistics Administration, U.S. Department of Commerce.

———. 1993b. *The Hispanic population in the United States: March 1993.* Washington, D.C.: U.S. Government Printing Office.

———. 1995. *Population projections of the U.S. by age, sex, race, and Hispanic origin: 1995 to 2050.* Washington, D.C.: U.S. Government Printing Office.

———. 1997a. *The Hispanic population in the United States: March 1997.* Washington, D.C.: U.S. Government Printing Office.

———. 1997b. *United States population estimates, by age, sex, race, and Hispanic origin, 1990 to 1997.* Washington, D.C.: U.S. Government Printing Office.

U.S. Department of Commerce. 1996. *School enrollment: Social and economic characteristics of students: October 1996.* Washington, D.C.: U.S. Government Printing Office.

———. 1998. *Educational attainment in the United States: 1998.* P20–505. Washington, D.C.: U.S. Government Printing Office.

U.S. Department of Commerce, Census Bureau. 1996a. *Health Insurance Coverage: 1996.* Washington, D.C.: U.S. Government Printing Office.

———. 1996b. *Money income in the United States: 1996.* Washington, D.C.: U.S. Government Printing Office.

———. 1996c. *Population projections of the United States by age, sex, race, and Hispanic origin: 1995–2050.* P25–1130. Washington, D.C.: U.S. Government Printing Office.

———. 1996d. *Poverty in the United States: 1996.* Washington, D.C.: U.S. Government Printing Office.

U.S. Department of Education. 1997. National Assessment of Educational Progress, NAEP in 1996 trends in academic progress. Washington, D.C.: U.S. Government Printing Office.

———. 1998. *No more excuses: The final report of the U.S. Hispanic dropout project.* Washington, D.C.: U.S. Department of Education.

U.S. Department of Education, National Center for Education Statistics. 1991. *The condition of education, 1991, Vol. 1: Elementary and Secondary Education.* Washington, D.C.: U.S. Government Printing Office.

U.S. General Accounting Office. 1994. *Limited English proficiency: A growing and costly educational challenge facing many school districts.* GAO/HEHS-94–38. Washington, D.C.: U.S. General Accounting Office.

U.S. Immigration and Naturalization Service. 1994. *Statistical yearbook of the immigration and naturalization, 1993.* Washington, D.C.: U.S. Government Printing Office.

Useem E. 1992. Middle schools and math groups: Parents involvement in children's placement. *Sociology of Education* 65 (4): 263–279.

Valdés, G. 1996. *Con respeto: Bridging the distances between culturally diverse families and schools—An ethnographic portrait.* New York: Teachers College Press.

———. 1998. The world outside and inside schools: Language and immigrant children. *Educational Researcher* 27 (6): 4–18.

Valdez, R. B., J. Da Vanzo, and L. Greenwell. 1993. *Social ties, wages, and gender among Salvadorean and Filipino immigrants.* Santa Monica, Calif.: Rand Corporation.

Valencia, A. A. 1994. The degree that parents and significant others influence Anglo American and Mexican American students to pursue and complete university studies. *Journal of Educational Issues of Language Minority Students* 14: 301–317.

Valencia, R., ed. 1991. *Chicano school failure and success: Research and policy agendas for the 1990s.* New York: Falmer Press.

Valsiner, J. 1989. How can developmental psychology become "culture inclusive"? In J. Valsiner, ed., *Child development in cultural context* (1–8). Lewiston, N.Y.: Hogrefe and Huber.

Valverde, S. A. 1987. A comparative study of Hispanic high school dropouts and graduates: Why do some leave school early and some finish? *Education and Urban Society* 19 (3): 320–329.

Varenne, H. 1982. Jocks and freaks: The symbolic structure of the expression of social interaction among American senior high school students. In G. Spindler, ed., *Doing the ethnography of schooling: Educational anthropology in action* (112–121). New York: Holt, Rinehart and Winston.

Velez, W. 1989. High school attrition among Hispanic and Non-Hispanic white youths. *Sociology of Education* 62 (2): 119–33.

Vernez, G. 1993. *Mexican labor in California's economy: From rapid growth to likely stability.* Stanford, Calif.: Stanford University Press.

Vernez, G., and A. Abrahamse. 1996. *How immigrants fare in U. S. education.* MR-718-AMF. Santa Monica, Calif.: Rand Corporation.

Vernez, G., A. Abrahamse, and D. Quigley. 1996. *How immigrants fare in U.S. education.* Santa Monica, Calif.: Rand Corporation.

Vernez, G., R. A. Krop, and C. P. Rydell. 1999. *Closing the education gap: benefits and costs.* Santa Monica, Calif.: RAND.

Villegas, A. M. 1991. Culturally responsive pedagogy for the 1990s and beyond. Princeton, N.J.: Educational Testing Service.

Vizenor, G. 1998. *Fugitive poser: Native American Indian scenes of absence and presence.* Lincoln: University of Nebraska Press.

Vobejda, B. 1987. Some colleges rethinking value of SATs: Administrators say test is taking on undue significance with high school students. *Washington Post,* June 27, A3.

Vogt, L., C. Jordan, and R. Tharp. 1987. Explaining school failure, producing school success: Two cases. *Anthropology and Education Quarterly* 18 (4): 276–286.

Vygotsky, L. S. 1956. *The genesis of higher psychological functions.* Moscow: Academy of Pedagogical Sciences.

Waggoner, D. 1991. *Language Minority Census Newsletter.* Washington, D.C.: Numbers and Needs.

Walberg, H. 1986. What works in a nation still at risk. *Educational Leadership* 44 (1): 7–11.

Waldinger, R., and M Bozorgmehr, eds. 1996. *Ethnic Los Angeles.* New York: Russell Sage Foundation.

Walker, C. L. 1987. Hispanic achievements: Old views and new perspectives. In H. Trueba, ed., *Success or failure? Learning and the language minority student* (15–32). Cambridge, Mass.: Newbury House.

Wallace, A. F. C. 1970. *Culture and personality.* 2nd ed. New York: Random House.

Walsh, D. October 12, 1990. Minority students in Santa Clara County continue to deteriorate academically. *San Francisco Examiner,* B1–4.

Warren, J. R. 1996. Educational inequality among white and Mexican-origin adolescents in the American Southwest: 1990. *Sociology of Education* 69 (2): 142–158.

Wehlage, G. G., R. A. Rutter, G. A. Smith, N. Lesko, and R. R. Fernandez. 1989. *Reducing the risk: Schools as communities of support.* New York: Falmer Press.

Weinstein-Shr, G. 1995. Learning from uprooted families. In G. Weinstein-Shr and E. Quintero, eds., *Immigrant learners and their families* (113–133). Washington, D.C.: Center for Applied Linguistics.

Weis, L., ed. 1988. *Class, race, and gender in American education.* Albany: State University of New York Press.

Wertsch, J. V. 1985. *Vygotsky and the social formation of the mind.* Cambridge, Mass.: Harvard University Press.

West, C. 1993. Learning to talk of race. In R. Gooding-Williams, ed., *Reading Rodney King, reading urban uprising.* New York: Routledge.

———. 1999. The new culture of politics of difference. In C. Lemert, ed., *Social theory: The multicultural and classics readings* (521–531). Boulder, Colo.: Westview Press.

Whiting, B. B., and C. P. Edwards. 1988. *Children of different worlds: The formation of social behavior.* Cambridge, Mass.: Harvard University Press.

Wiesner, T. S., R. Gallimore, and C. Jordan. 1988. Unpackaging cultural effects on classroom learning: Native Hawaiian peer assistance and child-generated activity. *Anthropology and Education Quarterly* 19 (4): 327–353.

Wigdor, A. K., and W. R. Garner, eds. 1982. *Ability testing: Uses, consequences, and controversies.* Parts 1 and 2. Washington, D.C.: National Academy Press.

Willig, A. C. 1985. A meta-analysis of selected studies on effectiveness of bilingual education. *Review of Educational Research* 55 (33): 269–317.

Wilson, W. J. 1978. *The declining significance of race.* Chicago: University of Chicago Press.

———. 1987. *The truly disadvantaged: The inner city, the underclass, and public policy.* Chicago: University of Chicago Press.

Winfield, L. F. 1986. Teacher beliefs toward academically at risk students in urban schools. *Urban Review* 18: 253–267.

Wong, M. C., G. D. Haertal, and H. J. Walberg. 1993. *Educational resilience in inner cities.* Eric Document No. ED 3999312. Philadelphia: National Education Center on Education in the Inner Cities, Temple University.

Wong-Fillmore, L. 1991. When learning a second language means losing a first. *Early Childhood Research Quarterly* 6 (3): 323–347.

Zentella, A. C. 1997. *Growing up bilingual: Puerto Rican children in New York.* Malden, Mass.: Blackwell.

Zhou, M. 1997. Growing up American: The challenge confronting immigrant children and children of immigrants. *Annual Review of Sociology* 23: 61–95.

Zuman, J. P. 1988. The effectiveness of special preparation for the SAT: An evaluation of a commercial coaching school. Paper presented at the annual meeting of the American Educational Research Association, New Orleans, April.

Index

Page references in *italic* indicate information contained in tables and figures.

About the Author

Eugene E. Garcia was born in Grand Junction, Colorado, on June 3, 1946. He is the son of settled-out migrant farmworker parents from northwestern New Mexico and worked in seasonal crops, harvesting sugar beets, cherries, apricots, peaches, apples, and pears on the western slope of Colorado. With nine brothers and sisters, the family became sharecroppers in one of the farms they would work in seasonally. Spanish was the native language for him and his family. He attended Appleton Elementary School and Orchard Mesa High School and graduated from Grand Junction High School, where he was captain of the basketball and the baseball teams and served as president of the Student Boys Council, graduating in the top 15 percent of his class.

Dr. Garcia is presently dean of the Graduate School of Education and professor of education and psychology at the University of California, Berkeley. He received his B.A. from the University of Utah in psychology and his Ph.D. in human development from the University of Kansas. He has served as a postdoctoral fellow in human development at Harvard University and as a National Research Council fellow in the National Academy of Sciences. He has been a recipient of a National Kellogg Leadership Fellowship and received numerous academic and public honors. He served as a professor at the University of Utah; the University of California, Santa Barbara; Arizona State University; and the University of California, Santa Cruz, before joining the faculty at Berkeley. He has served previously as a National Research Center director and an academic department chair and dean. Dr. Garcia is involved in various community activities and has served as an elected member of an urban school board. He has published extensively in the area of language teaching and development, authoring or coauthoring over 150 articles and book chapters along with eight book-length volumes. He holds leadership positions in professional organizations and continues to serve in an editorial capacity for psychological, linguistic, and educational journals and serves regularly as a proposal panel reviewer for federal, state, and foundation agencies.

In 1993, Dr. Garcia was asked by President Bill Clinton and Secretary of Education Richard Riley to serve as senior officer and director of the Office of Bilingual Education and Minority Languages Affairs in the U.S. Department of Education. He was appointed to that position by the president and served from 1993 to 1995. He assisted in the development and implementation of federal education policy and related programs that provide some $12 billion in resources to local schools throughout the United States.